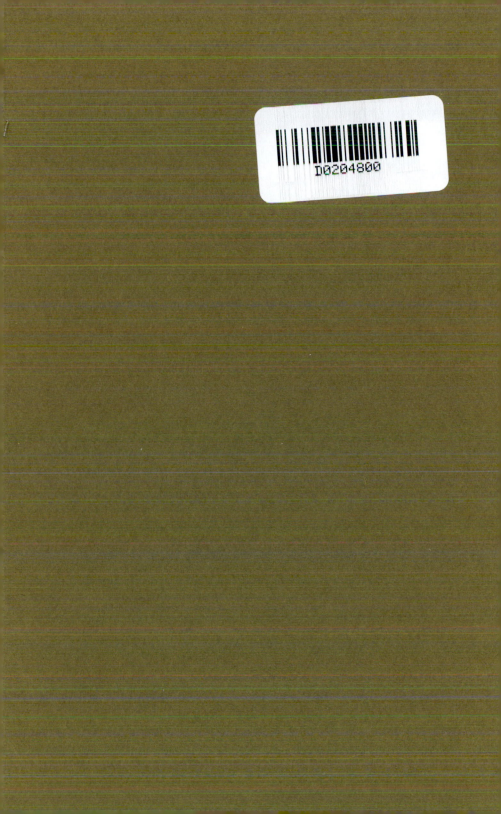
D0204800

Travels of a Genre

Travels of a Genre

THE MODERN NOVEL AND IDEOLOGY

Mary N. Layoun

PRINCETON UNIVERSITY PRESS

PRINCETON, NEW JERSEY

Copyright ©1990 by Princeton University Press
Published by Princeton University Press, 41 William Street,
Princeton, New Jersey 08540
In the United Kingdom: Princeton University Press, Oxford

All Rights Reserved

Library of Congress Cataloging-in-Publication Data

Layoun, Mary N., 1949–
Travels of a genre : the modern novel and ideology / Mary N. Layoun.
p.   cm.
Includes bibliographical references.
ISBN 0-691-06834-8
1. Fiction—20th century—History and criticism. 2. Literature,
Comparative—European and Asian. 3. Literature, Comparative—Asian
and European. I. Title.
PN3503.L376   1990 | 89–39388
809.3'04—dc20

Publication of this book has been aided by the Whitney Darrow
Fund of Princeton University Press
This book has been composed in Linotron Sabon

Princeton University Press books are printed on acid-free paper,
and meet the guidelines for permanence and durability of the
Committee on Production Guidelines for Book Longevity of the
Council on Library Resources

Printed in the United States of America by Princeton University Press,
Princeton, New Jersey
1   3   5   7   9   10   8   6   4   2

OLSON LIBRARY
NORTHERN MICHIGAN UNIVERSITY
MARQUETTE, MICHIGAN 49855

In memory of Labība and Tamām, to whose travels and narratives I am indebted.

For my traveling companions, Kyo of many questions and Odysseas of many stories.

For Nikos, without whose support and encouragement none of what precedes or follows would be possible.

Cultural treasures owe their existence not only to the efforts of the great minds and talents who have created them but also to the anonymous toil of their contemporaries. There is no document of civilization that is not at the same time a document of barbarism. And just as such a document is not free of barbarism, barbarism also taints the manner in which it was transmitted from one owner to another.
—Walter Benjamin, "Theses on the Philosophy of History"

CONTENTS

Preface   xi

CHAPTER 1
Fictional Genealogies   3

CHAPTER 2
The God Abandons the Murderess: or, Murder as
Opposition?   21

CHAPTER 3
In the Flickering Light of Umm Hāshim's Lamp   56

CHAPTER 4
Of Noisy Trains and Grass Pillows   105

CHAPTER 5
Doubling: The (Immigrant) Worker as (Exiled)
Writer   148

CHAPTER 6
Deserts of Memory   177

CHAPTER 7
Hunting Whales and Elephants, (Re)Producing
Narratives   209

CHAPTER 8
In Other Words, In Other Worlds: In Place of a
Conclusion   243

Bibliography   259

Index   269

PREFACE

The production of aesthetic or narrative form is to be
seen as an ideological act in its own right, with the
function of inventing imaginary or formal "solutions"
to unresolvable social contradictions.
—Frederic Jameson, *The Political Unconscious*

IN WHAT FOLLOWS, the modern novels of six writers—in modern Greek, Alexandros Papadiamandis and Dimitris Hatzis; in Arabic, Yahyā Haqqī and Ghassān Kanafānī; and in Japanese, Natsume Sōseki and Ōe Kenzaburo—are considered as narrative constructions of (im)possible solutions to social and historical contradictions. In the conjunction of narrative texts and analyses below, literature, literary theories, and their cultures presumably beyond the boundaries of "Western"* literary theory and those same "Western" theories are brought to

* This, I suppose, is the place to mark my unease with the conventional capitalization of the terms *east* and *west*. My argument here is rather explicitly *against* the attribution of definitive or fixed meanings to "east" and "west." They overwhelmingly suggest an implicit valorization and what is always presumably a primary term. Typically that primary position has been allocated to the "west" (although I'd suggest that to have it occupied by an "east" would be no real improvement). So, I had resolutely uncapitalized all references to "east" and "west" in a perhaps crabbed and pedantic attempt to indicate their diminished or at least distinctly *relative* referential capability. Ironically, according to convention again, it is only in reference to geographical direction that "east" and "west" are written with lower-case letters. And throughout, the argument is made that these "easts" and "wests" are not geographical references. And so, all "easts" and "wests" herein, which I so resolutely uncapitalized, were, in the editing process, just as resolutely recapitalized to comply with conventional usage and to avoid confusion on the readers' part. Still, as we avoid your confusion (?) and uphold our convention (?) I would like to insist that, at least for the consideration of texts and contexts here, "east" and "west" are decidedly slippery, elastic, relative categories always to be construed in ironic quotes and with lower-case letters.

bear on one another. This is not to impose literary theories from elsewhere on other cultures and literary texts. This would only be to repeat the maneuver that occurred in the imposition of the dominant form of the modern, realist, bourgeois novel on "non-Western" narrative genres and forms that preceded the "immigrant" genre of the novel. (When I began to write this book, I conceived of this "imposition" as essentially a metaphoric one. Recently and rather coincidentally, I learned that in one West African country, colonial officers paid local writers or literate storytellers to write novels in a deliberate attempt to promote the novel over other narrative or poetic forms. In this instance at least, the "metaphor" was more literal and far less figurative than I had suspected.) But, this is not an elegiac endeavor. I am more interested here in the cultural and textual response to hegemony than in mourning its occurrence. So, in what follows, early and contemporary Greek, Arabic, and Japanese novels are situated in terms of their relationship(s) to what was, and is, a dominant social and historical contradiction—early-twentieth-century imperialism, and the cultural accoutrements of that imperialism, and, more recently, multinational variations of that imperial scheme of unequal relations. At the same time, these books are considered in terms of their relationships to and participation in internal or intranational struggles for power and cultural hegemony. While the novel was not a particularly indigenous literary genre in the "third" or non-Western world, it quickly predominated as a privileged narrative construct. And yet, on the site of that hegemonic narrative form, there emerged counterhegemonic opposition as well. In this production of narrative forms, ideology, history, and culture intersect. This intersection in specific "non-Western" texts is examined here in an attempt to conjoin contemporary theories of narrative, of culture, of ideology, and of social, cultural, and political praxis. Inevitably perhaps, this conjunction cannot succeed. But it is an attempt that, with other attempts, points at (im)possible futures that I would like to insist on.

This is, then, an appropriate moment in which to express my gratitude to the many people who have contributed in various ways to this book. It seems to me that what are presumably most solitary endeavors—reading and writing—are in fact provoked, informed, and sustained not by solitary individuals but by intellectual, social, and political interaction and dialogue. I hope some sense of that dialogue and interaction is maintained in what follows. As is the convention, all errors and shortcomings are, of course, my own.

I would like to express my gratitude to a number of people for reading earlier versions of this work and for their suggestions, criticisms, encouragement, and example: Martin Jay, Eric Johannesson, Francine Masiello, Masao Miyoshi, Edward Said, Nanos Valaoritis, and Victoria Vernon. Special thanks also to Fredric Jameson and Susan Willis. And I am grateful to the two anonymous readers of the manuscript for their careful and astute comments. Many thanks also to my colleagues at the University of Wisconsin, Madison, for their support, encouragement, and companionship as well as to the students with whom I have read and discussed many of the books here and from whose questions and work I have learned a great deal. To my husband, collaborator, and critic, Nikos Ladopoulos, I am more grateful than I can say—for his willingness to discuss many of the issues in this book, for patiently reading and critiquing its many versions, and for his manifold support and encouragement.

Travels of a Genre

Chapter 1

FICTIONAL GENEALOGIES

IF GENEALOGY is typically the tracing of "natural," biological—and often patriarchal—lines of descent, *fictional genealogies* proposes the pluralization of that presumably singular generative line and its character as a fictional narrative. It also, of course, refers to the fictional genealogies of the genre of the modern novel. Much of what follows, then, will suggest that there was very little that was "natural" about the development of the modern novel. Rather, the suggestion is what should be by now a familiar one—that literary (and cultural) genres and texts are the site of active struggles and conflicts as well as of propositions about "resolutions" for those struggles and conflicts. Neither a culture nor its constituent "texts" are seamless, internally coherent, and essentialist but, as Eric Wolf points out in his *Europe and the People without History*, a "rough and tumble of social interaction"[1] between contending forces. And rather than assuming that interaction as causative in its own right—as, in other words, a self-propagating genealogy, it is perhaps more usefully considered as a complex network of relationships themselves in dynamic exchange with political, economic, and social contexts. So, while there are various genealogies cited for the modern European and English novel, one of the dominant categories for these genealogical discussions of genre has been the (perhaps equally genealogical) national.

Thus, the origins of the modern West European novel have typically been located within the national boundaries of the modern West European nation-state. Considerations of the novel as a genre, an endeavor admittedly fraught with difficulty, are far fewer than national cultural *histories* of the

---

[1] Eric R. Wolf, *Europe and the People without History*, 387.

novel—the history of the modern German novel, of the modern French novel, of the modern English novel, and, there, at what some consider the outermost edge of Western Europe, of the modern Spanish novel. The arguably unavoidable underpinning of such discussions is no doubt the attempt to account for the regional specificity of particular texts. But the extent to which such histories, not unlike the novels they describe, define and bound a regional or particularly national specificity is striking. National histories of the novel and the modern West European novel itself stake out the fictional terrain of a particular definition of the nation. This is not a totally coincidental maneuver. Bakhtin's magisterial linguistic and cultural history of the multiple discourses of the Western novel—which he traces as far back as the ancient Greek romances[2]—in spite of the broad inclusivity of its definition of the novel, posits a noteworthy threshold for the early modern, late seventeenth- and eighteenth-century European novel. That is the extent to which, at that point, the novel begins to delineate and make familiar (everyday or ordinary) the national landscape, both literally and metaphorically. Such novels are marked by their fictional postulations of what amounts to a national language, of national character, of an inclusive national culture, of national topos and history. Much of Bakhtin's critical work on the novel pursues the various narrative "voices" that make up Western "novelistic discourse." He traces a concatenation of those voices—the "dialogic imagination"—that marks his own critical history and prehistory of the novel as much as it does the novelistic discourses of which he writes. But, I would suggest, the symphony of those voices is, elsewhere, heard rather differently—selectively and not quite so symphonically.

If there is considerable critical divergence over the location of originary points and subsequent genealogies, there might be somewhat fewer differences over the relations of the modern European novel as a cultural and specifically literary form to its various historical and social contexts. So, the modern novel

[2] M. M. Bakhtin, "Forms of Time and Chronotope in the Novel," *The Dialogic Imagination*, 86–110.

is linked to the rise of a literate bourgeoisie with particular social and cultural values and narrative expectations; to the development of industrial capitalism; to the powerful claims of the Enlightenment; to the spread of printing presses, the increased circulation of magazines and newspapers, to circulating libraries; to the penetration of the vernacular and certain popular cultural forms—popular theater, storytelling, folktales—into what had been more exclusive or "high" literary genres. The emergence of the modern novel can also, at least in retrospect, be situated in the contexts of the picaresque "travelogues," the baroque rupture or distortion of the "real," the rise of a romantic individualism, and the assertion of the totalizing frame of history and of a "rational" thinking self in eighteenth- and nineteenth-century philosopical and historical narratives. No *one* of these contexts is necessarily the "correct" and essential one—the single answer to a multiple-choice question about the origins of the modern novel. It is far more useful to consider some configuration of the contexts above as the foreground of the modern West European novel.

But in the move to what is foregrounded, there would undoubtedly be more argument over the specific characteristics of the modern novel. What formally or structurally distinguishes the modern novel from earlier narratives? Terry Lovell's *Consuming Fiction*,[3] while acknowledging the significance of Ian Watt's location of coherent, rational, and orderly individualism and realism in the rise of the English novel,[4] astutely critiques that position for its disregard of the simultaneously dominant presence of the gothic, of the less-than-rational, and the desirous. Lovell's analysis also offers a crucial corrective to Watt's exclusion of the women who dominated not only the consumption of the early novel but also, until the mid-nineteenth century and the novel's entry into the fields of high literature, its production.[5] *Consuming Fiction* pays rather more careful attention to the initial status of the novel

[3] Terry Lovell, *Consuming Fiction*, esp. 19–45.
[4] Ian Watt, *The Rise of the Novel*, esp. 9–59.
[5] See also Dale Spender's *Mothers of the Novel* for a witty and informative feminist rewriting of the "rise of the novel."

as a "debased," "debasing," and just barely literary form. Steele's aside, "I am afraid thy Brains are a little disordered with Novels and Romances," in his early eighteenth-century newspaper *The Spectator*,[6] is an apt reminder of the novel's originally questionable status. For as Lovell and others have pointed out, it is only later that the novel comes to occupy a stable and exalted role in bourgeois literary culture. For Lukács, the novel emerges from and is characterized by the degradation, the problematization, of the epic hero and his collective social world. The novel is the literary form of a world marked by a metaphoric and literal "homelessness" and "exile."[7] It is a world and a hero that are no longer objects of contemplation for a Judaeo-Christian god, even less, as Walter Benjamin reminds us, objects of contemplation for the Olympian gods.[8] With encompassment in the divine look an impossibility, the novel is marked by the predominance of a narrative perspective that takes itself as the object of its own contemplation. The novel, in this definition, emphasizes the "rational" and phenomenal; its unifying element is the individual and her or his consciousness. But, in an interesting rereading of Lukács, J. M. Bernstein[9] replaces Lukács's location of Cervantes's *Don Quixote* as the originary moment of the modern novel with Descartes's *Discourse on Method*. For Bernstein, as in fact for Ian Watt some thirty years earlier, it is Descartes's *Discourse* that, like Defoe's *Robinson Crusoe*, marks the "moment of the narrative installation of the self" that is equally "the moment of the emergence of the novel."[10] Without foregoing Terry Lovell's qualification of the domi-

---

[6] *The Spectator*, #254. See also Michael McKeon's wide-ranging and impressive account of the historical and cultural struggles that ground the origins of the novel *before* a particular definition of it—that definition accounted for by Watt—gains hegemony: Michael McKeon, *The Origins of the English Novel, 1600–1740*.

[7] Georg Lukács, *The Theory of the Novel*, 86–93.

[8] "Mankind, which in Homer's time was an object of contemplation for the Olympian gods, now is one for itself."—in the conclusion to his "The Work of Art in the Age of Mechanical Reproduction," in *Illuminations*.

[9] J. M. Bernstein, *The Philosophy of the Novel*.

[10] Bernstein, *The Philosophy of the Novel*, 153.

nance of the realistic novel, the narrative perspective of and focus on a problematized individual and his life do distinguish the modern novel from earlier narratives. That fiction of the individual is not necessarily the preferred bourgeois (male) self-image—the coherent, orderly, and rational narrative perspective. As pleasing or reassuring as that image might be, it is one through which seep other images of repressed desires, of fancies and fantasies and fears that modern capitalism titillates but does not and cannot satisfy. Perhaps, though, one can characterize the early modern novel as a genre that focuses on the perspective and world of the "average" and "ordinary" individual who *attempts* to order, contain, and narrate his or her surroundings—human and nonhuman—without clear benefit of preexisting and socially agreed upon models and paradigms (i.e., with emphasis on the *novelty* of that individual and her perspective). It is an attempt that only occasionally succeeds. But it would seem to be precisely those occasional "successes" that are typically designated as literary exemplars of the modern novel.

It is not an attempt to draw a literary or social history of the modern European or "non-European" novel that will occupy the following pages. I would only suggest that what is presumably the naturalness or coherent internal development of the modern West European novel is far more a retrospective construct than an "objective" description. The emergence and subsequent literary predominance of the modern novel was attended by cultural, political, and social strife in which the discourse of the novel participated and by which it was shaped. Clearly, then, the novel was not and is not a singular, monolithic, and fixed genre but one that emerged in a particular conjunction of sociocultural and literary circumstances and that developed variously in relation to its circumstances. Within the various national definitions of hegemonic culture at a given historical moment, the modern novel assumed a dominant position. And, adapting to changing contexts, it arguably continues to occupy that position of dominance. The specific shape(s) of the novel are, ultimately perhaps, inseparable from those contexts. But there is, simultaneously, an organizing view that the novel proposes, modulated and modified though it is, that does distinguish the modern novel from earlier narrative forms—from epics, folktales, the lyric poem, salon drama, historical chronicles, or even, for here I would agree with Bernstein, from the picaresque novel. Whether, in the tracks of national histories, we locate the novel within the boundaries of a nation-state as, at least implicitly, a modern genre, or, with Bakhtin, we consider "novelistic discourse" from its ("Western") prehistory to the present as multiple and historically pervasive, there *is* a substantially different and diverse novel that begins to circulate in the late seventeenth and eighteenth centuries and that, ensconced in a by then hegemonic bourgeois culture, reigns relatively supreme in the nineteenth and early twentieth centuries. It is in this latter period that the modern European novel is introduced to the Middle East, Japan, and Greece. Specific textual consequences of this introduction and subsequent development, rather than the origins and developments of the modern European or non-European novel itself, will be the focus here.

·   ·   ·

If the modern European novel is the textual site (and cite) of cultural, linguistic, and social struggle, there is a crucial eighteenth- and nineteenth-century context of struggle in which the European novel was indubitably implicated and by which it was marked—but in a rather distinctly different way than other participants in that same context. That is the global, and distinctly *extra*national, context of imperialism. For the "non-European" or "third world" or "minor" novels examined in the following pages, imperialism and the distinctly unequal relations between the imperial and "imperialized" nations was a virtually unavoidable crisis. This is not to propose that imperialism burned its indelible imprint directly onto the pages of every novel produced in the "third world." Rather, the political, economic, social, and cultural fact(s) of imperialism pervade their modes of production, their structural frameworks, their formal concerns. For, there is no special privilege or sacrosanctity that would preserve literary production outside of that context. In fact, the analyses of the following chapters begin with the attempt to demonstrate just that point—that there *was* no such exclusion and further, to consider the specific ways in which that imperial inclusion informs the content and form of the novel "elsewhere." Thus, within a certain framework, what the novel as a genre actually *was* in Europe or England is very nearly beside the point. Setting aside for the moment in-fact generic history (if there is such a thing), the modern West European novel was apprehended and, at least initially, produced in Greece or Egypt or Japan as the paradigmatic genre of the rational, modern, and democratic West, as an "advanced" cultural technology. Of course, to designate a genre (or a text) as inherently and definitively anything ahistorically ignores the extent to which such designations are themselves historically situated and produced. So, then, the characterization(s) by other cultures of the modern European novel are not *mis*apprehensions or distortions of what the novel "really" was. What could seem "inaccurate" or static or even naive perceptions of the novel as a genre appear so only as they are isolated from the network of which they are a part—(grossly unequal) relationships between an imperially expanding West Europe and England in the eighteenth, nineteenth, and early twentieth centuries and the rest of the world. The ideology of an imperial "civilizing mission" rather explicitly designated its task as the bringing of an advanced and rational culture, and of course the "true" faith, to the rest of the world. That this was subterfuge for the rapacious conquest and control of what was consequently made the "underdeveloped" or "third" world does not negate what was the hegemonic power of modern Western culture and of the novel as one specific aspect of that culture. And so, perhaps ironically in keeping with imperialism's claims about its own cultural mission, the novel (variously defined) flourished as the dominant narrative mode in Greece, the Middle East, and Japan.

Not that there were no traditional narrative forms in the Arabic or Greek or Japanese cultures. Quite the contrary. But, in Arabic culture, for example, there was no single narrative form that was clearly preeminent. This is discussed in rather more detail in chapter 3 in the consideration of the fiction of the Egyptian writer, Yahyā Haqqī. But it should be mentioned here that, in something of a parallel to the situation in early twentieth-century Greece (see chap. 2), the folktale, religious hagiography, myth, chronicles, biography, and the essay all predate the modern novel. But, prior to the twentieth century, no one of these narrative forms predominates. The situation in Japan provides an interesting counterpoint, for there things were somewhat different. There is, of course, the famous Japanese exception of what is sometimes considered Murasaki Shikibu's tenth-century "novel," *Tale of Genji*. But, throughout Japan's literary tradition, there were many and varied narrative forms other than the *Genji*. Classical poetry was sorted and gathered into official imperial anthologies; the various poems of many of those anthologies were typically linked with prose headnotes that provided a distinctly narrative and often fictional framework for the collections. On the other hand, both fictional and nonfictional prose was frequently interspersed with poetry. In the Tokugawa era (1600–1860), prose narratives, often illustrated with wood-block prints, flourished in the rapidly growing merchant culture of the cities. There was even a prolific production of what we might call cartoon books, closer perhaps to the "fotonovelas" of contemporary Latin America—strip illustrations with accompanying narrative and dialogue. Whether or not Murasaki's singular narrative is considered evidence of a novelistic tradition, Japanese narrative in the late nineteenth century was scarcely dormant.

Yet, in spite of the multiplicity of possible narrative forms already in circulation in other cultures and regardless of whether it was heralded as a "liberating instrument"[11] or condemned as the narrative mode of a secularizing and degraded West, the novel did become the dominant literary narrative mode. From a certain perspective, the novel metaphorically

[11] Jacques Berque, *Cultural Expression in Arab Society Today*, 215.

"colonized" preexistent narrative production; already existent modes of narrative production were subjugated and refashioned in the image of the novel. But here there are at least
two qualifications. First, as one of the hegemonic cultural
trappings of an imperial Europe or Britain, as a challenge to
preexistent narrative forms, the novel also proposed radically
different ways of organizing narratives and perspectives. As a
particular form of narrative discourse, it made available certain narrative or discursive possibilities. At the same time, of
course, it foreclosed other possibilities and postulated them as
impossibilities or aporias. And also, the postulations of the
"imported" novel about its generic possibility and impossibility and its implication in the exercise of cultural imperialism—
through its self-proclaimed structural boundaries if nothing
else—occasion something other than "imitation," other than
narrative production in a mode defined elsewhere. They also
occasion opposition and resistance. That oppositional narrative practice challenges but does not necessarily refuse the
novel.

But some further clarification of the proposition made here
is still possible. There is no suggestion of some categorical
form—the novel—into which "third world" narrative content
is poured. This would only suspiciously repeat the imperial
model that posits the extraction of raw materials to be shaped
by technologies of production in the creation of surplus value
for an imperial center. If the form of the novel was simultaneously a new opening and a containment or closure, if the
novel hegemonizes or imperializes, it did not and does not do
so without resistances and infiltrations of various sorts. The
narrative "technology" of the novel was not forcibly imposed
on other worlds to give shape to their inchoate (literary) experience. Hegemony, after all, does not work by coercion but
by compelling "direction"—Gramsci's *direczione*. Instead,
the formal narrative assumptions of the novel-become-domi-
nant, while certainly shaping and limiting narrative discourses, also encounter forms of resistance and opposition to
that dominance. Or, the hegemonic narrative technologies of
the novel were confronted by counterhegemonics. If there was

no singularly definitive and "natural" novel in West Europe, there was certainly no singular and monolithic "third world" cultural response to the novel. Instead, the novel in other cultures has multiplied and reentered the center as plural challenges—literal *objects*—"thrown across" the path of a hegemony that likes to characterize itself as equally multiple. These challenges too constitute an impinging presence within the "center"; they force themselves into the discourse, the theories, the literary and cultural practices, and the political consciousness of the center.

· · ·

The perhaps irritatingly persistent enclosure, up to this point, of "first" and "third" worlds or "East" and "West" in quotation marks is not intended to suggest that these terms are only figments of a textual imagination but, rather, that they are resolutely *non*geographical coordinates. They designate, instead, the abstraction of relative relationships of power. In the "older" East/West construction—an example of what Edward Said has called "imaginative geography"[12]—it is the latter designation that is presumed primary and definitive. But this West or its necessary counterpart, East, is scarcely to be found fixed on a map. Obviously, a geographical East is always relative to where one stands. Historically, the dividing line between East and West has been conspicuously mobile. Instead, the East can be more usefully understood as a reference to an increasingly complex configuration of largely unequal relationships with the West. Something quite similar underlies the more recently coined designations of "first" world as opposed to the "third" and the "second." But this being said, and acknowledging as well that the extent to which the economic and military power to which those terms presently refer is not just a textual or literary construct but only too literal, there is no singular and self-same entity called "the third world." One of the things the third world does have in

[12] Edward Said, *Orientalism*, 54–56, 210–11.

common—the only thing it has in common some would argue—is precisely that unequal relationship with the first world, a history of colonialism and imperialism. The third world, then, was not and is not some preexistent category of social, intellectual, political, or cultural (under)development. It was made. It was created by the first world. This construction and its subsequent deformation have become the focus of an increasing number of astute critical studies in the last twenty years or so. But what has received less attention, what is only just beginning to emerge in such critical studies, are the cultural, social, and political responses in the third world to that construction. The imperative to think globally that has been recognized in some critical studies of socioeconomics, of, for example, capitalism as a "world system,"[13] is still a little more contentious in the critical consideration of culture. There, disciplinary and linguistic boundaries of national area specializations still predominate.

Yet, it will, I hope, become increasingly unacceptable, even impossible, to consider first world culture in isolation, as sufficient unto itself. For, historically, it never has been. And, it is hoped, the fixed arrangement and ordered display for consumption of third world culture, whether carried out by "orientalists" or their latter-day manifestation as academic specialists or native informants, will be rejected as equally unacceptable. The national fixation that bounded much critical commentary on the modern novel has served a similar function in critical theory and cultural or literary criticism as well. But, if the dangers of a grand totalizing scheme—of which imperialism itself was one, after all—have become only too apparent, the retreat to the "safe" confines of a dubiously retrenched isolationism is also unacceptable. And, in fact, one of the central propositions of the "world system" theorists is precisely the global implication within one economic system— capitalism. So, as the concluding chapter of Peter Worsley's

[13] See Immanuel Wallerstein, *The Modern World-System*, esp. vol. 1, 7–8 and 300–345. See also Wallerstein, *The Capitalist World-Economy* (London: Cambridge University Press, 1979).

The Three Worlds: Culture and World Development makes explicit, "One World or Three?" is no rhetorical question.[14] In a thoughtful and more-explicit-than-usual response to Aijaz Ahmad's astute critique of his "Third World Literature in the Era of Multinational Capitalism," Frederic Jameson identifies the tactical assumptions of his article as "teaching third world literatures; the recognition of the challenge they pose to even the most advanced contemporary theory; the need for a *relational* way of thinking global culture . . . a comparative study of cultural situations."[15] In fact, the latter two propositions imply that the very designations of first, second, and third world(s) must necessarily be historicized, situated (but not necessarily obliterated from the page) as constructs of imperial power, as examples of Said's "imaginary geography." But, we would do well to remember that imaginary geography, like ideology, is never some totally false fabrication, as opposed to the truth of a presumably nonideological sphere. In spite of the more dubious contentions of some of his work, Louis Althusser's definition of ideology as the "representation of the imaginary relationship of individuals to their real conditions of existence" remains seminal.[16] And, as he asserts later, ideology does not magically self-destruct. As Fanon cautions in another context—and in retrospect, almost poignantly, "Independence is not a word which can be used as an exorcism, but an indispensable condition for the existence of men and women who are truly liberated, in other words who are truly masters of all the material means which make possible the radical transformation of society."[17]

. . .

[14] Peter Worsley, *The Three Worlds: Culture and World Development*, 296–344.

[15] Frederic Jameson, "A Brief Response." See references for Jameson's original article and Ahmad's article-in-response in Bibliography.

[16] Louis Althusser, "Ideology and Ideological State Apparatuses," in *Lenin and Philosophy*, 162–70.

[17] Frantz Fanon, *The Wretched of the Earth*, 310.

We always eventually find, at the edge of the text, the language of ideology, momentarily hidden, but eloquent by its very absence.[18]

The implication of ideology in a discussion of the workings of the modern novel "imported" to other cultures is not fortuitous or rhetorical. In this consideration of the critical workings of the modern novel in Greece, the Middle East, or Japan, the interactions between ideology and culture—or here specific texts—are a central focus. The complexities of that relationship are the critical object of much recent theory.[19] And a similar concern marks the earlier work of the Frankfurt School as well. In this attempt to map the terrain of ideology and culture, to locate the subject and the text in relation to ideology, Frederic Jameson, in a lengthy essay on the psychoanalytic theories of Jacques Lacan, has located two major movements. One is "the hegelianizing and dialectical current which, emerging from Lukács' *History and Class Consciousness*, found its embodiment in the work of the Frankfurt School." That hegelian and dialectic direction is distinguished from "that structural and scientific reading of Marx which, combining the heritage of Saussure and the lesson of Mao Tsetung's *On Contradiction* (and also with Lacanian psychoanalysis), informs the theoretical practice of Althusser and his group."[20] (The unspoken critical presence hovering at the edges of this schema, particularly of its latter component, is,

[18] Pierre Macherey, *A Theory of Literary Production*, 60.

[19] As, for example, the work of Althusser, Jameson, Macherey, Worsley, cited above. Other useful critical works: Catherine Belsey's *Critical Practice*; Lennard Davis's *Resisting Novels: Ideology and Fiction*; Terry Eagleton's *Criticism and Ideology*; Stuart Hall's "Signification, Representation, Ideology"; Peter Hulme's *Colonial Encounters*; Gayatri Spivak's *In Other Worlds*, which includes "The Politics of Interpretations," an essay to which I often return; Michael Sprinker's *Imaginary Relations*; *Ideology and Cultural Production*, Michele Barrett, ed.; *The Ideology of Conduct*, ed. Nancy Armstrong and Leonard Tennenhouse; the Center for Contemporary Cultural Studies' *On Ideology*; Argument Sonderband's *Rethinking Ideology*, Sakari Hanninen and Leena Palden, eds.

[20] Frederic Jameson, "Imaginary and Symbolic in Lacan: Marxism, Psychoanalytic Criticism, and the Problem of the Subject."

of course, what has been rather grossly designated as deconstruction or, more recently, as postmodern criticism.) These distinct but not necessarily mutually exclusive critical currents offer useful directions for an inquiry into the mutual interaction of ideology and culture. The urgency of such an inquiry and the complexity with which it is forced to deal have grown as the movements of ideology have become increasingly camouflaged.

Implicating the workings of ideology in and around the text in a consideration of the modern non-Western novel is not a proposal for typological or classificatory gymnastics. "This work is conservative and that one progressive"—however the content of those categories might be defined. Nor is there some tidy notion lurking in the wings of ideology as false consciousness. But, having said this, let me specify further that one of the particular notions here about ideology and its relation to literary texts, and the novel in particular, is that both as an instance of narrative discourse and as an attempt at situation within the tantalizing (and elusive) boundaries of history, the modern novel, like ideology, presents itself as an "unreal" (Althusser's "imaginary" or Macherey's "false") aesthetic solution to only-too-real sociohistorical dilemmas. Not that the relationships between the socio-historical and the aesthetic or literary are direct ones by any means. But as heavily mediated or overdetermined as they are, they nonetheless implicate the not-only-literary concerns of structures, of history, of collectivities to the individual, to the personal, to the psychological and then attempt to negotiate a course amidst those concerns. In this context, Stuart Hall's observation, in an essay on ideology, culture, and Althusser,[21] on the limitations of the theoretical "bifurcation" that emerges from the very structure of Althusser's essay on "Ideological State Apparatuses" is most pertinent. Hall points out that Althusser's formulation of ideology results in the allocation to a "psychoanalytic (feminist) pole" of the question(s) of subjectivity—the personal, the sexual, the psychoanalytic—and to a "marxist

[21] Hall, "Signification, Representation, Ideology."

(male) pole" of the questions of ideological reproduction—social relations, production, and systems of reproduction. It is not only Hall who urges the necessity of negotiating this divide—one that informs other equally bifurcated notions such as of public and private or of theory and practice as well. Gayatri Spivak, in "The Politics of Interpretations"[22] insightfully "reads" the ideology pervading some texts of cultural interpretation in the context of indicating the necessity of formulating the movement between the subject and collective subjects in and of ideology. In addition, her analysis of Wayne Booth or Stanley Cavell or Donald Davie suggests the almost humorous and certainly ironic fashion in which notions of ideology themselves take on that pervasive commodification that characterizes one of the predominant ideologies of consumer society—as if an ideology could be picked up from a selection on the shelf on which it had been arranged to appeal to our self-image of the moment. What this "consumer" notion of ideology avoids—and here there are fewer humorous implications—is the extent to which we are always, as Althusser insists, *in* ideology—or, more properly, ideolog*ies*—and also the extent to which it, or they, are not just of our own choosing.

Finally, if ideologies are not laying on a shelf awaiting purchase and consumption, neither are they free-floating or innocently abstract above the "ground" of practice. Ideologies disseminate their effects in the world and not just on or in the word. Nor are they, as Marx reminds us about history, "made just as we please."[23] Like the image of learning new languages that concludes the same paragraph, they are always already there before us and it is into them that we insert ourselves. And yet, there is no self-propelled machine of history dragging us along in its wake. It was in this sense that I proposed above that there is no self-evident and self-propagating genealogy of the novel. But if there are no fixed and self-propelled and propelling reproductive machineries, neither is there some perpet-

---

[22] Spivak, "The Politics of Interpretations," 118–33.
[23] Karl Marx, *The Eighteenth Brumaire of Louis Napoleon*, 15.

ually fluid position open to either texts or folks in the world. At a given moment, from within our various ideologies that do, but not entirely, define our individual and collective constitution, we *do* intervene or insert ourselves or make our own histories. In other words, and perhaps obviously, if ideology is not free-floating and innocently abstract or transcendent above the ground, neither are we or our cultural or literary (or critical) productions. Given this, the ways in which we are in and of, producers and productions, of ideology are scarcely equally or universally distributed.

Althusser's example of being "hailed" by ideology in the person of a policeman shouting "Hey you!" is a useful case in point.[24] For, on the hypothetical streets of Althusser's Paris, my own response, that of the policeman, of onlookers and passersby, and finally of the police station and city and state law in whose name and under whose authority I am hailed will be substantially different depending on the intersection of ideologies and of race, class, and gender distinctions by which I am marked. If I am a young, white, male French citizen, well dressed and carrying a briefcase, the various possibilities provoked by this situation in which I am called out will be distinctly different than if I were a not-so-young, Arabic woman with a temporary visa, carrying a small child, and speaking accented French. I do not, at this given moment, choose "my ideologies" any more than I do the other things that mark me to a greater or lesser degree, regardless of whether I am able to choose or modify them. I am "hailed" by a history, by ideologies, by personal and collective subjectivities—by narratives, if you will—in which I participate, which (perhaps) I shape, but not under circumstances only of my own choosing.

In this context of ideologies by which we are marked and from within which we operate, of contexts that impinge on texts and that perhaps might even be impinged on by texts, the critical commentary in the following pages on six non-Western novels for a largely Western or at least English-speaking audience, published and circulated by an American aca-

---

[24] Althusser, "Ideology and Ideological State Apparatuses," 174–75.

demic press is hardly exempt from contexts, academic and otherwise, in which the "novel" world is arrayed and represented for the consumption of the usually Anglo or European purveyor. Whether or not, as Lenin proposed in his *Imperialism: the Highest Stage of Capitalism*,[25] imperialism by the early twentieth century was still searching for investment in the rest of the world, it *was* seeking the raw materials, cheap labor, and, most essentially, the markets of the non-European worlds. Thus one of the primary goals of imperialism from the early twentieth century can be postulated as the *ex*traction of (surplus) value, rather than the *in*vestment of capital. This is an admittedly dangerous, not to mention frightening, metaphor for literary *or* academic production. The extent to which the organizing perspectives and goals of imperialism hover in the margins of the literary production of the eighteenth, nineteenth, and twentieth centuries *in* Europe, America, and Britain cannot be mitigated by claiming some special exempt status. Yet in that context, as illustrated by Althusser's example of being hailed by ideology, there are more than a few determinate possibilities. The directions of the novel in the non-West, in other worlds and in other words, metaphorically suggest those possibilities that are more than just a determinate few. So, perhaps the relation of the novel as a narrative genre to non-European or "non-Western" cultures is not of merely coincidental significance beyond those cultures or worlds. If the formative (and deformative) impact of a genre introduced and fostered through the channels of imperialism's distinctly unequal relationships is explored in texts "outside" of the European domain, perhaps the equally necessary critical analysis of literature and imperialism "within" that domain can be hastened.

In the conclusion to his *Literary Theory*, Terry Eagleton, in commenting on societies "like our own which have no time for culture," cites (rather expansively) those times and places in which literature and culture are "charged with a signifi-

[25] V. I. Lenin, *Imperialism: The Highest Stage of Capitalism* (New York: International Publishers, 1984).

cance beyond itself," in which "culture is so vitally bound up with one's common identity. . . ."[26] It is this significance that marks the six narratives of the following chapters. I hope they vitiate just a little the indictments of "third world" or "non-Western" culture for not being "developed enough"—indictments that come from within those cultures as well as from without. For the contemporary texts in particular, that "sufficient development" is suggested not only from within the text but from without it as well. If within the United States that seems a too-literary or grossly cultural call to action that is always bound to fail, perhaps that is more of a comment on American culture and its possibilities than on culture or texts elsewhere. And if that "significance beyond itself" exceeds a little the societies and cultures for whom it is primary, perhaps that is one small indication of Eagleton's claim that "they are not all a thousand miles from our doorstep." But if we ignore them, or if we insist on casting them as the same, or as exotic and unapproachable except to some variation of orientalist narrative, they might as well be a thousand miles away. There are other possibilities however, as Gabriel García Marquez suggested on receiving the 1982 Nobel Prize for Literature:

> We, the inventors of tales, who will believe anything, feel entitled to believe that it is not too late to engage in the creation of a utopia of very different kind. A new and sweeping utopia of life, where no one will be able to decide for others how they die, where love will prove true and happiness possible, and where the races condemned to one hundred years of solitude will have, at last and forever, a second opportunity on the earth.[27]

[26] Terry Eagleton, *Literary Theory*, 215.
[27] Gabriel García Marquez, "The Solitude of Latin America," *Granta* 9 (1983): 60.

Chapter 2

THE GOD ABANDONS THE MURDERESS: OR, MURDER AS OPPOSITION?

> listen—the final pleasure—to the sounds,
> the exquisite instruments
> of the strange troupe of traveling actors,
> and bid farewell to her,
> to the Alexandria that you are losing.
> —C. P. Cavafis, "The God Abandons Antony"

IT IS NOT CLEAR whether this ironic counsel of stoicism offered to a defeated Mark Antony was accepted. Whether or not Mark Antony accepted the counsel, the sense of irretrievable loss that underlies that ironic counsel, which is arguably the impetus for it, is "accepted" in the fiction of the mainland Greek novelist and short story writer, Alexandros Papadiamandis (1851–1911). The ironic poetic commentaries of the modern Greek poet C. P. Cavafis (1863–1933) might at first seem a strange introduction to the work of Alexandros Papadiamandis. For Cavafis's poetry situates itself in the margins, so to speak, of ancient Greek, Hellenistic, and Byzantine texts. And it was written from what were the margins of the early twentieth-century Greek world in Alexandria, Egypt. But the work of both Cavafis and Papadiamandis is marked by the dislocation, the loss or slippage, of a past, of a sense of self and community, that "have surrendered" and "failed," that seem "illusions now."[1] It is in that context, that Cavafis's poem counsels ironic restraint or stoicism. It is in that context that Papadiamandis's fiction constructs narratives that alternate between the stoicism and restraint suggested by "The

[1] Constantine Cavafis, *Poiemata*, vol. 1, 20.

God Abandons Mark Antony" and a doomed resistance to that dislocation suggested by Papadiamandis's *The Murderess*, discussed below.

Papadiamandis was born on the small and impoverished island of Skiatho, the oldest son of a Greek Orthodox priest. As the island's only town had no secondary school, the boy left Skiatho at the age of sixteen for the island of Khalkis and then for Piraeus on the mainland. He returned to Skiatho only for brief holidays and for the last few years before he died in 1911. The remainder of his life was spent in Athens, eking out a living by doing numerous free-lance translations of novels, short stories, and articles from French and English into Greek for Athenian newspapers, by writing short stories and novels that were published in various newspapers and periodicals, and by borrowing from friends. He attended school intermittently after leaving Skiatho but never obtained a degree; his knowledge of languages and literature was largely self-taught. As virtually the sole support of his parents, three maiden sisters, and the wife and children of his younger brother, who died insane at a young age, Papadiamandis—with little formal education, shabbily dressed, provincial in manner and speech, always short of money—scarcely fit in with the presumably sophisticated and quasi-European circles peopled by the Athenian literati. Nonetheless, it was in Athens that Papadiamandis lived most of his life and wrote virtually all of his fiction. The popular image of Papadiamandis trapped in an alien city while pining away for his rural island homeland can be only partially accurate.[2] For Papadiamandis must have recognized, if only intermittently, that the rapidly changing urban landscape to which he claimed such opposition afforded him both the impetus and the freedom from his "beloved island" to write. But finally, regardless of the conscious stance of the biographical Papadiamandis, the ambivalent relationship both

---

[2] Although it was a stance that Papadiamandis himself cultivated, as is clear in his letters: "from that place of poverty and suffering and of small pleasures [Skiatho], I came to this place [Athens] to be condemned—where for such a long time I have borne my cross, scarcely able to endure—in this city of plutocrats and slaves."

to Skiatho and to Athens, to the simple islanders and to the Europeanized bourgeoisie, is nowhere more clearly expressed than in Papadiamandis's fiction.

A bound edition of Papadiamandis's work was never issued in his lifetime, the sole forum for his work being the daily and periodical press. His first fiction, "The Expatriate" (1879–1880), serialized in the Constantinople newspaper *To Neologo*, and "The Traffickers in Nations" published in the Athenian press under a pen name, are rather undistinguished. They were followed in 1884 by a historical novel, *The Gypsy Girl* and, in 1885, by a long short story based on a folk song, "Christos Milionis." From the appearance of "Christos Milionis" until his death, Papadiamandis wrote some two hundred short stories of varying length and a few full-length novels. Influenced by his friend Papadiamantopoulos—or, as he was later known, Jean Moreas—he also tried his hand, rather disastrously, at French verse. It is with this fiction, from "Christos Milionis" on, that Papadiamandis earned his name as an ethographic writer. Recreating the contemporary village life of Skiatho in his own peculiar linguistic style, Papadiamandis was misunderstood both by the demoticists of his time and by the linguistic purists. By the latter he was lauded as a symbol of the conservative traditionalism for which they stood; by the former he was "identified with the forces of obscurantism and reaction."[3] Contemporary criticism of Papadiamandis has been little more conclusive or analytical. He has been characterized as a "conservative" with "a hatred for the Franks and a horror for every kind of innovation. . . . His novels were juvenalia. . . . Later, what we still call short stories were only short narratives . . . composed only of descriptions." As for Papadiamandis's language, the same critic continues: "It is cursorily written and lacking in limpidity; the distribution of parts is defective. . . . We have the absence of the principal after a hypothetical proposition. Adverbs are often placed at random; adjectives are poor and conventional or

---

[3] Thomas Doulis, *Disaster and Fiction: Modern Greek Fiction and the Asia Minor Disaster of 1922*, 39.

so rare and elegant that they evoke no response in the reader."
And finally, Papadiamandis "lived outside the problems and
distresses of the Greeks of his generation."[4]

But then, Yiannis Kordatos, a cultural and political historian of modern Greece, characterizes Papadiamandis as "a
prose writer of great talent. . . . not only the most accomplished interpreter in his works of the ethographic life of his
island of Skiatho but the negative critic of the socio-political
Greek life of the last twenty years of the nineteenth century."[5]
And Thomas Doulis, in his *Disaster and Fiction*, in pointing
out the lack, until very recently, of critical recognition in the
modern Greek tradition of Papadiamandis, cites him as "the
greatest prose writer of his time . . . who accurately described
while transcending the life most characteristic of the Greece of
his time."[6]

Finally, the linguistic purists and conservative traditionalists who claimed Papadiamandis as their own and the liberal
demoticists and Europeanized bourgeoisie who rejected him
as a Byzantine throwback were both wrong. The former
looked to the past for both their authority and their sociopolitical and cultural models, the latter to the future and the expanding West. But Papadiamandis's texts were the voice neither of the one nor of the other. It is probably more accurate
to say that both he and his fiction were caught somewhere
between these two poles, a location more distinctly marked by
the present than by either past or future. Papadiamandis's fiction articulates the restrictions and limitations of the traditional way of life as well as the posturing and hypocrisies of
the new bourgeois order.

Here some reply can be made to his critics' charges that Papadiamandis, and we can assume his fiction as well, were
"outside the problems and distresses of the Greeks of his gen-

---

[4] Constantine T. Dimaras, *History of Modern Greek Literature*, trans. Mary
Gianos (Albany: State Universtiy of New York, 1972), 391–92.

[5] Yiannis Kordatos, *Istoria tis Neoteris Elladas* (History of modern Greece),
4: 655.

[6] Doulis, *Disaster and Fiction*, 39.

eration."[7] Papadiamandis was not a part of the coterie of Athenian intellectuals who dominated the social and cultural forefront of his day. He was a regular of neither camp—not of the crusading demoticists nor of the strident purists. Instead, he frequented a small church near the Acropolis, where he liked to chant psalms, and a traditional Greek café—as distinguished from the French-style cafés that were very much in vogue at the time—where his fellow islanders gathered.[8] Unlike his demoticist contemporaries, Grigoris Xenopoulos or Giorgos Theotokas, whose fictional settings "reflect an older and hierarchial communal system that is unrepresentative of Greece as it was then" (Doulis, 39), or those writers who openly imitated European prose literature or those traditionalists who attempted to write in a language and with a form that would presumably duplicate the Attic classics, Papadiamandis's fiction remained firmly grounded in the present of the Greek countryside. To that extent, his prose affords, better than most, an approach to some of the cultural and social conflicts and tensions of late nineteenth- and early twentieth-century Greece.

It is true that, in the midst of a raging controversy over language in postrevolutionary Greece, Papadiamandis wrote everything but three short stories[9] in a rather peculiarily personal blend of demotic, *katharevousa*, and Byzantine or ecclesiastical Greek. But unlike some of his purist contemporaries, Papadiamandis consistently maintained the vernacular in his

---

[7] Dimaras, *History of Modern Greek Literature*, 392.

[8] Such cafés have been a significant facet of Athenian life since the modern rebirth of the city. Small traditional cafés scattered throughout the capital served as unofficial cultural centers for Greeks who had migrated from the islands or the provinces. At one café, all those who had immigrated from, say, Khios, gathered to hear news of the island, to send letters home with the next outgoing ship, to sing regional folk songs, to eat the pastries that are a specialty of that area, or to seek work from or with their compatriots. On the contemporary persistence of this, "E 'Presvies' tis Ellenikis Eparkhias" ("The 'embassies' of the Greek provinces"), *Apodimos* (The emigrant) (November 1982): 45–46.

[9] "Manas Thigatera," "To Nisi tis Uranitsas," and "To Thavma tis Keserianis."

OLSON LIBRARY
NORTHERN MICHIGAN UNIVERSITY
MARQUETTE, MICHIGAN 49855

characters' dialogue—faithfully reproducing various rural dialects, the lisping speech of a young child, or the clipped pronunciation of the Macedonian Greeks. It is equally true that, though he lived most of his adult life in the capital of Athens, Papadiamandis wrote almost exclusively of village life on his native island of Skiatho, apparently at least, ignoring the rapidly changing political, social, and cultural context in which he lived. But, in fact, rather than ignoring that modern urban context, it is just that context that is the crucial if just-off-stage pretext for Papadiamandis's fiction. It is just that context without which the narrative constructions of Papadiamandis's fiction are impossible.

The insistent emphasis on Papadiamandis's choice of literary over colloquial language and of rural over urban subject matter, then, is scarcely a sufficient basis for a critical examination of his fiction. It is clearly inadequate for a consideration of the role Papadiamandis's novels and short stories play in the development of modern Greek fiction, in the creation of an emerging narrative of modern Greek culture, or in the literary-ideological response to a specific sociohistorical context. In fact, the linguistic and thematic formalism[10] that typifies so much of modern Greek literary criticism, and Greek cultural analysis in general, tells us as much, if not more, about the ideological underpinnings of modern Greek society and culture as it does about the specific literary text.

Thus, the ferocious battles between the purists and the demoticists—the former claiming to be the standard-bearers of the great classical Greek tradition, the latter claiming to be the democratic champions of the common Greek and his common language—that were the focus of much cultural, social, and political attention from shortly after the 1821–1829 War of Independence to, in a mitigated form, the present day, can be seen as a perhaps unwitting camouflage for the more essential struggle for economic, political, and cultural power between the autochthonous ruling class and the diaspora bourgeoisie.

[10] Nicos Mouzelis, *Modern Greece: Facets of Underdevelopment*, esp. chap. 8, "Modern Greek Formalism: Political and Cultural Aspects of Underdevelopment."

The former were the *kotzabasides*, the landed heads of groups of Greek villages (*eparchias* or provinces) under Ottoman rule, and the *fanariots*, the wealthy Greeks of the *fanar*—the headquarters of the Greek Orthodox Patriarch in Constantinople. And they were in direct conflict over control of the newly emerging nation with the European Greeks, the Greeks of the diaspora—those who had left Greece during centuries of Ottoman rule for the more profitable and secure life of Western Europe. It should come as no surprise that these two groups, the *kotzabasides* and the *fanariots* on the one hand and the European Greeks on the other, engaged in a struggle for power over so much else, should also find themselves on opposite sides of the language issue in the new Greek state. But it would be a mistake to assume that the contest between the purists and the demoticists, as emblematic as that struggle became in the eyes of the Greek people, was in any real sense a struggle between the ruling classes and the people. Neither the purists nor the demoticists, the indigenous ruling elite nor the diaspora bourgeoisie, represented the interests of the Greek people. Douglas Dakin in his *The Unification of Greece: 1770–1923*, though obviously valorizing the "civilizing mission" of the Europeanized diaspora bourgeoisie, acknowledges nonetheless the exclusion of the Greek people themselves from the power struggle between the two elites.

> The lower orders desired to improve their lot, to own and increase their holdings, to escape exactions. . . . Between rich and poor there was a latent conflict, but there was never a united front of the lower orders against the upper classes. The poor had no leaders of their own; they were not a uniform mass; and there were no intellectuals to tell them that they were. In so far as they had leaders they followed local worthies higher up the social scale to whom they were tied by the complex bonds of Greek society.[11]

The demotic movement, made up by and large of the diaspora European Greeks, represented itself as a modern and democratizing force in opposition to the traditionalism of the

[11] Douglas Dakin, *The Unification of Greece: 1770–1923*, 44.

purists. And this was not a claim without some basis. For the diaspora Greeks had been educated in and influenced by the ideas of the French revolution, the Enlightenment, and the liberal humanism of modern Europe. They saw, in the popular Greek overthrow of the Ottoman Empire, an opportunity to return to their homeland and establish a Europeanized bourgeois state. They could hardly be expected to have any interest in returning to Greece as subordinates of the *fanariots* and *kotsabasides* under essentially the same system of rule that had dominated Greece for the preceding four centuries. In the context of Greek history, the development of a liberal bourgeois state would, in principle at least, have been an improvement over the oligarchic domain of the *kotzabasides* and the *fanariots* who had flourished under Ottoman rule[12] and who had no intention of giving up their privileges—not to the newly returned diaspora Greeks and most especially not to the Greek people who had actually fought the war of independence. The indigenous Greek ruling class wanted "Ottoman society without the Turks"[13] even though, initially, they had not supported the war of independence in any manner, or at best, were ambivalent about it. Some of the *kotzabasides* and the *fanariots* had, in fact, actively opposed the struggle for independence, openly siding with the Ottoman rulers in the war. Needless to say, this did not particularly endear them in popular conception. But the presence or absence of popular support for the ruling elite under the Ottoman empire was of as little concern to that ruling elite as it became for the newly arrived European Greeks. The popular leaders of the Greek revolt were quickly jailed, exiled, or executed. The stage was then relatively clear for a power struggle between the indigenous and diaspora Greeks.

There was another dimension to the struggle between these two factions that is of particular significance in a consideration of the fiction of Papadiamandis. That is the extent to which the diaspora Greek bourgeoisie saw itself as, and no

---

[12] Mouzelis, *Modern Greece*, chap. 1, sec. 1, "The Ottoman Period."
[13] Dakin, *Unification of Greece*, 44.

doubt was, the herald of a new alliance between Greece and Western Europe, the harbinger of a modern European-style state. And so in one more way the diaspora bourgeoisie set itself apart from the *kotzabasides* and *fanariots* who were fervently opposed to the Westernization of the new Greek state. The traditional oligarchy wanted to preserve the structure of the Ottoman state minus the Turks, as Dakin so aptly acknowledges. And so that struggle in much of the underdeveloped world typically (if somewhat misleadingly) characterized as one between "East" and "West," between "tradition" and "modernization," was played out on the stage of the emerging Greek nation. It was a struggle that characterized the political, economic, cultural, and even linguistic makeup of the new Greece. And the foreground for much of this struggle was the nascent capital city.

That newly designated capital city, Athens, was virtually nonexistent before 1860—a pile of ruins and a few houses. But, as the site of the once great classical city so valorized by European neoclassical thought and its heirs, the new capital, Athens, was to rise from its classical ashes as "the cradle of Western civilization" and step forth into the light of a new and decidedly European day. Thus, the cities already existing within the boundaries of the Greece of 1820—indelibly marked by Turkish, foreign, or class influences—were not considered suitable as the site of the new capital. The decision to build the capital of the new state on the site of the ancient city of Athens was made by Ludwig I, the Bavarian regent whose son, Otho, was to become the first "Greek" king. German and French architects were quickly called upon to create plans for the new capital. And, inspired perhaps by a European fervor for their own version of the classical Greek past,[14]

[14] See Martin Bernal, "Black Athena Denied: The tyranny of Germany over Greece and the rejection of Afroasiatic roots of Europe: 1780–1980," *Comparative Criticism* 8 (1986): 3–69, or his *Black Athena: The Afroasiatic Roots of Classical Civilization* for a detailed exposé of the neoclassical European "re-formation" of the classical Greek past. In a gesture that suggests something of the hold of that "aryanized" neoclassical version of the classical Greek past, Otho, the first "Greek"/Bavarian king of Greece, called himself

they chose to build the new capital in the immediate environs of the ancient city—"the worst of all possible proposals."[15] In distinct antithesis to the larger and more developed, if also more "oriental," city of Salonika to the north,[16] Athens

> with its press and cafés had become the miniature Paris of the Levant. Here a growing body of literary men imitated in verse and prose, and *especially in prose*, the outstanding French writers. Here, too, as in Paris, there were political and literary cafés. . . . Here journalists and politicians talked; here they read their newspapers, of which in 1863 there were over twenty published in Athens, to say nothing of periodicals, pamphlets and occasional broadsheets.[17]

In spite of their marginal control over local Greek resources—that power was in the hands of the *kotzabasides*—the Europeanized Greeks succeeded in imposing their sociopolitical and cultural framework on the emerging state. For not only did the diaspora bourgeoisie possess the requisite administrative and legal skills for the functioning of a new state but, more important, they enjoyed the strong support of the Western powers.[18] Still, the Europeanized Greeks were able to achieve only a partial victory over the traditional oligarchy. From the beginning of the new Greek state there were persistent attempts to organize national life—political and cul-

---

"King of the Hellenes"—in reference to the far-flung ancient empire—rather than "King of Greece"—a rather more contained and nationally bounded title.

[15] E. K. Stasinopoulos, *Istoria ton Athinon* (History of Athens), 366.

[16] In fact, Salonika was outside of the boundaries of the newly formed Greek state. But the city of Salonika was nonetheless the antithesis, both literally and metaphorically, of everything that Athens was established and cultivated to be. Salonika, with its large foreign—Arab, Turkish, Armenian, Jewish—though Greek-speaking population, its strategic location in relation to the eastern Mediterranean and the Arab world, and its decidedly Eastern, as opposed to European, milieu was everything that Athens was *not* intended to be, everything against which Athens was conceived by her modern reformers.

[17] Dakin, *Unification of Greece*, 95. Emphasis added.

[18] The active intervention of France, England, and czarist Russia decisively shaped the outcome of the Greek Revolution.

tural—along liberal bourgeois lines. But a dominant capitalist economy, like an autochthonous bourgeoisie, was virtually nonexistent in Greece throughout the nineteenth century. The Europeanized Greeks managed to transport and impose a European-style political framework on the new Greek state. But, like much importation, the content, if not the very framework itself, was changed in the process. The struggle for power between the two elites persisted. The traditional oligarchy, recognizing necessity, acquiesced in the creation of a centralized state power and military and then proceeded to work their way into the state apparatus and wield it from within to promote their own interests. For the remainder of the nineteenth century, bourgeois democracy never really prevailed in Greece. Instead, clientelism distinguished Greek political and social life. The economy and social organization remained predominantly agrarian. There was not the typical exodus of peasants into the cities because of the almost total absence of any industry until well into the next century. Those who did migrate from the countryside to the capital were absorbed instead into Greece's mushrooming state bureaucracy, creating almost from the beginning a huge and unwieldly public sector.[19]

In this context, the development of the modern Greek novel is an interesting and essential component in the construct of the modern Greek nation-state and its culture. The novel as a presumably modern, foreign, and Western genre was introduced to Greece through the auspices of the diaspora bourgeoisie newly arrived in Greece and through the many, widely available translations of French, English, German, and Russian novels published not just in book format but serialized or excerpted in newspapers and periodicals. Papadiamandis himself was one of these translators. Parallel to this literary, liter-

---

[19] Mouzelis, *Modern Greece*, 17: "It has been calculated that towards the end of the period examined [1830–1880], the number of civil servants per 10,000 of the population was approximately seven times higher in Greece than in the United Kingdom." This is a staggering comparison if we remember that toward the end of this period, the United Kingdom was the dominant imperial power, with all the civil servants that such domination entailed.

ate, and Europeanizing cultural influence were the popular narratives, oral tales, songs, and epics of folk culture. Perhaps ironically, the first attempts at a modern, postindependent Greek novel disdained Greek narrative traditions and folk culture while utilizing the "folk" themselves as narrative material for the production of the novel. In the absence of an established bourgeois culture and its notions of the "coherent" and "orderly" individual and the "meaningful" details of that individual's life, the early modern Greek novel attempted an "orderly" narrative purveyance of the "disorderly" peasant and his or her village life.[20]

The question of whether or not there is a relation between the failure of Western-style social and political models to reproduce themselves in Greece and the (im)possibility that the European novel would take root and flourish in the same fashion as it had in the industrial, bourgeois societies of Western Europe is a tempting if potentially reductionist one. In his still timely *The Rise of the Novel*, Ian Watt makes clear the integral relationship between the ascendancy of the bourgeoisie as a class and of industrial capitalism as its dominant mode of production and the development and rise of the modern British novel. But then, what becomes of the modern novel when it is transplanted to a society in which there exists neither an indigenous, let alone ascendant, bourgeoisie nor a developed capitalist mode of production? There is no longer any doubt that the cultures of the "non-European" worlds, with economies and political systems underdeveloped by the expanding West in numerous ways, managed to produce and reproduce the modern novel in astonishingly manifold variations. In fact, weary purveyors of the Anglo-American and European canon of great texts are increasingly fascinated by the novel in other worlds. The contexts of the "rise of the novel" in England or France or Germany or even the more peripheral prerevolu-

---

[20] For example: *O Zetianos* (The beggar) by Andreas Karkavitsas, *O Patouhas* by Ioannis Kondylakis, *O Pyrgos tou Akropotamou* (The tower of Akropotamos) by Konstantinos Hatzopoulos, *E Zoe kai o Thanatos tou Karavela* (The life and death of Karavelas) by Konstantinos Theotokas, and, of course, Papadiamandis's *E Fonissa*.

tionary Russia are not quite the contexts of the "rise of the novel" elsewhere. Here, the domains of the sociohistorical and the cultural, and in this instance the specifically literary, are not proposed as parallel to one another, with the sociohistorical providing an "auxiliary" backdrop for the literary. Instead, the sociohistorical and the cultural interact, both in fact and symbolically or ideologically. So, while the rise of the novel in West Europe was tied to the rise of a particular ascendant and soon-to-be hegemonic class and to the dominant ideology of that class, the rise of the novel in a place like Greece was tied to its dependent and underdeveloped social, economic, and cultural position vis-à-vis an expanding and hegemonic West. It is this international as well as intranational interaction that is a crucial context for a discussion of the novel, the literary text, or the developments of a culture in general. For the moment, we will look at the fiction of Papadiamandis, and in particular his novel *E Fonissa* (The murderess),[21] as a literary and cultural participant in this interaction.

Papadiamandis wrote what is undoubtedly one of his finest works and one of the significant achievements of modern Greek prose—*The Murderess*—in 1903–1904 for serial publication in the Athenian periodical *Panathinea*. Khadoula, the character on whom the novel focuses, is the village herbalist, an impoverished grandmother, a weary mother of three daughters and of four sons—all but one of whom have left Greece to find work in Europe or America—and the widow of John the Frank (Frangoyiannou).[22] Khadoula, whose mother

---

[21] Alexandros Papadiamandis, *E Fonissa* (The murderess), in *Ta Apanda* (The collected works), 417–520. Unless otherwise noted, all translations are my own. For an English translation of *E Fonissa*: Alexandros Papadiamandis, *The Murderess*, trans. Peter Levi (London: Writers and Readers, 1983). See also Elizabeth Constantinides's translation of selected short stories by Papadiamandis, *Tales from a Greek Island* (Baltimore: John Hopkins, 1987).

[22] The *frangos*—Frank—of Frangoyiannos' name refers not just to the "west–Germanic peoples who conquered the Roman Empire in the 3rd century AD," as it does in the standard English definition, but to Europeans, Westerners in general, and/or to the Western or Roman Catholic Church. So, if we are to attach any significance to the literal meaning of the names of Papadiamandis's characters, Khadoula Frangoyiannou's fate is even linguis-

was accused of being a witch, is a devout adherent of Christianity but of a Christianity heavily imbued with paganism. And she is, of course, the murderess of the title. The novel opens with a third-person description of Khadoula half asleep at the cradle of her newborn and sickly granddaughter while her daughter, the mother of the sick child, dozes fitfully in the next room. Several of the images that dominate the novel are already apparent in the opening lines:

The literal and metaphoric darkness of poverty:

> The small hanging lamp flickered under the mantelpiece. It cast shadows instead of light on the room's few pieces of wretched furniture, which appeared cleaner and more acceptable by night. (417)

Frangoyiannou's life of servitude and hardship as a woman:

> Aunt Khadoula, also called Yiannou the Frank, wasn't sleeping; she was sacrificing her sleep at the cradle of her sick granddaughter. . . . Thinking back over the whole of her life, she realized that she had done nothing but serve others. When she was a child, she waited on her parents. When she married, she was a slave to her husband—and yet, because of her character and his weakness, she was at the same time his guardian; when she bore children, she became their slave; when her children bore children, she became once more the servant of her grandchildren. (417)

> The old woman sang a lullaby to the infant; she could as well have chanted "her songs of suffering" over the baby's cradle. (418)

And an ironic, almost ascerbic, narrative stance toward the characters that people the text:

> Khadoula, known as the Frank, or Frangoyiannou, was a woman of about sixty, well-built, with clear cut features, a mas-

---

tically linked to the foreigners, the Europeans, of her husband's surname. It will, in fact, be "a gendarme in Frankish dress" who pursues Frangoyiannou to her watery death at the novel's end.

culine temperament, and a faint moustache on her upper lip. (417)

Amersa [Frangoyiannou's second daughter] was unmarried, already an old maid, but hard-working and known for her ability as a weaver. She was dark, tall, mannish—her dowry, and trousseau and embroidery, all of which she'd made herself, had been locked away for years in a big, dowdy chest—food for worms and moths. (422)

Dadis [Frangoyiannou's son-in-law] appeared at the door of the chilly room. He was broad-chested, with a graceless, clumsy body—a "hick", as his mother-in-law referred to him—and virtually beardless. (423)

There is no romanticized depiction of idyllic village life here. There is nothing of the pastoral in the dim, shabby cottage of Frangoyiannou's daughter and son-in-law; in the sickly girl-child who has kept the old woman awake at the side of her cradle for eleven cold, wintry nights; in the poverty and illness of both mother and child that make of the festivities and feasting typically surrounding the birth of a new child ("even a girl-child") an ironic joke; in the rough and clumsy son-in-law whose capture for her eldest daughter had demanded all of Frangoyiannou's skills at finagling; in the old woman's grim memories of her past; or in the providence of a God who apparently bedevils even the most devout of His flock. And so it is not totally unexpected that after five chapters of alternating between memories of a desolate past and the reality of an equally desolate present, Frangoyiannou kills the newborn girl who is her grandchild and namesake. The newborn Khadoula[23] has no future, literally or metaphorically; she is doomed. And neither does her grandmother. The old woman has committed a double murder with the suffoca-

[23] There is no small irony in the name that the old woman and the newborn girl-child share. "Khadoula" recalls the vernacular "khadi"—caress. Needless to say, the "caresses" the newborn child receives at the hands of her grandmother are deadly. And the old woman herself could not have either received or bestowed many caresses in her lifetime, as her memories of her childhood illustrate.

tion of the infant. It is not only that Frangoyiannou will be killed in the end as retribution for her actions. And, it is a testament to Papadiamandis's consummate skill in portraying the old woman that one hesitates to call her actions "crimes." She has cut herself off from, is dead to, the sources of sustenance on which her life is predicated. Her world is silent.[24]

> The dimly lit room was overcome with a complete and utter stillness after the infant's final wailing cough was so suddenly cut short. Frangoyiannou, her face bent down and her forehead resting on her two hands, had stopped thinking. It seemed to her that she had stopped living as well. (453)

In something of an overdetermining narrative gesture, not only is the room deathly still, but it is ominously dark—"the small lamp in front of the icons had long since gone out and the shapes of the saints were scarcely visible" (453). In spite of Amersa's prophetic dream that the baby died and that Frangoyiannou's hands as she dressed the tiny corpse turned black, in spite of the black marks on the newborn's throat, in spite of the baby's official examination by a pompous young medical student doubling as village coroner, Frangoyiannou is not openly suspected of her granddaughter's murder. Only Delkharo, the baby's mother, and Amersa, Frangoyiannou's second daughter, have any inkling of what the old woman has done. But they say nothing.

It is not until two chapters later that Delkharo learns of her infant daughter's death, though in chronological time no more than a few minutes have passed since the old woman smothered the child. In the interim chapter, Amersa, through the omniscient narrator, recalls her own stabbing at the hands of her brother, his flight from the village to work as a ship's hand, his murder of a fellow shipmate, Frangoyiannou's frantic but fruitless attempts to bribe the judge and jurors, and the subsequent sentencing of the young murderer to twenty years in Khalkida prison. For the moralistic, and perhaps for the

[24] The pretext of silence here is an interesting contrast to that of Natsume Sōseki's *Kusamakura* or *Kokoro*. See chap. 4.

fatalistic, this provides a clear justification for Frangoyiannou's actions. She is the mother of a murderer. Is it any wonder that she herself commits murder as well?

There is an irony in the simplistic determinism that therefore sees Frangoyiannou as "a force of evil" with a "predisposition to murder."[25] The greater part of the novel is occupied with making Frangoyiannou's reasoning and actions plausible and comprehensible, if not actually evoking sympathy for them. The official valorization of Papadiamandis's fiction by the conservative Greek literary establishment is then rather amusing—to institutionalize and designate as required reading in Greek primary and high schools the works of a writer who elicits understanding of, perhaps even sympathy for, a crazy old woman who murders girl children. And then, why, even on the face of things, does she murder girl children exclusively? Because they live in a grossly unequal patriarchial society that deems them, especially when they are of the "multitudinous females of the poor classes," little more than slaves. Because, according to Frangoyiannou's vision of things, the lives of "girl children of this class are a torment [to themselves] and to their families" (447).

In fact, it is not only the proliferation of girl children among the poor that provokes Papadiamandis's ironic dismay but the abundant production of children at all. In the short story, "*Mavromandilou*" (1891), the childlessness of the heroine is a blessing—"Fortunately, she hadn't borne any children of her own." And in "*Farmakolitria*" (1900), when a boy child is born in the neighborhood, one of the men in the story exclaims, "Rejoice all of you. Another beast of burden has come into the world." This scarcely seems a glorification of Greek peasant life and traditions. Papadiamandis's fiction suggests the necessity of radical social change rather than the defense and preservation of Greek tradition. Nonetheless, the official reading in Greece of Papadiamandis has been as the simple,

[25] Apostolos Sahinis, *To Neoelleniko Mythistorema* (The modern Greek novel), 162.

devout, austere preserver of an idyllic, premodern Greek tradition.

Here it is useful to trace both what Papadiamandis's text, is in opposition to and what it is in support of. Clearly, the refusal of, the opposition to, some unacceptable sociohistorical and cultural context implies an attempt, however unstable and provisional, to resolve that same unacceptable context. In *The Murderess*, the textual rejection of the Western, European, liberal bourgeois scheme for Greece is accompanied by the construction of an impossible alternative in what is presumably the valorization of the semifeudal, Eastern, Orthodox society of Skiatho. The clear impossibility of such a solution to the challenges facing the traditionalist stance is nowhere more obvious than in the structure of the novel *The Murderess* and in the very character of Frangoyiannou herself. That this old woman, who takes it upon herself to murder girl children to save them and their parents from a life of misery and poverty, must be done away with at the novel's end goes without saying. (There would be an interesting problem of narrative closure if this were not the case.) This necessity becomes increasingly clear two or three chapters into the novel. But between the opening descriptions of the poverty and weariness, both past and present, that induce the old woman's "mental lapse" and her watery death—caught between the rising tide, that makes impossible her search for refuge and forgiveness in a small chapel, and the approaching policemen and villagers—we see the oppression and hardship of Greek peasant life that makes Frangoyiannou's actions, if not laudable, at least eminently comprehensible. *The Murderess* opens in a grim and foreboding present and moves between that moment and a past that is little better. From the moment that Frangoyiannou strangles her first victim, her own grandchild, there is no future for the way of life that she embodies. Beset from within by hardship and poverty and from without by the encroaching foreignization of Greek society, the protracted present of Frangoyiannou and her fellow villagers can only be altered by radical change. And, in a way, Frangoyiannou does effect a "radical change"; but it is an obviously unacceptable one. Perhaps, though, the issue is not really the literal viability of the radical change that Frangoyiannou attempts, but the recognition that a radical change is in fact necessary. In spite of the persistence and arguable convenience of formulating the situation described in *The Murderess* as one of confrontation between tradition and modernization, between memories of the past and designs for the future, it might be more useful to consider the opposition differently—as rather that between tradition and revolution, between social and cultural nostalgia and the need for a radical restructuring of the narrative present. In fact, it might not be modernization that is opposed here but the specific structure and definition of that modernization.[26] In Papadiamandis's fiction, and this novel in particular, there is little doubt of the necessity for an elemental change in the scheme of things. But there is a distinct textual reticence both about the character of that change and about the scheme of things that this change will encompass. For *The Murderess*, the divine scheme of things is decidedly not subject to alteration. That is Frangoyiannou's hubris—to attempt to change things in the name of God, to even assume that she might have any inkling of the will of God, of the divine scheme of things.

> And Christ said, as Frangoyiannou had heard her confessor explain, that whoever loves his soul will lose it and whoever hates his soul will preserve it in eternal life. Didn't it follow then that if people weren't blind they would help the plague that strikes with the wings of angels instead of asking for deliverance.
>
> What else can one do for the poor? The greatest kindness one could render them would be to have some 'barren weed' to give them all—God forgive me for saying it.
>
> Frangoyiannou's mind actually began to slip. She had lost her

---

[26] John Berger, "Historical Afterword," in *Pig Earth*, 208–10. Berger suggests that it is not modernization or change per se that the peasant opposes. After all, change might well benefit the peasant's way of life. It is rather a specific definition of modernization that the peasant opposes—one typically imposed from the outside, from the city, and one that frequently entails the end of peasant life rather than its improvement.

reason at last. It was only natural since she had exalted herself
to the consideration of higher matters. (446–47)

So much for changing the divine scheme of things. But this
position is hardly surprising at a time when the major alternative to the secular, Europeanizing trend of modernization
was seen as embodied by the traditional oligarchy and the *fanariots* whose ties to the Orthodox church were direct and intimate. Nor is it surprising for the son of a devout, village
priest, transplanted though he may have been to the capital
city, to seek refuge in the "unknowable" will of God. Clearly
neither the biographical Papadiamandis nor his fiction are exempt from historical and social exigencies. Papadiamandis's
short story "The Teacher" can scarcely camouflage in its fiction what would appear to be the distinct manifesto of its author.

> The ecclesiatic platform—the pulpit—is austere, exclusive and
> authentic. Of that only I speak. It is presumed that whatever is
> said, is not data [information], but conclusive, unquestionable,
> exemplary, dogma. . . . Piety should not be prostituted by
> worldly lay people with their twisted moustaches and their
> starched collars. What innovations, what foreign imitation and
> nonsense is this? Are we Protestants here? ("*O Didakhos*"
> [1906])

It is perhaps not as paradoxical as it might at first seem that
this conservative, traditionalist view can at the same time offer
a trenchant indictment of the oppressive conditions generated
by its own bases of power and of the imminent encroachment
of bourgeois European hegemony. But the formalistic denunciation of Papadiamandis for his use of language, the insistence on the choice of language as the measure of literary and
political worth, has precluded much reasonable critical commentary on Papadiamandis's fiction. That Papadiamandis
writes about the peasantry in a language that they could
hardly understand, that he appropriates folktales and
traditions to flesh out the alien form of the novel, or even that
his work can be said to participate in the distinction between

popular and elite art—these observations are true enough. But these are not the definitive characteristics of Papadiamandis's fiction. One of its most remarkable features is rather its ability to evoke the disarticulation of modern Greek society, and perhaps of the modern Greek novel, in an attempt to solve the conflicts that just such social and cultural disarticulation engenders.

One of Papadiamandis's most frequently quoted and most misconstrued statements is from the novel *The Gypsy Girl* and is on the inescapability of the class into which one is born and, therefore, the futility of any attempt to change things.[27] Yet, almost in spite of itself, Papadiamandis's fiction reveals less a romanticization of the peasantry than the urgent need for change in their condition. And if Frangoyiannou demonstrates the impossibility of changing, or even understanding, the divine scheme of things, her fate does not necessarily preclude change in that scheme that is not immediately within the realm of the divine. There are, for example, only two households in the village of Skiatho that are not dominated by darkness, poverty and hardship. One is the house of Anagnostis Benidis, "in his time, the most important personage in the area. He had been an elder of his province before the War of Independence [under Ottoman Rule] a deputy in the first Assembly of Troizin, Pronias, Argos etc. and mayor before the Constitution was enacted. Afterwards, he was a high-ranking bureaucrat in many places" (480). The other is the house of Alexandros Rosmais, a *kotzabasis* and the present head or elder of the province. It is in the courtyard of Rosmais's estate, washing his family's clothes with her younger daughter, that Frangoyiannou is witness to the accidental drowning of a young neighborhood girl. Ironically, it is with this young girl's death—a drowning of which Frangoyiannou is not guilty—that the village begins to suspect her of murder. The Rosmais

---

[27] "She must remain in the class into which she was born, however humble and impoverished it might appear, for it is better to choose an eternity of honorable poverty than the disgrace and conceit of decadence and luxury." Or, in a letter written ten years earlier to his father: "We should remain in honorable poverty so that God can help us."

garden stands in sharp contrast to the dimly lit, impoverished
surroundings of Frangoyiannou and her fellow villagers. It is
a veritable paradise: "Near the well, [where] a huge, blossom-
ing mulberry tree extended its great, dark green branches, like
a blessing in the form of a cross, bestowing its cross-like visage
upon the worthy and unworthy, the small garden enclosed by
a picket fence [where] multicolored and fragrant blossoms un-
furled in sweet dew, a feast for the eyes of all God's creatures"
(469).

Here Papadiamandis's sentences are long, complex, full of
modifying clauses—linguistic plenitude a marker perhaps for
natural plenitude of the benign landscape. The courtyard is
bathed in sunlight, open, airy, in bloom. An "immense
wooden olive press that resembled drawings of Noah's Ark,"
an oven, and a masonry tank for pressing grapes all bespeak
of wealth and power. There are no "rotting, worm-eaten and
ill fitting windows" (499). Nor does this house resemble that
of Lyringos the shepherd—"a hut of once white stucco that
appeared none too prosperous or clean from the outside and
looked as though it hadn't been white-washed for many
years" (461–62). Whether or not Papadiamandis intended
this disparity to be justifiable is not really the issue here. For,
if there is any attempt at justification for the wealth and comfort of the *kotzabasides* in the face of the impoverished misery
of the peasants, the text itself belies the effort. There is an implicit indictment of the circumstances that compel Frangoyiannou's actions and that create the hardship and inequality
that she confronts. But there is, as well, a textual ambivalence
in the representation of the island peasantry. They are the
source and basis of the practice of the "imported" genre of the
novel. At the same time, they encompass a way of life from
which the biographical author has had to escape. If, in his
prose, Papadiamandis attempts to construct a refuge in the
peasant tradition from the impingement of the new and the
foreign, in reality Papadiamandis had to have recognized the
impossibility of the life's work he had chosen—writing fiction—in that same peasant setting. His persistent reluctance
to return to Skiatho from Athens can be little other than this

recognition, to which his letters to his parents and sisters in *Ta Grammata* attest.

For the villagers and peasants of Skiatho in *The Murderess*, the new centralized Greek government and its officials were little, if any, improvement over the previous Ottoman rulers and their administration. The change from foreign, infidel rule to rule by fellow Greeks certainly did not alter a great deal in the day-to-day lives of the peasants. If there is an implicit opposition in Papadiamandis's text between the privilege of the traditional landed gentry and the peasantry, there is as well an underlying conflict between the villagers and *any* outside power—Greek or foreign. It is the imposition of taxation on the islanders by Sultan Mahmout that brings an end to the raids of the Greek *klefts* (literally "thieves" but more properly bands of mountain guerillas) and "by the grace of God, bestows peace on the island. . . . The raids were replaced by taxation, and from then on, the fortunate people continue to work for the ravenous, central belly that 'hath not ears' " (420).

The officials of the postrevolutionary Greek government fare little better than their Ottoman counterparts in Papadiamandis's textual rendering of them. The pretentious young medical student who signs the death certificate of Frangoyiannou's granddaughter; the court clerk in *fustanelles*; the clerk of the Harbor Authority in baggy breeches; an officer of Treasury Division N. who was an old bachelor; a dandified sergeant with "a slender waist" and "a hooked moustache"; a customs officer with an "income three times his salary"; "two or three agents of foreign business firms" who attempt to seduce young village women; "the magistrate in conjunction with the assistant judge from the police department who always said 'yes' to every declaration of that inspired functionary of justice and the sergeant who never said 'no' " to the magistrate"; and the gendarmes, "those brilliant luminaries" who had pursued and captured Frangoyiannou's son and who were close on the trail of the old woman herself—all of these officials are foreign to Skiatho, for all that they are nationally and ethnically Greeks. It is in the representation of these functionaries of the state that the textual irony is most clear. They are almost ridiculously out of place on the island. And the villagers offer little help to them, stubbornly resisting and obstructing them in their pursuit of Frangoyiannou, more from deeply ingrained distrust and suspicion than from any particular loyalty to the old woman. Frangoyiannou, at the close of the novel, calculates aloud as she spies a local man with the two gendarmes pursuing her,

> if one of the men was a peasant from her parts . . . it could mean that he was taking part in the chase only drudgery forced upon him and that he would perhaps slow down the gendarmes. It was not altogether improbable that he might even feel a sneaking sympathy for the unfortunate old fugitive, the woman they were pursuing who was fleeing over the rocks on bleeding feet, the unfortunate woman, about whose guilt he was not even certain. (517)

If the *kotzabasides* live in comfort and plenty in the midst of misery, these officials of the modern Greek state are emissaries of the new quasi-bourgeois order that the text postulates as an even more primary threat to the village, its peasants and their way of life.

The ambivalent narrative position of *The Murderess* toward the class conflicts it represents, however inadvertently, is difficult to avoid. This in spite of the biographical Papadiamandis's pledge of alliance and sympathy with the *kotzabasides* and with "traditional" village life and customs. That textual ambivalence gestures to an extratextual ambivalence as well. To privilege a text as an individual, authorial utterance cannot obscure the extent to which that same text is also a participant in broader, social discourse(s). And the positions occupied by the same text are not inevitably coterminous; they may well be contradictory. For example, much is made by Papadiamandis's critics of his reliance on the manners and customs of Skiatho in his fiction.[28] And so, that fiction, with few

---

[28] Alexandros Papadiamandis, *Autobiographoumenos* (Autobiographical writings), 21: "I simply write of the memories and impressions of my childhood."

exceptions, is classified as "ethographic." Papadiamandis's significance in the Greek literary tradition is something like that of a grudgingly admirable if occasionally verbose and difficult recorder of a "vanishing" society. But there is little contradiction noted between Papadiamandis's authorial reliance on a traditional isolated rural island life and his almost uninterrupted residence in an Athens that was established and cultivated as virtually the precise antithesis of everything of which Papadiamandis wrote. His nostalgic longing for and detailed reminiscences of the island life of Skiatho do not preclude his social and cultural immersion in a milieu that consciously turned away from indigenous Greek traditions and a history of cultural alignment with the Mediterranean and the East for a most deliberate emulation of West European social, political, and cultural models. In fact, a crucially absent element in virtually all of Papadiamandis's fiction is the European- and particularily Parisian-inspired Athens.[29] And by extension, the absence of Athens suggests as well the absent center of the imperial city of Paris itself. With few exceptions, Papadiamandis does not mention the European capitals, nor even the Greek capital of Athens in which he lived most of his life. Yet his fiction is an (unspoken) invocation against the secular, Western, bourgeois way of life that those cities, and of course Athens in particular, represent. The capital city of Athens and the foreign metropolis to which Athens is linked are there on the shadowy fringes of Papadiamandis's fiction. They are the strange places that swallow up so many young Greek men. Frangoyiannou's sons have all immigrated to America, never to be heard from again. Those cities stand for a huge and unknown continent that is almost beyond the reach of imagination and language. The old illiterate villager of "Letter to America" comes regularly to ask the narrator to write a letter to his long-departed son who is somewhere in America—North America, South America, or Central America, the

[29] See Stasinopoulos, *Istoria ton Athenon,* for an unwitting account of the construction of the dependent periphery and later semiperiphery in the image of the core.

old man is not sure. But he is convinced that since the narrator can write, surely he is capable of locating the old man's son. The magical power of inscription should surely be able to penetrate the far reaches of the center. Perhaps the old illiterate villager's fanciful conception of the power of language is not quite so far as it might seem from what informs Papadiamandis's fiction.

The Murderess presents a society that, traditional and precapitalist, has nonetheless indubitably come into contact with the outside—that is, modern, non-Greek—world. Frangoyiannou's three sons have left the island of Skiatho, and Greece as well, in search of work that they are unable to find in their own country. This export of labor to the developed countries has been a dominant facet of modern Greek life and economy since (and even before) the early nineteenth century. That it remains so today is evident in *The Double Book*, by Dimitris Hatzis, discussed in chapter 5. This aspect of modern Greek life, of modern Greek underdevelopment, this essential point of contact with the modern outside world, is already apparent in much of Papadiamandis's fiction and in *The Murderess* in particular. There is no attempt to represent the life of the island peasant as timeless and idyllic. *The Murderess* is, instead, a narrative of a society in sometimes violent transition, disrupted by an urban, modernizing movement that remains at the periphery of the novel but that, in its literal absence, is nonetheless metaphorically omnipresent.

Papadiamandis's prose reveals not the descriptive conservation of customs and manners, but rather the sometimes violent confrontation of the peasant way of life with change, with history. To this end, Papadiamandis does not send his island peasants and shepherds to the capital city as in *The Lamp of Umm Hāshim* by the Egyptian writer Yahyā Haqqī, discussed in chapter 3. Papadiamandis's fiction leaves the villagers there where most of them actually were at the time—in the village. The dilemma of a traditional way of life in conflict with the movement of history does not need to be set on the stage of a modern city to be apparent. Whatever the overt authorial reason that Papadiamandis focused on the island life of Skiatho, the textual focus of that fiction reveals a society and a way of life in transition. The transitional nature of peasant society in *E Fonissa* is evident in the ambivalence of that text's peasants, and of the text itself, to their own way of life and to the possibility of change in that way of life. It is an ambivalence that is unavailable in what is frequently the romanticized representation of tradition and the peasantry in modern Greek fiction. And in those representations, though the peasant is typically valorized as the repository of some notion of "national authenticity," she is simultaneously a member of a more or less frightening and unsavory mass of people.

To write about the peasant way of life is not by definition to write for the peasants, or for those peasants who can read. *E Fonissa*, with its peculiar and difficult blend of demotic, Byzantine, and purist Greek is ample evidence of this. But if the demoticists of Papadiamandis's day wrote in a language that was arguably not inaccessible to the literate Greek peasant, the subject matter of their texts was an esoteric mystery. The villager, peasant or even worker of the early twentieth century would scarcely have recognized himself in the fiction of Xenopoulos or Theotokas.[30] Writers such as these were compelled to situate their fictions in a more distant past to afford their pastoral perspective. Distinctly nonpastoral, Papadiamandis's fiction reveals the poverty, superstition, and hardship of the Greek peasant way of life as well as their strong bonds with one another, their "simple" goodness, patience, and perserverance.[31] But there remains a certain omi-

---

[30] A notable exception is the fiction of the demoticist Demosthenis Boutiras. Twenty years Papadiamandis's junior, he wrote of life in Athens among the workers and newly arrived peasants with masterful simplicity. He can be seen, to some extent, as a forerunner of the contemporary Greek novelist, Dimitris Hatzis, whose work is examined in chap. 5.

[31] Berger, *Pig Earth*, 10. Berger's description of the "peasant character," of what is presumably peasant simplicity, is an appropriate caveat here: "In a village the difference between what is known about a person and what is unknown is slight. There may be a number of well-guarded secrets but, in general, deceit is rare because impossible. The village's knowledge of an individual is not much less than god's—though its judgement may be different. . . . [the peasant] is not 'simple' or more honest or without guile, it is simply that

nous quality to the scenario that Papadiamandis's fiction presents. If the reference to the traditional peasant way of life is a utopic gesture in the face of an unacceptable sociohistorical dilemma,[32] the utopia is an insistently negative one. It is a utopia—a most literal no place—that exposes the qualification of its own utopic attempt.

In *The Murderess*, the traditionalist refuge in the face of an unacceptable Western-defined modernization is clearly untenable. Frangoyiannou is, after all, a murderess. The society in which she lives is one dominated not by rustic simplicity and plenitude but by hunger, fear, superstition, and poverty. Her fellow villagers are not really any better off than Frangoyiannou herself; they've just not reached the point of desperation and weariness that she has. The sickly wife of Perivolas the gardener, with her "five or six daughters—I don't know if any of them's died"; Lyringos the shepherd and his wife with three daughters in five years, all three of them "come into the world to live a life of suffering and misery"; the wife of Kambanakhmakis the goatherd, struck dumb with nervous shock and unable to care for her small children; Frangoyiannou's own children—one in jail for murder, three sons far away in search of work, two unmarried daughters, and the third married to a lout—the life of Papadiamandis's peasants is a constant struggle for survival, a struggle that is almost unbearably grim.

Certainly Papadiamandis's fiction displays a distinct ambivalence in its depiction of peasant society. Regardless of the fact that he was the son of the village priest and so somewhat better off than his fellow villagers, life on Skiatho, for all that Papadiamandis presumably sees it as some sort of refuge from the Athens "of plutocrats and slaves," was at least constricting. Papadiamandis was none too eager to return to the bosom of his family or to the traditional confines of his village. In his occasional overemphasis on the poverty, superstition, and fear of the peasants' life; in his sometimes essentialist physical de-

---

the space between what is unknown about a person and what is generally known—and this is the space for all performance—is too small."
[32] Frederic Jameson, *The Political Unconscious*, 289.

scription of them, in his apparent consignment of them to an unalterable life of misery, Papadiamandis's text betrays a more complex and equivocal authorial stance toward its subject matter than Papadiamandis himself might have been willing to admit. And so perhaps it is not quite so coincidental that the text also betrays the instability of the peasant way of life, its susceptibility to, even its own ability to foment, change—a far more elemental and potentially radical change than the *kotzabasides*, the diaspora bourgeoisie, or even Papadiamandis himself would care to imagine. And the danger of the peasantry escaping the bounds of its role as the repository of national tradition, or escaping the bounds of bourgeois nationalism altogether, is not unfounded, in the text or outside of it. The change from Ottoman to Greek rule did not concern the early-nineteenth-century peasantry as much as the desire for concrete improvements in their way of life. If their lot remained a miserable one, it made little difference to them whether the state was Ottoman, Greek, or Bavarian for that matter. The popular leaders of the War of Independence were quickly dispensed with at the arrival of the diaspora Greeks and the assimilation of the traditional autochthonous oligarchy into the new state administration. The development of a vehement and narrow nationalism served no one quite so well as the new ruling elites, whether they had only just arrived from Europe or whether they were the indigenous landed gentry.[33] It is perhaps a further symptom of the sociopolitical disarticulation of the new Greek state that so much of this crucial (and essentially class) conflict was subsumed under the language issue or the clientelism of the intraruling class struggle for power. And it is not surprising that these issues signifi-

[33] See Ellis Goldberg, "Bases of Traditional Reaction: A Look at the Muslim Brothers," *Peuples Mediterraneens* 14 (1981) in which he suggests, in a discussion of the development of the trade union movement in early-twentieth-century Egypt, that the specific dimensions of nationalism in third world or underdeveloped countries are shaped at least in part by the desire of the indigenous ruling elites to maintain their internal sociopolitical control and to act as brokers for the hegemonic foreign powers. This suggestion does not seem at all incongruous with the situation of the developing modern Greek state.

cantly marked the practice of the novel as well. The choice of language, the choice of audience, the subject matter of the novel, even narrative voice, were inextricably bound to this larger sociopolitical context. Papadiamandis's *E Fonissa* clearly seems an attempt to deal with these issues. An examination of the specific solution(s) of *E Fonissa* makes apparent just how provisional that solution is. If the grimness of village life is overemphasized, so is the punishment and isolation of Frangoyiannou. The very landscape of the island itself, the earth to which the peasant is presumably inexorably linked, turns against her. There in the secret hollows in which her mother hid from the *klefts* after working magic against them, Frangoyiannou finds herself hiding from the gendarmes. But the earth offers Frangoyiannou no protection; it rejects her.

> The rocks danced demonically in the night. They arose as if alive in pursuit of Frangoyiannou and pelted her as if hurled by invisible avenging hands. (512)

> She stepped on the pile of rocks at the edge of the chasm. Then they would begin to move as if in anger. (513)

Even the all-encompassing solace and protection of the Church and its ministers appear to have failed the old woman. For when Frangoyiannou encounters Father Yosephat at a mountain spring, the spiritual consolation he offers to the troubled old woman is almost laughable. She tells him of her "torments and sufferings," of her wish to "escape from this world," and the kindly but ineffectual old monk responds with ready-made lines from the Psalms that Frangoyiannou can neither understand nor relate to her spiritual condition. The old monk does slightly better in terms of physical aid, for he offers Frangoyiannou some lettuce and peas from his garden. This is a sustenance that is at least of concrete use.

Finally, at the close of the novel, Frangoyiannou is unable to reach the small chapel toward which she is struggling so that she might confess her sins. Does she fail to reach the chapel because her sins are so great or because the chapel and its presumably devout priest can offer her no solace or forgiveness? Frangoyiannou, in her attempt to alter an untenable situation, has violated both worldly and divine law. The text will allow her only a fleeting thought of escape on a passing boat bound for the mainland. But Frangoyiannou cannot go free. Her tiny revolt against the established order of things must be punished.

It is remarkable that, at the conclusion of the novel as well as at various moments throughout the text, the delineation of the third-person narrator is hardly distinct. At times the narrator's commentary merges with the tortured wanderings of Frangoyiannou's mind. At other moments in the novel, the narrator assumes a position of objective observation, the familiar third-person voice. And, occasionally, the narrator openly displays a narrative equivocation with phrases such as, "If she were there, Amersa might have said . . ." or, "She could have thought to herself at that moment that . . ." Did or did not Amersa say something? Did she think what follows or is it the speculation of the narrator? What and who is this narrator who has trouble maintaining his position as distinct from his characters? Unlike Yahyā Haqqī's *Qindīl Umm Hāshim*, *E Fonissa* is not framed by the convention of a first-person narrator who attempts to assume the role of the traditional storyteller. The narrative voice of *E Fonissa* is that of the third-person, but it is a third person voice that is distinctly provisional and unstable. The text lapses into authorial speculation of what a character might have said if she were there or what she might have thought if she knew. It is interpolated by what is clearly authorial approval or denunciation of the characters' actions or the circumstances that affect their lives. The wandering thoughts of the ostracized and outcast old fugitive, Khadoula, seep into and stain the third-person narrative until, at times, it verges on the first person. And too, the text of *E Fonissa* is intercalated with bits of information and explanation reminiscent of the traditional Greek folktale or story that suggest Walter Benjamin's definition of the storyteller—the origins of place names, tales connected with natural sites, explanations of peasant proverbs, sayings, and customs.

Every real story . . . contains, openly or covertly, something useful. The usefulness may, in one case, consist in a moral; in another, in some practical advice; in a third, in a proverb or
maxim. In every case the storyteller is a man who has counsel
for his readers.[34]

Not so unlike the counsel of Homer's *Odyssey*, a copy of
which Papadiamandis was never without, or of that other
Greek travelogue, *The Expedition of the Argonauts*, Papadiamandis's text provides signposts and explains origins for what
was as far away in his time as Kolkhis or the island of Phaiacia
were to a much earlier audience. To a people only too ready
to ignore, if not to altogether abandon, a culture and way of
life that were presumably corrupted, oriental, and backward;
to an intellectual and political elite engaged in a tug-of-war
that they formulated as a choice between a glorious classical
past that needed to be recaptured and a beckoning, modern
future that must necessarily be built on the European model,
E Fonissa elicits the far away—the present. It is in its manipulation of narrative voice, as well as in its insistence on retelling tales about the meaning of place names or the superstitions
and myths that surround certain parts of the island landscape,
or in the morals and proverbs slipped into the dialogue, that
Papadiamandis's text reveals a relationship to the folktale and
story that is not yet totally effaced. *E Fonissa* is witness to yet
another transitional moment, another opposition, in the situation of modern Greek fiction—the subsumption of the more
properly communal tale or story into the privatization of the
novel and the domination of oral, or at least colloquial, "experience" by written and literary "information."[35] In a similar
fashion, the folk tradition, the peasant experience, is appropriated to and dominated by the genre of the modern novel,
foreign in both cultural and class origin. From this perspective, what is presumably Papadiamandis's rejection of all
things Western, foreign, and secular situates itself in all its

---

[34] Walter Benjamin, "The Storyteller," in *Illuminations*, 86.
[35] Benjamin, "The Storyteller," 83–109, for his distinction between the
novel and the tale.

complexity. Papadiamandis, for example, cannot quite be the vehement enemy of all things "Frankish," as his critics have suggested. His own use of the modern novel form would then have to be considered a telling self-indictment.

The conflicts engendered by the contradictory sympathies of *E Fonissa*, by the problems it raises and the textual resolutions it proffers, mark both the content and structure of the text. On the one hand is the peasantry, characterized in the extreme by Frangoyiannou, with their misery and poverty, their recourse to anti-Christian or at least pre-Christian magic, their fertility—all these signs for their potential, if suppressed, power. In somewhat passive but nonetheless concrete opposition to the peasantry is the oligarchy of the traditional large landowners, the established social and political power represented by Rosmais and Benidis. It is alignment with this class of powerful landowners that the Papadiamandis the biographical author professes for himself and claims for his texts. But it is a projected extratextual alignment indelibly marked and compromised by Papadiamandis's textual representations of the peasant way of life. *The Murderess* is simultaneously drawn to, informed by, and fearful of the suppressed or unarticulated power that Frangoyiannou represents. A third position opposed to both of these two is that of the diaspora bourgeoisie. In contrast to the oligarchy, they are the ascendant political power and without the traditional ties of the former to the immediate past of Ottoman rule and its forms of dominance. The diaspora bourgeoisie are perceived by the peasants, however, as an equal, if not greater, opponent—foreign, not-really-Greek and as oppressive as Ottoman or traditional oligarchic rulers. The textual scorn for the diaspora bourgeoisie and their state functionaries is complicated by the very form in which that scorn is presented—the novel, foreign, imported, secular, and consumed by the very class on which the text showers its disdain. But there is still another position, if only one of implicit potential, in *The Murderess*. That is the unsuppressed power of the peasantry, the possibility of radical change in the situation of the peasantry rather than the textually mediated rebellion of Frangoyiannou. It is a change that challenges equally the traditional oligarchy and the newly ascendant diaspora bourgeoisie. Whatever its possible form, this fourth position is a radical questioning of the distribution of power, of the proverbially timeless peasant way of life, of the role of the Church, and, finally, of the institution of the state itself. For the implicit textual suggestion of this radical change implicates the very nature of the state and of its narrowly defined nationalism. Regardless of the claims of the real author, neither the oligarchy nor the bourgeoisie within the text, nor, of course, the murderous solutions of the old peasant woman, are capable of resolving the textual contradictions in *E Fonissa*. It is then scarcely surprising that Frangoyiannou must be done away with. That, as the dominant textual symbol of the potentially unsuppressed power of the peasantry and of the radical change that the realization of that power would effect, she must be decisively eliminated. Or that the peasantry of Skiatho are relegated to an unalterable eternity of grim poverty and superstition. Or that all those foreign to the island contribute only to the corruption of its morals and ethics. Or that the traditional oligarchy represented by Benidis and Rosmais remain a passive source of light and good in the novel even though they are implicitly guilty of the peasants' misery and poverty.

The contradictions of *E Fonissa* prove too much for the text to manage. Frangoyiannou drowns in the rising tide, halfway between the unwilling peasants and zealous "Franks" who are chasing her and the "divine forgiveness" of the Church she cannot reach. But if Frangoyiannou's tiny revolt is decisively contained, the solutions of the "Frankish" bourgeoisie and of the traditional oligarchy are textually impotent. The bourgeoisie evoke overt textual disdain, and the oligarchy, for all that they are presumably enshrined as the passive source of textual good, are forced to remain silent, peripheral, and passive in the novel. The houses and gardens of the oligarchy speak for their persons, for the ease and wealth of their lives. But to the extent that they speak of these things, they implicitly speak as well of the causes of the poverty and grim misery of the peasants who surround them, who work their farms, clean their clothes, and tend their children. The contrast is stark between the language of the houses and grounds of Benidis and Rosmais and the language of the huts and hovels of the rest of the island. *E Fonissa* is unable to formulate the syntheses, however facile, that characterize the Egyptian novel, *Qindīl Umm Hāshim*, examined in the next chapter. So, in a virtually inevitable gesture, Frangoyiannou is eliminated. For what would become of the text and its careful hierarchy of power if she were allowed to live? But her death neither eliminates nor resolves the symptoms or the sources of the problems that she indicts.

Chapter 3

IN THE FLICKERING LIGHT OF UMM
HĀSHIM'S LAMP

> I bring you news of death, my friends, of the old
> language
> of the old books
> I bring you news of death
> of our speech full of holes like an old shoe
> —Nizār Qabbānī, "What Value Has a People
> without a Tongue?"

THE WORK of the Egyptian novelist, short-story writer, and critic Yahyā Haqqī (b. 1905) spans more than half a century of Egypt's turbulent history. Haqqi's work is implicitly informed by the conflicts and aspirations of Egyptian and Arab writers and intellectuals from the first half of the twentieth century. His fiction, as well as his social commentary and literary criticism, are emblematic of the political and cultural attempts of Egypt and the Arab world to confront and respond to an expanding West and to the social, cultural, and political turmoil that confrontation with the West caused within Egypt. In this context, Haqqī's *Qindīl Umm Hāshim* (The lamp of Umm Hāshim)[1] is an exemplary text. Characterized, rather misleadingly but persistently, as predominantly the fictional representation of "the intellectual between East and West,"[2]

---

[1] Yahyā Haqqī, *Qindīl Umm Hāshim* (The lamp of Umm Hashim) (Cairo: Dār al-Kitab, 1973). Unless otherwise noted, all translations are my own. For an English translation of *Qindīl Umm Hāshim* see Yahyā Haqqī, *The Saint's Lamp and Other Stories*, trans. M. M. Badawi (Leiden: E. J. Brill, 1973).

[2] See, for example, M. M. Badawi, "*The Lamp of Umm Hāshim*: The Egyptian Intellectual between East and West," *Journal of Arabic Literature* 1 (1970): 145–61 or Issa J. Boullata, "Encounter between East and West: A

Qindīl Umm Hāshim participates in the crucial social and cultural dilemmas of the years between the two world wars in Egypt.

Yahyā Haqqī was born in 1905 in the Harat Mida district of Cairo near the Sayyida Zainab quarter in which his fiction is so frequently situated. His parents were ethnically Turkish, his grandfather having immigrated to Egypt from the Greek Peloponnesus in the 1860s. Haqqī attended law school in Cairo, graduating in 1925; he joined the government service and began working in the local (*ahli*) courts, which, unlike the mixed or foreign courts, conducted their proceedings in Arabic. Then, from 1927 to 1929, Haqqī was sent to Manfalut to work among Egyptian peasants on behalf of the government (uncomfortably enough for Haqqī) administering Egypt's agricultural laws. In 1919, he was transferred to Jeddah and for the next twenty-five years worked as a career diplomat. During that time, with the exception of the period from 1939 to 1945 when he returned to Egypt, Haqqī served in various diplomatic capacities in Istanbul, Rome, Paris, Ankara, and Libya. From 1962 to 1970, Haqqī was the influential editor of the Cairo literary periodical *Al-Majalla* and was also instrumental in introducing the work of younger generations of writers.

Haqqī's years of travel and extended residence in Europe and the Arab world undoubtedly influenced his thought and writing. But it was his two years in Manfalut that profoundly shaped his view of Egypt, her people, and her past and future. Shortly after leaving Manfalut, Haqqī wrote five short stories on the Sayyidis, the peasants of upper Egypt. On his return to Egypt from Rome in 1939, he wrote *Qindīl Umm Hāshim*, which traces the trajectory of a young Egyptian, Ismā'īl, and his peasant family from that family's migration to Cairo from the countryside and the achievement of their goal of educating

Theme in Contemporary Arabic Novels," *Middle East Journal* 30 (1976): 49–62. Miriam Cooke's *The Anatomy of an Egyptian Intellectual: Yahya Haqqi* is an affectionate and insightful critical account of Haqqi's work—including *Qindīl Umm Hāshim*—which explores the complexity of his fiction rather than casting it as primarily emblematic of the "East"/"West" confrontation.

their son, Ismāʿīl, who spends seven years in school in London. Haqqī's narrative preoccupation with the life of Egypt's peasants, and, frequently, with those who have left the countryside behind for the city, marks much of his fiction. Here it is particularly his *Qindīl Umm Hāshim* that is the focus—for its accomplished manipulation of the novel form, its structure and linguistic style, its thematic development, and, as mentioned earlier, for its participation in the crucial social and cultural problems of its time. By his own account, it is somewhat to Haqqī's dismay,[3] that *Qindīl Umm Hāshim* has been located in the literary canon of the Arab world and, of course, of Egypt for its linguistic style, as occasionally difficult as that style might seem, and for its resolution of a postulated opposition between (Western) science and (Eastern) spirituality. In spite of, or in addition to, this valorization within the definition of a national or Arabic culture, it is impossible to consider the early twentieth-century Arabic novel without considering *Qindīl Umm Hāshim*.

One of the sources of the modern novel in the Arab world lies in the nineteenth-century *nahda* or "literary renaissance." The importance of this political and cultural movement, the "Arab awakening"[4] to the succeeding century cannot be underestimated. For, though it was ultimately overcome by European occupation,

> though it did not manage to formulate a coherent and efficacious programme of social transformations, as would have been necessary to resist the imperialist aggression, it was nonetheless a decisive factor in the formation of modern Arab feeling. For it reestablished the flow of ideas between the provinces of the Arab world, and uniformly remodelled the language by adapting it to the common need for modernisation—in short, it revivified the main instrument of Arab unity.[5]

The two centers of this Arab cultural renaissance were the cities of Cairo and Beirut. Not unexpectedly, they were also

---

[3] Cooke, *Anatomy*, 7.

[4] See George Antonius's history of the Arab world from 1847 to the period following World War I: *The Arab Awakening*.

[5] Samir Amin, *The Arab Nation*, 33.

the two major points of contact with the expanding West. Cairo, as all of Egypt, was the goal of Napoleon's expedition of 1798 and the Egyptian capital became the center of France's three-year occupation of Egypt. With the exit of the French in the early nineteenth century, Egypt came under the increasing dominance, and finally in 1882, the direct occupation of the British. In Lebanon, Beirut and its surrounding areas had, as far back as the eleventh century, been a gateway for the Crusades and, in the centuries that followed, was the nexus for the relatively uninterrupted relationship of its Marionite Christian community with the Roman Catholic church. Both capitals were of what today we euphemistically call "strategic importance." And both countries have been, and continue to be, arenas for much of the struggle between the West and the Arab world—a struggle in which culture frequently assumes as significant a role as the more conventionally political. Both countries have also been the focal point for many of the intra-Arab struggles over the last century. Thus they have been important centers of Arab thought and action both vis-à-vis the outside world and within the Arab world itself.

The three-year occupation of Egypt by the French, in addition to being "the beginning of a period of great battles, terrible events, disastrous occurrences, ghastly calamities, ever growing misfortunes . . . and general devastation,"[6] was also a catalyst for the introduction of notions of European humanism, the French Revolution, and post-Enlightenment science and technology. The French occupation also saw the establishment of the first newspapers and of the concomitant printing presses in Egypt, including one in Arabic. The importance, then and now, of the popular press in Cairo and, when it was established later, in Beirut, in the dissemination of ideas, both political and cultural, and in the publishing of novels, short stories, poetry, and criticism cannot be overemphasized.[7] Newspapers and periodicals remained the primary forum for

---

[6] From al-Jabartī. Quoted in: John Haywood, *Modern Arabic Literature: 1800–1970*, 31.

[7] See Albert Hourani, *Arabic Thought in the Liberal Age: 1798–1939*.

political and cultural publication until well into the present century. The widespread availability of inexpensive, bound books issued by independent publishing houses is for the most part a post–World War II phenomenon not only in Egypt but throughout the Middle East. This factor influenced not only the audience for Egyptian literature but its form as well. The predominance of the short story and the serialized novella over the longer novel form is undoubtedly related to the easier access to publication available in daily newspapers and periodicals and the concomitant constraints of that publishing format. But there were other constraining factors on the development of Egyptian prose fiction. The absence of independent publishing houses for the printing and circulation of literature was a characteristic of early literary production in more than one underdeveloped country—as in late-nineteenth- and early-twentieth-century Greece.

And as it was in Greece, so in Egypt the modern novel was an "imported" genre, an accoutrement for Egypt, at least initially, of first French and then British hegemony. (It is interesting to consider whether later, in both Greece and Egypt, the novel became an accoutrement of indigenous ruling class hegemony.) The modern novel, like modern theater, was accounted for in the late-nineteenth- and early-twentieth-century Arab world as one of the cultural manifestations of modern, scientific, and democratic European and British societies. In spite of the variety of existing narrative traditions in Arabic—the *maqāma, qissa, hadīth, sira*—"no one seems to have become, as the European novel did, the major narrative type" prior to the early twentieth century.[8] In fact, the relationship of the novel to these existing narrative traditions was an uneasy one, for all that this new and foreign genre might have appeared "to the anxious sons of the East as a liberating instrument."[9]

From what was the novel perceived as a liberation? One of the dominant written prose forms of premodern Egypt, as of

[8] Edward Said, "Introduction," *Days of Dust* by Halim Barakat, xiii.
[9] Jacques Berque, *Cultural Expression in Arab Society Today*, 215.

much the premodern Arab world as a whole, was the *ma-qāma*—short pieces of ornate, rhymed prose. Although there are *maqāma* that are anecdotal or didactic, concern with form and style predominated. Throughout what are called the Dark Ages—from the death of the historian Ibn Khaldūn in 1406 to the early nineteenth century—the *maqāma*, particularly those of al-Hamadhāni (968–1007) and al-Harīrī (1054–1122), with their emphasis on style and language, remained a primary model for literary prose.[10]

For the novel, the predominance of the *maqāma* style presented a number of problems. Although literary Arabic remained essentially stable from the time of the *Qurān* (the seventh-century model for the written language), the colloquial language had changed a great deal. And so, in the nineteenth century, if literature were to be written for more than just a small educated elite, it would be forced to use a language that its audience could understand. The colloquial language differs noticeably from the Mashreq to the Maghreb and even from one neighboring country to another. And thus to use an entirely colloquial language meant that prose, or any written text, would be confined by national boundaries. But pan-Arab nationalism—an attempt at unity that supersedes national boundaries—was a definitive part of the *nahda*. And Islam and its language, classical Arabic, were the sine qua non of that movement. But, since the Arab world included a substantial population that was not Muslim, it was the Arabic language that was arguably the crucial link.

There was another predecessor from which the modern Egyptian and Arabic novel drew—the *sira* or folktale. But as a narrative source for the novel, the folktale exacerbated the language issue. Oral folktales in any culture are, by definition, in a language that is understood by their primary audience—the common people. But the modern novel in Egypt, not unlike the rest of the Arab world, drew from the content and

---

[10] This was so much the case that Haywood notes: "Early attempts at novel and short-story writing tended to be in rhymed prose, full of *balagha* (rhetorical) devices. . . . Even translations of French and English fiction were frequently written in ornate prose" (18).

structure of the folktale rather than from its language. The reluctance until very recently to admit the collection of tales, anecdotes, fables, and travel journals—*Alf layla wa layla* (A thousand and one nights) into the Arabic literary canon is in no little part based on that text's "mixed language"—in which the colloquial is used intermittently with a version of a more literary Arabic. Reluctant to forgo one of the crucial bases for pan-Arab nationalism, the *nahda* produced its own modified version of the classical Arabic language—modern standard Arabic. But the divorce between the common, spoken language and the still-purist, though modernized, literary language remained. This presented an inevitable division in the character of modern Arabic culture. For the importation of foreign, bourgeois art forms was not necessarily accompanied by the importation of foreign, bourgeois educational levels and literacy rates.[11] Interestingly enough, in nineteenth-century Japan, widespread illiteracy was not so distinct a problem and yet, for other reasons, a similar rift between the literary and the spoken language made the use of language in the early novel a crucial issue (see chap. 4). In spite of such problems of language and form—problems that marked the early European novel just as distinctly—from the early years of this century, the novel in the Arab world was a participant in the broader cultural and political attempt to remake the present. It was in this respect then very much of the spirit of the nineteenth-century *nahda* or renaissance.

For the *nahda* was an attempt to encourage the overthrow of the crumbling Ottoman regime that controlled most of the Mediterranean and Middle East and then to come to terms with the rising industrial, political, and social challenge of Europe. Success in the former goal was aided by the already de facto disintegration of the control of the Ottoman Empire and by the only-too-willing assistance of various European powers, most notably France and England, themselves anxious to

---

[11] One estimate places the literacy rate of Egypt in 1927 at scarcely 14 percent. (A. H. Ebeid, "National Policy and Popular Education in Egypt: 1919–1958" [Ph.D. diss., Oxford University, 1964], 230–34.)

divide the spoils of the "sick man of Europe." But precisely for these reasons, the latter goal entailed considerable struggle. That European assistance to the Arab world in throwing off Ottoman rule had a price is something of an understatement.

Unlike much of the rest of the Middle East, Egypt has a long history of predominantly agrarian, rather then merchant, economy and a firmly ingrained peasant culture. Egypt's urban mercantile trade, when it did develop, was predominantly the provincial extension of "commercial empires based elsewhere"[12]—whether Hellenistic, Byzantine, or Arab. The premodern history of Egypt was based on "the unfolding dialectic between its permanent peasant base and the occasional integration of the country into a much larger economic whole."[13] Because of its long and relatively unbroken history, its singular socioeconomic base, and the centralized organization that grew up around that base, Egypt maintained a comparatively distinct regional identity and geographic unity even prior to colonial rule. In addition, initial attempts at modernization and social reform were made while Egypt was still nominally under Ottoman rule, with the efforts of Mohammed Alī (1805–1849) and, subsequently, of the Khedives, most especially Ismā'īl (1863–1879). Mohammed Alī initiated a process of modernization based on his recognition of the need for a strong military and economy in dealing both with the Ottoman Porte and with the West.[14] But the Anglo-Turk-

---

[12] Amin, *Arab Nation*, 19.

[13] Amin, *Arab Nation*, 19.

[14] Mohammed Alī instituted an agrarian reform of sorts that restructured property rights and that, with concomitant changes in taxation, managed to wrest control of the agricultural surplus from the hands of the traditional landed elite and into the hands of the state. Mohammed Alī became, in effect, the sole landowner of one huge farm—Egypt. He introduced a nascent industrial complex in three major sectors: military production, textiles, and agricultural processing (envisioned largely as a means to supply and equip his army). He instigated the large-scale construction of irrigation works, a standing army raised by conscription, military and secular schools patterned on the European system, educational missions of Egyptians (rather than of the existent Turko-Circassian ruling elite) sent abroad for technical and academic

ish coalition of 1840 stopped Mohamed Alī's move toward independent development.[15] Mohammed Alī's successors hoped to reform and modernize Egypt not independently but with the help of European capital and by integrating Egypt into the world market.

The dangers this turn toward dependency on the West entailed were felt most clearly not by the Egyptian ruling class, which profited rather handsomely from the development of a cotton monoculture for export to England.[16] It was rather those sections of the population ruined by the domination of British and ruling-class Egyptian interests that were, for obvious reasons, most aware of the dangers of foreign colonization. Clerks, artisans, remnants of the merchant world, small manufacturers and, in the rural sector, the village notables:

> As heirs to their cultural tradition . . . this Third Estate was the mainstay of the renaissance from 1880 onwards. . . . Faced with the imperialist menace, the aristocracy, out of self interest and also because of their own Turkish origins, had rejected the traditions wholesale, although without achieving any counterbalancing real assimilation of European culture. The "Third Estate," on the other hand, clung desperately to the traditions, in order to save its own personality.[17]

But conservatorship over traditional culture soon became a consolation prize for the absence of any possibility of real economic or political power. And by the time of the ill-fated Urabi Revolt in 1882, and the subsequent occupation of Egypt by the British, it was clear that the impetus of the *nahda* was waning. Caught politically and culturally between loyalty to Egyptian tradition and to some sort of independence and fascination with Western power and progress, the *nahda* was as much the victim of its own contradictions as it was of the en-

---

training. All this, however, proved to be a false dawn for the autonomous capitalist development of a modern Egyptian state.

[15] The development of Egypt up to this point is an interesting parallel to the similar attempts at reform of Meiji Japan. See chap. 4.

[16] Mahmoud Hussein, *Class Conflict in Egypt: 1945–1970*, 20.

[17] Amin, *Arab Nation*, 31.

suing British occupation. There are reverberations of this position in Haqqī's *Qindīl Umm Hāshim*, with its formulation of and attempt at resolving the impossible opposition of Western science and Eastern spirit. But in the short time between its inception in the mid-nineteenth century and its obstruction by the foreign occupation of the country, the *nahda* did manage to arouse a political resistance to foreign domination, culminating in the Urabi Revolt, and a cultural resistance that took the form of the revitalization of the Arabic language, the development of a critical reevalution of traditional thought, and the rebirth of national, and pan-Arab, sentiments.

With the military defeat of the Urabi Revolt, the demise of the *nahda*, and the British occupation of Egypt, the third estate, which had constituted the driving force of the *nahda*, was eliminated politically, economically, and culturally. The new generation that succeeded them, a decidedly compromised urban petite bourgeoisie, resorted to a "riskless opposition" (Amin) of accepting foreign domination and refusing modern values. But with the continuation of British occupation, an Egyptian nationalist movement began to take shape. For "although unsuccessful, the Urabi Revolt marked the beginning of political agitation on a mass scale in Egypt."[18]

The role of the burgeoning Egyptian press, and of the intellectuals, journalists, and literati who wrote for this press, in the formation of nationalist feeling was significant[19] in spite of the periodic imposition of censorship by the British. After 1890, a number of opposition newspapers appeared—Abdallāh al-Nadīm's *al-Ustādh* and Shaikh 'Ali Yūsuf's *al-Muaiyid*, whose pan-Islamic ideas were inspired by the earlier periodical *al-Urwa al-wuthqā* published for a short time in Paris by al-Afghāni and his disciple Mohammed Abduh to attempt to explain the weakness and decline that had made it possible for Egypt and other Muslim countries to fall under European domination.

At the same time, because of the steadily increasing number

[18] P. T. Vatikiotis, *The Modern History of Egypt*, 172.
[19] Vatikiotis, *Modern History of Egypt*, 173–75.

of landless peasants resulting from the tax increases and debt peonage,[20] there was a constant stream of peasants into the cities. By 1907, with the continuing occupation and the further weakening of the dependent Egyptian economy caused by worldwide economic crises, there was another demand for social and political reform arising from among a growing Egyptian working class. The cultural and ethnic composition of this class was distinctly rooted in the disinherited peasantry. As is clear in *Qindīl Umm Hāshim*, the ranks of the urban working class, and occasionally of the petite bourgeoisie, or alternatively of the lumpen and subalterns, were continually swollen by immigration from the countryside into the city. The novel's central figure, Ismā'īl, and his family are some of the countless Egyptian peasants who immigrate to the capital in search of work and an escape from the hardships, taxation, forced labor, and land loss of the countryside. *Qindīl Umm Hāshim* opens with the scent of fenugreek and milk and earth and with the fervent devotion of unquestioning faith—with an almost archetypal representation of the peasant. It is this view of the world of the peasant, half profound uneasiness and half idealized affection, that determines the fate of Haqqī's Ismā'īl. Ismā'īl differentiates himself from the collectivity of the Egyptian peasantry and of the lower-working-class district of Sayyida Zainab; he rises above his circumstances, goes to England, becomes an ophthalmologist and returns to single-handedly save the eyesight of his country. Ismā'īl is afforded the narrative opportunity to go beyond his traditional, impoverished peasant environment not just through his own individual effort but because "the whole of the family's life and efforts were devoted to increasing Ismaī'īl's comfort. An entire generation was exhausting itself so that a single one of its children might succeed" (9).

---

[20] By the early 1870s and even before the British occupation, more than a third of the rural population of Egypt was landless. See Joel Beinin, "Formation of the Egyptian Working Classes," *MERIP* 94 (1981), 14–23. And, for a more extended treatment: Joel Beinin and Zachary Lockman, *Workers on the Nile: Nationalism, Communism, Islam, and the Egyptian Working Class, 1882–1954.*

The ties of the new Egyptian working class and petite bourgeoisie to the countryside, to peasant traditions and identity, were definitive.[21] And if this class, in its peasant origins, did not recognize itself as the repository of some authentic, national identity, the intellectuals and writers of the growing national bourgeoisie, and even of the traditional landowning elite, were only too willing to create such an equation. Nor was the creation of this equation an isolated incident. It is questionable to what extent the "great chasm" between Eastern spirit and Western science so dominant in the works of the early, pre–World War I writers was in fact a reality of the day-to-day life of the Egyptian peasant or worker. The extent to which the ideological creation of such equations, and of the definitive terms of the confrontation between East and West, reinforces the exalted position and absolute mediating necessity of the same intellectual elite who did the creating is an irresistable speculation. Such creations can also be seen as a deliberate move to contain and curtail the potential for some more properly revolutionary social and political change. The dissolution of larger political and social issues into questions of demotic versus purist language in the modern Greek state is another case in point. For the peasant and working classes of the colonized country, and even occasionally for the lower middle and petite bourgeoisies, there is a double move to exert dominance over them—that by the foreign imperial power and subsequently by the national elite, at first in conjunction with the foreign power, and later, as the national elite grows in economic and/or political strength and after the endowment of some sort of independence by the colonizer, in the place of the foreign power. But in the case of both Egypt and Greece, recognition of this essentially conservative maneuver comes only later with the actual coming into power of a national bourgeoisie. Clearly, the development—or underdevel-

---

[21] This is, for example, in contrast to the peasants who immigrated to America and were subsequently proletarianized. A definitive element of their situation as immigrants to America would seem to be precisely that their ties to peasant culture and tradition were rather more "effectively" sundered if for no other reason than that of geographical distance.

opment—of both the sociopolitical and economic structure of these countries is a conspicuously disjointed one; the composition and functions of the classes that make up Egyptian or Greek society do not parallel, following some neat evolutionist paradigm, those of West Europe, England, or the United States.

In spite of the repressive policies of the British preceding and during World War I, the Egyptian nationalist movement grew in strength from the early years of the twentieth century. This growing strength found its voice in the press with the founding in 1907 of the moderate nationalist *Umma* party's newspaper *al-Jarida*, edited by Ahmad Lutfi al-Sayyid. It examined various aspects of contemporary Egyptian life—government, education, social structure—and proposed what it considered essential reforms for an independent and modern national society.[22] At the end of 1907, the anti-British nationalist newspaper *al-Liwa'*, edited by Mustafā Kāmil, gave birth to the Nationalist party. Kāmil died shortly after the founding of the party, and was succeeded by Muhammad Farid as both party head and newspaper editor. Farid brought another dimension to the nationalist debate because of his interest in socialist ideas and his acquaintance with a number of figures in the Socialist International. The ideological split between the trend for a reform phrased in secular terms and that in terms of a traditional Islamic heritage, referred to earlier, continued, the latter movement characterized by the writings of Ahmad Lutfi al-Sayyid (1872–1963) and the former by the work of Muhammad Abduh (1849–1905) and his disciples. Since Egypt was still nominally under Ottoman rule, in spite of the de facto British occupation of the country, there was a yet more conservative traditional trend in political and intellectual thought—that which sought to continue and strengthen alignment with the ruling Turkish Khedive as a valid form of Islamic government. Unlike Mohammed Abduh and his dis-

---

[22] Vatikiotis, *Modern History of Egypt*, 215: "What is significant about the *Umma* is that its newspaper was more important than the actual activities of the Party organization itself. In fact, the founding of a publishing house for the *Jarida* . . . preceded the formal organization of the *Umma* party."

ciples, or his mentor, the famous Islamic reformist al-Afghānī, these intellectuals and political figures saw no need to reform Egyptian society except to be rid of British domination and to return to a "truly Islamic" form of rule. The formation of a number of nationalist political parties representing various elements of the Egyptian bourgeoisie and, not unlike the situation in Greece, backed by different European governments, accelerated a period of nationalist and economic struggle that culminated in the 1919 Revolution and in the emergence of the Wafd party, which dominated official Egyptian political life until the Officers Coup of 1952. The movement for Islamic reform, which had managed to stay more or less abreast with that for the secular reform of Egyptian society, was now decidedly peripheralized in favor of the latter. Militant Islamic traditionalist reform assumed the form of the Muslim Brotherhood, founded in 1928, and functioned almost exclusively as an opposition force, though one of no small following.

The period from the 1919 Revolt to 1952 was characterized by power struggles between the Wafd and the monarchy. On December 18, 1914, the British declared a protectorate over Egypt—a largely superfluous measure given their military occupation and de facto control of the country for nearly twenty years. The following day they deposed the Ottoman khedive and appointed a monarch/sultan to succeed him, beginning the royal line that extended to 1952 and King Fārūq. Martial law was declared and British repression intensified. The end of World War I brought economic crisis for the Egyptian people or, for most of them, that is. For Egyptian capitalism had grown rapidly as a result of the sharp reductions in imported European goods. There began a period of social unrest and conflict that culminated in the Revolt of 1919, with widespread strikes, demonstrations, and uprisings. The British had refused to allow a group of nationalist leaders to go as a delegation—*wafd*, hence the party of the same name—to London to set forth the case for Egyptian independence. They had also refused, at the end of World War I, to allow American President Wilson's Fourteen Point Plan to be applied to Egypt. Popular sentiment against British occupation and for Egyptian in-

dependence found a symbolic representative in the figure of
Sa'ad Zaghlul of the Wafd. When he was arrested and
deported in March of 1919, a wave of strikes, mass protests,
and sabotage against the British intensified. A month later,
Zaghlul was allowed to return and from then on managed to
present himself as the personification of the popular struggle
against foreign occupation. Yielding to continuing pressure,
the British in 1922 issued a unilateral recognition of limited
Egyptian independence, while maintaining their military occupation and de facto rule. The first Wafd government assumed power in January of 1924 and thereafter engaged in an
ambivalent alternation between dependency on, and power
struggles against, both the British and the monarchy—a vacillating stance that continued for almost thirty years. The period between the two World Wars in Egypt was marked by the
increasing impoverishment of the countryside, attendant peasant uprisings, and an even greater increase in the number of
landless peasants who swelled the ranks of the unemployed in
the cities. Egypt's primary export crop remained cotton, and
with the dramatic drop in cotton prices in 1928 and the economic depression of the early 1930s, the situation in the countryside was devastating.[23] The small gains made by Egyptian
workers prior to World War I were largely eliminated and the
trade union movement was repressed by both British and
Egyptian ruling interests. The living and working conditions
of the urban working class declined in spite of the rapid development of light industry from 1920 to 1945—a process
that instead benefited the growing national bourgeoisie.

The degree to which Egyptian independence was compromised became increasingly clear during this period. The dominant tone of both political and intellectual discourse began to
change. Emulation of the European paradigm had not repro-
duced the same social, economic, or cultural formations. Instead, the situation for the great majority of the Egyptian people had actually deteriorated. Though they managed to

[23] The novel *al-Ard* (The earth) (Cairo, 1954) by 'Abd al-Rahman al-
Sharqāwi is a singularly impressive treatment of these years in rural Egypt.

articulate in their opposition to both the monarchy and the British the demands of the masses of the Egyptian people, and to appear as defenders of the interests of the entire nation, by the time the Wafd negotiated the Anglo-Egyptian Treaty of 1936, which failed to gain the national demands of Egypt, the bankruptcy of the Wafd's conciliatory and vacillating stance was generally recognized. Once again the issue of what would constitute an "authentically Egyptian" path of development became central. If the construction of a quasi-European political and social framework was unsuccessful, a return to the Islamic past might manage to produce an acceptable alternative. And so, in the late 1920s, the bourgeois exponents of a European-style secular liberalism began extolling as truly Egyptian what was also truly past.

But this turn to a particular definition of tradition followed a period in which a number of new and potentially radical intellectual trends had been introduced to Egypt.[24] *Fasl al-maqal fī falsafat al-nushū' wa'l-irtiqā'* (An introduction to the philosophy of evolution and development) by Hassān Husayn had appeared in 1924. In 1926 Tāhā Husayn's *Fī al-shi'ir al-jāhilī* (On pre-Islamic poetry), questioning the traditional religious interpretation of the *Qurān* and the *Sharī'a* on the basis of pre-Islamic poetry and urging the development of a Cartesian rationalism and other philosophical methods in literary criticism, was published. In 1930, Ismail Mazhar's translation of Darwin's *Origin of the Species* appeared, as well as a dis-

---

[24] Vatikiotis, *Modern History of Egypt*, 303. He notes with scarcely concealed satisfaction that "whereas at the end of the nineteenth century, the literary quarrel between the old and the new was largely over style, now the concern of the modernists was the transformation of the whole conception of literature. . . . [initially] interested in discovering the truth via uncompromising rationalism. . . . Their followers in the 1920's and 1930's emphasized the role of science in the modern world. Technology and industrialization became the two major characteristics of modern civilization. . . . They proclaimed Western civilization as the highest stage of man's spiritual and material development; declared Islamic civilization dead and useless; and advocated the adoption of Western civilization and culture without reservation as the only way for the advancement of their country."

cussion of the theory of evolution, *Nazarīya al-tatawwur wa asl al-insān*, by Salāmah Mūsā.

Earlier, in 1922, the discovery of the tomb of Tutenkhamen aroused a new interest among Egyptian intellectuals in the Pharaonic past, a past that revealed, according to Tāhā Husayn in *Mustaqbal al-thaqāfa fī Misr* (The future of culture in Egypt), the links of Egypt not with the Orient, to which it owed little, but to the Hellenic and Mediterranean world and thus to Europe. If this view was not quite shared by the general population of Egypt, it definitely had its appeal in intellectual circles. It is clear that with the steadily increasing contradictions in Egyptian economic and social life, the unabashed exhortation to emulate the West and to proclaim tradition as useless was bound to have repercussions. The conservative reaction was not only to the failure of the Egyptian adaption of secular liberalism, but a response as well to the *successes* of the modernizing tendencies of the colonial and liberal Egyptian regimes. For if the economic and social misery of the countryside and of the swelling urban proletarianized masses not only did not improve but actually worsened under colonial and then semi-independent Egyptian rule, there was another stratum of traditional popular leaders, the *ulama*—village sheikhs, teachers, students, small shop owners—who were permanently displaced by the successful instigation of a system of secular and impersonal law. It is these people who formed the recruited core of the Muslim Brotherhood—an organization whose membership grew into the hundreds of thousands toward the end of the interwar period.

The appeal of the Muslim Brotherhood, the call to "militant nostalgia"[25] in the face of a massive and foreign disruption, did not fail to affect the dominant writers and intellectuals of the period as well. Their expedient retreat to the Islamic bases of Egyptian society, to a rediscovery of the rational and scientific roots of Islam, suggests some measure of nervous re-

[25] Goldberg, "Bases of Traditional Reaction." See also his more extended treatment in: Ellis Goldberg, *Tinker, Tailor, and Textile Worker: Class and Politics in Egypt, 1930–1952.*

grouping in the face of a rising tide of popular anger over the failure of either foreign-dominated or nationally officiated modernization to effect any real improvements in their lives and over the only-too-real and alien disruption of the traditional bases of their lives. In what can be seen as an attempt to appropriate and contain a potentially explosive popular movement that had social, political, and intellectual implications, some of the leading liberal secularists of but a few years earlier revealed a newfound faith. Tāhā Husayn, laying aside the methods of critical scholarship of his *Fi al-shi'ir al-jāhilī*, wrote a three-volume study, *'Alā hāmish al-sīra* (On the margin of the Prophet's life, 1937–1943) in which he "attempts to re-tell the story of Islam in ways which will appeal to the modern Egyptian consciousness. . . . to minds formed by Western education."[26] Mohammed Husayn Heikal, editor of the Liberal Constitutional party's newspaper *al-Siyāsa*, in a series of books on the life of the Prophet (*Hayāt Mohammed*, 1935), attempted to show the rational and ethical content of early Islam, its validity as an ideological foundation for a modern Egypt, and the inadequacy of reason and science alone to insure the happiness and well-being of society.

Both Tāhā Husayn and Mohammed Husayn Heikal were, in addition, authors of two of the first, accomplished Egyptian novels. One of the first modern novels of Egypt and of the Arab world was Mohammed Husayn Heikal's *Zainab: manāzir wa akhlāq rīfiyya*, published anonymously in 1914 by "an Egyptian peasant"—rather a fanciful stretch of the imagination, for Heikal was the son of a wealthy landowner studying law in Paris when he wrote the novel. The novel's subtitle, *Rural Scenes and Customs*, belies somewhat the actual content of the work, though it is in many respects a romanticized and idyllic depiction of peasant life in the Egyptian countryside. Hamid, the main character of the novel, is the initial paradigm for a figure that reappears in a great deal of modern Egyptian and Arabic fiction—the intellectual caught between

[26] Hourani, *Arabic Thought*, 334.

two cultures, his own and that of the foreign colonizer.[27] *Zainab* also demonstrates the uneasiness with which the ideas of social reform popular in the intellectual circles of the early twentieth century[28] took on fictional form or content. Heikal was forced to violate Egyptian peasant life in his fictional representation of it to enable his novel and its characters to voice the ideas with which he was concerned. Nonetheless, Heikal establishes a number of precedents for the Arabic/Egyptian novel with *Zainab*—the valorization, at least for the first thirty years or so, of the countryside and the peasantry, the already mentioned postulation of the intellectual caught between two worlds, the position of women, and the use of colloquial dialogue in a text otherwise dominated by literary Arabic. Perhaps some of the shortcomings of *Zainab* suggest as well the shortcomings of that liberal intellectual trend that saw a national revival engendered simply through the spread of education and reform of the status of women.

Tāhā Husayn, like Heikal, was an associate of Luftī al-Sayyid and, after graduating from al-Azhar University, studied in France. His two-volume, largely autobiographical, *al-Ayyām* (The Days) is a watershed in the development of Arabic fiction. Part I, describing Husayn's village childhood in Upper Egypt, appeared in 1927; Part II recounts his life and education at al-Azhar and was published in 1939. In spite of the obvious relationship to his own life, Husayn's text is a third, rather than a first-person narrative. But, in a gesture that attempts familiarity and collective identification that includes both the narrator and implied reader, the third-person narrator refers to the young blind boy growing up first in the rural village and then in Cairo as "our friend." This inclusive narrative gesture is foiled though by Husayn's idiosyncratic language, with its long redundant sentences halfway between the elaborateness of classical Arabic and the greater simplicity of

---

[27] There is an interesting parallel in African fiction—the "been-to" convention. For West African fiction, see William Lawson, *The Western Scar: The Theme of the Been-To in West African Fiction.*

[28] Heikal himself was a member of the intellectual group formed around Luftī al-Sayyid and the newspaper that he edited, *al-Jarida.*

the modern language. Contradictory narrative gestures notwithstanding, Husayn's essays and his novels and plays have profoundly influenced liberal Arab thought. In a critical celebration of his bourgeois humanism, the French cultural historian Jacques Berque pointedly remarks "that the antibourgeois regimes which have followed [Husayn] have not produced a message of this quality."[29]

It is in this set of contexts that the fiction of Yahyā Haqqī and *Qindīl Umm Hāshim* in particular must be situated. For in spite of the critical commentary that insists on Haqqī's work, and particularily *Qindīl Umm Hāshim*, as an example par excellence of the conflict between East and West, Haqqī's texts are at least equally concerned with the stance of the Europeanized intellectual, member of a growing bourgeois elite, vis-à-vis the increasingly impoverished Egyptian people. *Qindīl Umm Hāshim* searches for a compromise between what it presents as a contradiction—Western medical science and Eastern peasant authenticity and spirituality. This is clearly an impossible dilemma when posed in these terms. And, at least theoretically, science and peasant authenticity are not necessarily in contradiction with each other at all. In fact, the hero of *Qindīl Umm Hāshim*—Ismā'īl—seems less an "Egyptian intellectual between East and West"[30] than an Egyptian bourgeois intellectual caught between class alliances—to the peasantry from which he has emerged and to the new bourgeoisie of which he is becoming a part. The need to resolve science and spirituality within the text is then as much a need to resolve class alliances. The basic opposition underlying *Qindīl Umm Hāshim* is not simply that of East and West, however those terms are defined, but also that of the peasantry and the emerging bourgeoisie. That the specific characteristics of the Egyptian bourgeoisie are, in fact, indelibly linked to the European colonization of Egypt, or that the worsening condition of the peasantry was the result of integration into and subordination to the world market, does not preclude the concur-

---

[29] Berque, *Cultural Expression*, 218.
[30] Badawi, "*The Lamp of Umm Hāshim.*"

rent existence of struggles within Egyptian society over the character of dominant Egyptian culture. Haqqī writes in the established Egyptian tradition of focusing on the peasantry and its traditions as a landmark of national identity and authenticity. At the same time, he is compelled to resolve, to recontain, those elements of peasant behavior and tradition that are unacceptable in his version of a "modern, enlightened" society.

Qindīl Umm Hāshim's Ismā'īl rids himself of the simpleness, superstition, coarseness, and "blind" resignation of the peasant (Ismā'īl will become an eye doctor, after all). But in doing so, he also rids himself of the solidarity and the security of peasant identity. He returns from seven years in England, educated, liberated, and, of course, alienated. Within the world constructed in *Qindīl Umm Hāshim*, there is no possibility of return to Ismā'īl's earlier existence. Ismā'īl's unobstructed reintegration into the world of the Sayyida Zainab district would violate the textual representation of the Egyptian peasantry on the one hand and its carefully constructed dichotomy between East and West on the other. It is the peasantry that is made the emblem for all that is native and authentic. And on the basis of this depiction of the Egyptian peasantry is constructed a refuge from which to refuse modern—and, to a certain extent, Western—values. So, Ismā'īl, in conclusion, will abandon his plans for "a private clinic in the most affluent residential quarters of Cairo" to work among the poor. "He adhered to the spirit and basis of his learning and, abandoning elaborate techniques and instruments, he relied first on Allah and only then on his learning and [the skill of] his hands" (57).

It is a rather familiar observation that situates the third world intellectual between a traditional and presumably plenitudinous past and a beckoning future of modernization, technology, and material plenty. Whether the historical context is one of colonization or of a revolution against that colonization, though, determines to a great extent the manner in which the future, as well as the past or present, is defined. Eqbal Ahmad notes about the dynamics of "transitional societies" in

the third world that "one judges the present morally with reference to the past, to inherited values, but materially in relation to the future. Therein lies a new dualism in our social and
political life."[31] During the interwar years in Egypt, the popular sentiment against the presence of the British, or of any
foreign occupying power, was strong. But among the dominant political parties and figures that took over leadership of
the nationalist struggle, there was little thought or planning
given to the specific dimensions of a future without the British.
For the reigning intellectuals and politicians, independence
was desirable but so was British tutelage. There was, on the
part of the ruling elite, no concept of or struggle for an autonomous and independent Egypt, free of European influence and
intervention—if such an alternative was even an objective possibility.

Qindīl Umm Hāshim's Ismā'īl, a fictional product of this
dilemma, wages a battle on two fronts then. He struggles for
some sort of acceptable self-definition against the onslaught of
a colonizing foreign power and for a position of power and
dominance over the threateningly volatile lower classes of his
own society. The seductive constraints of a traditional past
and of the class that presumably embodies that past—the
peasantry—must be qualified, contained, so as not to engender a danger from below. It is in this sense that Haqqī's *Qindīl
Umm Hāshim* is not merely the story of confrontation between East and West, but of confrontation between East and
East as well. And, the particular narrative compromise that
Ismā'īl represents is a specifically literary one rather than some
sort of overarching and programmatic resolution of the concrete Egyptian struggle with colonialism, dependence, and internal social organization. It is more the narrative's articulation of the dilemma itself and the attempt at a resolution that
is of interest than the specifics of the resolution or its merits as
a "real" possibility.

Some suggestion of the contradictions engendered by this

[31] Eqbal Ahmad, "From Potato Sack to Potato Mash: The Contemporary
Crisis of the Third World," *Arab Studies Quarterly* 2.3 (1980): 225.

fictional compromise are immediately apparent in *Qindīl Umm Hāshim*'s inclusion of a "modern" resolution within a narrative framework that gestures to, that attempts to recreate, some more properly premodern narrative format. An earlier, storytelling or anecdotal mode, and the sense of collective identity that it presumed, is evoked in *Qindīl Umm Hāshim*, as it is in much of Haqqī's fiction. The narrative voice is frequently awarded, not to an omniscient third person, but to a first-person speaker who, if the story is not his own personal experience, was himself witness to the events about to be related or had heard of the story from a fellow villager, family member, or friend. In *The Lamp of Umm Hāshim*, the narrator is Ismā'īl's nephew. As such, he shares both Ismā'īl's peasant origins and, presumably, his upward mobility. One generation removed from Ismā'īl, the narrator is a passive benefactor of his uncle's struggles and presumably the validation of whatever counsel Ismā'īl's story has to offer.

The novel opens with an account of the narrator's grandfather, Ismā'īl's father, coming from the countryside with his family to visit the Cairo mosque of Sayyida Zainab, the granddaughter of the Prophet and the patron saint of the poor and unfortunate. Later, the narrator's grandfather moves to Cairo in search of work. The familial relationship of the narrator to the characters of his story is itself an invocation of a collectivity—and a safely non-class-based collectivity—that presumably weathers the passage of time. To state the assumptions of *Qindīl Umm Hāshim*'s narrative stance rather crudely, the narrating nephew is a witness to the endurance of the family unit, to its resistance to "modernization," atomization, and meaninglessness. The frequent interjections of the narrating nephew in the story that he recites testify to the sustaining meaning that the story of Ismā'īl's life *must* have to his successors. The narrator recounts the migration of Ismā'īl's parents (the narrator's grandparents) from the countryside to the city, and their subsequent struggle to provide an education for their son, Ismā'īl. In doing so, the narrating nephew argues the case, from the beginning, for the power of the past, of tradition, and of some elemental "authenticity" that they both share.

> Whenever I imagine those distant days, my heart trembles with emotion at the thought of them and the face of my grandfather, Sheikh Rajāb, appears to me surrounded by a halo of brightness and light. And my grandmother, Adīla, with her simplicity and goodness, what feeble-minded person would consider her human, for if she were, what would angels be like? How much more ugly and loathsome the world would be without faith and resignation like hers. (9)

It is not only the narrator's relationship to his uncle's story and thus to the past that is evident in this passage but a particular definition of their mutual origins and of the Egyptian peasant as well. It is the viewpoint of one at a carefully constructed remove from the exigencies of peasant life. The narrator recalls—or imagines—the smell of fenugreek, milk, and soil that Sheikh Rajāb and his family exude when they come from the country to visit the mosque of Umm Hāshim in Cairo; the halos of brightness and light that surround his grandfather's face; and the sense of his grandmother as a living embodiment of goodness, simplicity, and faith. But these "memories"—imaginary or not—speak more clearly of alienation and distance from the countryside, the peasantry (even if they are of one's own family), and the "traditional" past, than they do of their eminent presence or essential characterization. It is a view that, ever more apparent as *Qindīl Umm Hāshim* unfolds, suggests an underlying distaste for, and at the same time a curious envy of, rural peasant life. It is also a narrative view framed by the pretext of the storyteller and the shape of his or her tales.

This assumption of the format of the narrating storyteller shapes much of Haqqī's fiction. The narrator lays claim to a special and privileged relationship to the characters and story of which he speaks. In a perhaps similar gesture, through the craftsmanlike use of language and carefully shaped narrative structure, a claim is laid to the solidity, the materiality, of a manual skill or craft. The text seeks to display the tangible workmanship of an artisan. Artifice or not, it is a relationship perhaps reminiscent of Walter Benjamin's essay, "The Story-teller: Reflections on the Works of Nikolai Leskov."

> Experience which is passed on from mouth to mouth is the source from which all storytellers have drawn. . . . Storytellers tend to begin their story with a presentation of the circumstances in which they themselves have learned what is to follow, unless they simply pass it off as their own experience. . . . Thus his tracks are frequently evident in his narratives, if not as those of the one who experienced it, then as those of the one who reports it.[32]

It is to a very similar tradition that Haqqī's texts consistently refer in a sociocultural context in which those same traditions and the way of life that they entailed are under seige from without and from within. The narrator in *Qindīl Umm Hāshim*, as the narrators in "*al-Salahfah tataira*," "*Umm 'Awajiz*," and much of Haqqī's other fiction, draw a great deal of their efficacy from this adoption of the storyteller's mantle, from this formal evocation of a more traditional relationship between the speaker of the story, the objects of his story, and the audience to whom he speaks. So, in "*al-Salahfah tataira*" ("The turtle flies"), the narrator begins,

> This story is imaginary but not a fairy tale; its events are likely occurrences and its hero not altogether inconceivable. Who knows? He might actually exist. And as a matter of fact, I know him. I am bound to him by ties more powerful and pleasant than those of kinship or marriage—we live in the same neighborhood. And what's more, we belong to the same alley. (59)

Or, again, the opening of "*Umm 'Awajiz*" ("Mother of the destitute")—another name for Sayyida Zainab, the grand-daughter of the Prophet, and the same Sayyida Zainab of *Qin-dīl Umm Hāshim*):

> Praised be He whose dominion extends over all creatures and who knows no opposition to his rule. Here I have no wish but to recount the story of Ibrahim Abu Khalil as he made his way

[32] Walter Benjamin, "The Storyteller," *Illuminations*, 84, 92.

down the steps of life, like the leaves of spring, which, though lifted a little by the wind, contain, even at their height, their inevitable descent until at last they are cushioned and trampled down into the earth. I was a witness to his descending the last steps of the ladder, but I learnt only later that he was an orphan.[33]

But the assumption here of some more intimate, traditional and premodern relationship to the stuff of the narrative, and the accompanying refusal implicit in that assumption, is brought into question by the content of that same fiction. If content determines form, as Georg Lukács has argued, then the content of Haqqī's fiction necessitates a formal subterfuge. For if Alexandros Papadiamandis's *E Fonissa* effects an impossible refuge from the modern dependent situation of an emerging Greek state, Haqqī's *Qindīl Umm Hāshim* postulates an equally impossible compromise between tradition and the modern. For both writers and for their narratives, the problem is made considerably more complex by the fact that the modern is inextricably linked to a foreign and hegemonic power. And if, for Papadiamandis, the foreign, Westernizing spirit was a relatively popular one at the time, for Haqqī the opposite was true.

Although first published in 1944, *Qindīl Umm Hāshim* was actually written some five years earlier, between 1939 and 1940. It was these interwar years in Egypt that saw the failure of Western-style liberalism and the mounting popular tension that years of increasing poverty and British domination had produced. The textual dichotomy between the simple faith and resignation of the Egyptian peasantry and the rational and advanced technology of the West is at best a questionable construction. As with the ideology of the trustees of the *nahda* movement earlier in the century, this dichotomy is as much a victim of its own contradictions as of foreign hegemony. It postulates the necessary preservation of a traditionally defined "authentic" national identity, while accepting, even advocat-

[33] Yahyā Haqqī, *Modern Arabic Short Stories*, trans. Denys Johnson Davies (London: Heinemann, 1967), 95.

ing, the technological and social superiority of the foreigners. Haqqī's fictional Egypt is truly an illustration of that "transitional society" of which Eqbal Ahmad speaks—evaluating the present morally and ethically in reference to the past, but materially in reference to the future and, perhaps inevitably, to the West.

And yet Haqqī's fiction, not unlike its characters, demonstrates a noticeable equivocation about the contemporary constituents of that ethical and moral link to the past. The people who populate the peripheries of Haqqī's fiction—the peasants newly arrived in Cairo from the countryside, the beggars and destitute, the peddlers and small shopkeepers, the prostitutes and petty thieves—are sketched in with a characteristically keen eye for detail that makes them at least as interesting as the main characters. And yet they are almost neutralized by an insistent narrative imposition of their simple faith and endurance, of powerless resignation and acquiescence.[34] And so the description by Ismāʿīl's narrating nephew of the square of Sayyida Zainab and its inhabitants in *Qindīl Umm Hāshim* is hardly surprising.

> Gradually the square fills anew. Figures with pale and exhausted faces, dull eyes, all of them dressed in anything they could manage, or, if you wish, in anything they could lay their hands on. . . . What is this hidden injustice from which they suffer? And this burden which weighs on their breasts? And yet, there is a kind of calm and contentment in their faces. How easily they forget. . . . Rows of people sit on the ground leaning against the walls of the mosque, some of them using the pavement as a pillow. A mass of men, women and children—no one knows where they came from nor where they go. Fruit fallen from the tree of life, they rot in its shade. This square is a school for beggars. (11–12)

The metaphors that characterize the people of Sayyida Zainab—fallen fruit rotting underneath a tree, a falling leaf

---

[34] John Berger's comment on what is presumed to be "peasant simpleness" is again an appropriate caveat. See chap. 2, footnote 26.

picked up for a moment by the wind only to fall again—posit their condition as an unarguably natural process. Leaves fall, fruit rots, ants swarm, and the lumpen poor are miserable. Thus invoked, nature mystifies and at the same time affords a face for an oppression that is frequently experienced as faceless. For oppression, unlike exploitation, is not the direct result of someone deriving profit from another's labor. In the latter case, there is another identifiable as the source of exploitation and against whom it is possible to struggle. Oppression is felt, individually and collectively, as a more generalized experience of the suppression of a social group within an economic, political, or social structure. Precisely because it is experienced as faceless and generalized, oppression does not necessarily engender collective group action against its cause. The characterization of those who people the narrative and their social and economic situations as part of a "natural" process disallows from the beginning the possibility of collective or individual action. The narrative representation of the residents of Sayyida Zainab square and district suggests a class that has not yet recognized itself as such, a class-in-itself and not yet for-itself. There is at least a linguistic recognition of this fact in the text of *Qindīl Umm Hāshim*, for there, invariably, *dull*—oppression—is used to describe the situation of Ismā'īl's family and the inhabitants of the Sayyida Zainab district. Only once does the word exploitation—*istiglāl*—occur and that is in reference to life in Europe. The text itself provides some structural basis for this distinction. The people of *Qindīl Umm Hāshim* or of Haqqī's other fiction display little consciousness of their collective identity or power. Nor are they in a situation—as factory or railroad or mine workers— that would presumably make such a consciousness a more likely possibility. And, to be sure, they are fictionally subsumed by persistent metaphors—drops of water in the sea, swarming ants, rotting fruit. And in addition to their narrative metaphorization, or metamorphosis, they people a square as yet relatively untouched by the laws of modern capitalism. "Here there are no laws or standard weights and measures or controlled prices. Rather there is custom, favors, and haggling; the weight of what you buy can be either over or under what it is supposed to be" (11).

This characterization of the transactions that take place in Sayyida Zainab square is a classic description of a precapitalist marketplace—a typical enough situation even in the early twentieth century, given the underdevelopment of Egypt's economy and its uneven integration into the world market. The sociopolitical reality that this description implies, and that *Qindīl Umm Hāshim* "verifies" in its fiction, is not one of self-conscious class development and affiliation. That kind of collective identity, rooted in a different if coexistent socioeconomic reality, could only be threatening to the position that *Qindīl Umm Hāshim* proffers. And so the temporal moment of the novel is, almost must be, not the Cairo of the late 1930s but that of the turn of the century.

Turning back the setting of this narrative by thirty or forty years, sidestepping what was the decidedly different reality of Egypt in the late 1930s, can only be a most ideological narrative shift. For what would have been a potentially radical threat to the text's vision of compromise is neatly avoided. So, the focus of Haqqī's fiction remains that of the uprooted peasant, the lumpen proletariat or, more rarely, the petite bourgeoisie. It is a world—with no clearly defined sense of class identity, uprooted more often than not from the countryside—more amenable, at least on the face of things, to the workings of Haqqī's textual compromise. And that compromise is only peripherally the one embodied by the character of Ismā'īl himself.

Although, as in Papadiamandis's *The Murderess*, the urgent necessity of social change in the way of life that *Qindīl Umm Hāshim* describes is apparent, it is hardly a possibility within the text. It is, rather, striking in its impossibility. Unlike Khadoula, who is compelled (and allowed the textual license) to effect a substantial change in her society, even if it is by murdering young girl children, neither Ismā'īl nor anyone else in *Qindīl Umm Hāshim* represent any such radical alternative. For Haqqī's novel is truly one of compromise. It is a linguistic compromise in the skillfully crafted utilization of the literary language into which the colloquial surfaces only at certain moments in the dialogue. It is a formal compromise in his manipulation of the narrative conventions of the folktale or story within the context of a novel. And it is a compromise of content in his mystification of the peasant origins of his characters and of the causes of the urban hardships into which they are thrust. But this latter compromise is most obvious, of course, in his depiction of Ismā'īl as some sort of halfway house between the alternately repugnant and entrancing "traditionalism" of the peasant and the seductive if "foreign" lure of bourgeois rationalism, order, and progress.

The convenience of *Qindīl Umm Hāshim*'s resolution is not obscure. And in this context, even the explicit formulation of the confrontation of East and West is a tendentious one. What is far more interesting, and a clear testament to Haqqī's skill as a writer of fiction, is the perspicacious creation of the minor characters of his novel and his gently ironic descriptions of life in the Sayyida Zainab district. In a touchingly comic passage, Ismā'īl's father announces his decision to send his son to study in a frighteningly distant England. "And his mother, from that moment on, shook in terror at the thought of the sea and shivered from the cold [of England]. She imagined that place as the summit of a high flight of stairs ending in a land blanketed with snow, and inhabited by a race that had the cunning of demons as well as their vices" (25). Ismā'īl's cousin, Fātima, to whom he has been engaged, recalls having heard "that European women run around half naked." Passages such as these suggest just how foreign, how incredibly different, Europe and the Europeans must have been to the average Egyptian. Here, for the moment, halos of brightness and light and the elemental goodness of archetypical peasants are dispensed with. And the overdetermination and stylization, which marks the depiction of Ismā'īl or of the largely symbolic and barely believable Englishwoman—Mary—who nurtures, seduces, and, of course liberates Ismā'īl, is not so overwhelmingly dominant. It is the people who populate the Sayyida Zainab square who enliven the pages of *Qindīl Umm Hāshim*—the crippled beggars "exposing their maimed and distorted bodies which are to them an honest means of earning a living like having a proper skilled trade"; the prostitutes who come to the mosque "in the hope that God might pity them and change the fate that was in store for them"; the blind condiment seller who insists on reciting the religious formula for buying and selling (the opening sura of the *Qurān*) before he will deal in his wares; the beggar weighed down by a bulging sack of bread, who nonetheless calls out, "For the love of Allah, good people, just one piece of bread for a starving man"; or the mosque attendant, Sheikh Dardīrī, who stands in the midst of the women who came to the mosque "like a cock among his hens" and who gathers the money he earns by selling the oil from the lamp of Umm Hāshim as a cure for the eye diseases of the faithful, not to hoard it under the floor tiles or spend it on hashish, as his colleagues speculate, nor to use it to replace his ragged *galabiya* and dusty turban, but to satisfy his penchant for frequent marriages—"a year didn't pass without [Sheikh Dardīrī] taking a new young wife." It is these narrative characters that are comments on what is presumably the novel's central conflict—that between East and West, the intellectual and spiritual displacement of Ismā'īl because of his Western education. If this is a major conflict in *Qindīl Umm Hāshim*, it is only one among a number of others. Or, more precisely, it is only the most apparent one—and an indication itself of some more essential conflict. For, it is at least a little ironic that these uprooted peasants and urban lumpen are postulated as the textual source of plenitude. At the same time, they are a striking indication of the stylized depiction of Ismā'īl. Within the narrative, these characters represent what is "authentically Egyptian" while simultaneously postulated as Egypt's, and Ismā'īl's, greatest obstacle to progress. They are both the source of plenitude and of backwardness.

But, though ambivalent, the staging within the text of the confrontation between the peasantry and the nascent bourgeois intellectual is meticulous. The novel is divided into twelve sections followed by a brief epilogue. The first six sections lead up to and encompass Ismā'īl's fateful stay in England; the remaining six are the account of his reentry into the district of Sayyida Zainab and a reintegrated identity. That Ismā'īl's parents are immigrant peasants links him to what is posited as the authenticity of Egyptian tradition—but also to what the text enunciates as its torpor, superstition, conservatism, and emotionalism. That they have come to the city and settled in the square of Sayyida Zainab links Ismā'īl to the momentous changes facing his country. That he is given a secular education and later sent to England for medical training links him to the Western world of what is presumably progress, rationalism, and individual liberty. Thus Ismā'īl is truly a textual locus for the disparate and conflicting modes of being that characterize *Qindīl Umm Hāshim*. But Ismā'īl is a curiously vacuous locus rather than the presumably plenitudinous one of the individual subject. The fictional construct of an individual and autonomous subject free to play in the fields of the Other was, in the West, a "key functional element in the bourgeois cultural revolution, the reprogramming of individuals to the 'freedom' and equality of sheer market equivalence."[35] But this assumption about individual autonomy, amputated from the sociohistorical context that is its crucial justification, clearly flounders in *Qindīl Umm Hāshim*. For the text is an indictment of the bourgeois European concept of the individual, not least of all in the development of the character of Ismā'īl. Ismā'īl's unmediated assumption of a foreign bourgeois individualism occasions the conflict that is the main focus of the novel. The source of Ismā'īl's individualism is textually posited in his stay in England and his Western medical education. The development of that individualism was cultivated by his English lover and mentor, Mary. It is this individualism, textually acceptable perhaps in England but not in Egypt, that suggests an indictment of bourgeois European concepts of the individual. But, perhaps because this deterioration of the concept of autonomous individuality was never rooted, politically, economically, or socially, in a precedent hegemony of either the bourgeoisie and its concomitant ideology of the individual, the indictment of individuality re-

[35] Frederic Jameson, *The Political Unconscious*, 221.

mains distinctly grounded in what amounts to a simultaneous fetishization of it. It is, after all, his separateness and individuality that Ismā'īl discovers in England, with the help of Mary. The implicit castration imagery in his account of their relationship and her insistence on his individuality is striking: "Ismā'īl felt Mary's words like a knife severing vital parts of his body that bound him to others. . . . The human soul seemed to him unable to find nourishment and for that reason it knew happiness only when it was separated from the crowds. To be one of the masses was a weakness and an affliction" (32). It is this concept of the individual subject, a presumably distinguishing characteristic of Western progress and rationalism, without which the compromise of *Qindīl Umm Hāshim* is impossible. It is the other pole against which is posed the traditional, if repressive, authenticity and collective identity of the peasant. The end of *Qindīl Umm Hāshim* might leave Ismā'īl a rotund, good-natured, and rumpled old man, working in the ghettos of Cairo and affectionately remembered by all, in spite of his vices. (He had an eye for women. "It is almost as if," his nephew confides, "his love for women was a manifestation of his love and devotion for all of mankind.") The text might also caustically refer to those European-educated Egyptians who return to their own country and, unlike Ismā'īl, seek only to "amass wealth, buy land, and own huge blocks of flats." Nonetheless, Ismā'īl is irrevocably affected by and drawn to the greater personal freedom he found in bourgeois English society. But this greater personal freedom is expressed as little more than a conventional symbol: "He lost his virginity and he took up drinking, dancing, and leading a dissolute life. This descent was matched by an ascent no less interesting and novel. He learned to appreciate the beauty of nature, to enjoy sunsets (as if in his own country there were not sunsets just as impressive). And he delighted in the biting cold of the north" (29).

Qindīl Umm Hāshim metaphorizes the conflict of individuality and a traditional social identity and affiliation, camouflaging, for all practical purposes, what is an even more essential sociohistorical conflict. The alternatives can be recast as not just between "Western" individuality and "Eastern" collective nonidentity, although that is not to deny the power of traditional forms of social organization. But hovering on the peripheries of Haqqī's fiction, as it hovers on the peripheries of Papadiamandis's fiction, is the specter of a more properly revolutionary response to the sociohistorical conflicts that inform the works of both writers—the specter of a nascent class consciousness. It is this specter on the margins of the text that the privileging of the East/West dichotomy so assiduously avoids. And thus the construction of that dichotomy implicates itself as a conspicuously loaded narrative maneuver.

Qindīl Umm Hāshim constructs a dichotomy between an "Egyptian" Ismā'īl—metaphorized as a "drop of water in the ocean," "a grain of sand that merged with countless other grains and was lost in them, separate but indistinguishable from them,"—and the Ismā'īl who returns from England, caught in and repelled by the poverty and misery of Egypt, of Sayyida Zainab Square, and of his old way of life. It is this opposition that the text so carefully overconstructs. This idea—the confrontation of East and West—commands the formal organization of the text. Divided into two almost exactly congruent halves, the midpoint of the text is marked by Ismā'īl's seven-year stay in England. With this as a demarcation line, what appear to be incidental details and encounters in the first half of the work are reiterated in the second half as signifiers of loaded meaning. Thus, Ismā'īl's mother, the narrator's grandmother, is likened, in the opening of Qindīl Umm Hāshim, to an angel, with "her simplicity and goodness . . . her faith and resignation." But she is recast, immediately upon Ismā'īl's return from England, as "totally devoid of personality. . . a lump of negative goodness." As an isolated incident, this reversal of perspective might not seem noteworthy. But juxtaposed with the other instances of careful and almost symmetrical repetition and reversal, this change becomes emblematic.

Before his departure for England, a sexually awakened Ismā'īl wanders through Sayyida Zainab Square to the mosque. Surrounded by the crowds of women who frequent the mosque, he delights in the smell of their sweat and perfume, "sniffing like a dog following a scent." This same image of a dog is repeated in Ismā'īl's first foray into the Square after returning from England and arguing with his family about their use of oil from the lamp of Umm Hashim to treat the diseased eyes of his cousin and future wife Fātima. But this time, "bodies hadn't known water for years. Soap was as real as a mythical creature. . . . Men began brushing up against her [a provocatively dressed woman in the Square] like dogs who'd never before seen a female" (44). Before Ismā'īl's departure for England, the people who populate the square, "sad, weary figures" though they might be, "came together in affection and the heart forgot its troubles." The beggars and street hawkers, prostitutes and artisans, surround Ismā'īl on every side and he is absorbed into them "like a raindrop in the sea." But on his return, these "sad, weary figures" appear to him as "poor and wretched beings, their feet heavy with the chains of oppression. They weren't human beings . . . but a mass of dead and crippled bodies weighing on his chest, smothering him, and straining his nerves" (45). The presence of the foreign Egyptian resident is referred to in the first half of the work with the mention of "Anastasi's Bar, called another name by the local people to suggest the kind of good time which it provided." The drunkards who emerge from the bar are more comic than anything else. But the same non-Egyptian resident is represented, on Ismā'īl's return from England, by the "fat and greedy Greek landlady, Madame Iftalia," whose smile makes him feel, in a wonderfully ironic image, "as if her fingers are rifling in his pockets."

There is another reference to a foreign presence in Egypt— a presence different from that of the Greek and Italian migrant workers and small shop owners, or their wealthier countrymen who owned factories and mills in Egypt of the time. As Ismā'īl's ship docks at the port in Alexandria, in a strange and ambivalent image, "a bell rang announcing the death of the ship and its corpse became prey to an army of human ants— soldiers and officers, our brothers the occupiers." This is, curiously enough, the only mention of the British presence in

Egypt. And it is enunciated in a tone distinctly different from that used to describe the Greek presence, for example. It is a passage that almost slips by unnoticed. But then, perhaps Haqqī's writing is more satiric than is usually acknowledged.

There are two more examples that are central to the text's formulation of Ismā'īl's conflict and ultimate resolution, a delineation and resolution that are almost too meticulously constructed, too loaded with meaning. The same Sheikh Dardīrī whose kindness and gentle antics made Ismā'īl smile with affection at the sight of him, appears to Ismā'īl, when he returns to the mosque after his sojourn in England, as a surreptitious smuggler of the oil from the lamp of Umm Hāshim, catering to the ignorance and superstition of the faithful. It is only Naīma, the beautiful young prostitute who frequents the mosque of Umm Hāshim to pray for salvation from her "fate" (her occupation), who is spared Ismā'īl's critical gaze. Ismā'īl singles her out from the other prostitutes who visit the mosque "because of her silence and slim figure," "her olive complexion, curly hair and delicately shaped lips." The night before Ismā'īl's departure for England, he finds her in the mosque and is strangely stirred at the sight of her beseeching the aid of Umm Hāshim: "Why did he tremble at the sight of her of all women or did he imagine it? No. There was a voice hidden in his heart that wanted to speak, to talk and lead him to the secret. And yet a thousand things drowned out this voice, muffled it, and hid its intensity" (24).

The libidinal secret that Ismā'īl cannot or must not discover is never textually disclosed. But then why introduce a character like Naīma at all? She is a strange and shadowy figure who reappears at each crucial juncture of Ismā'īl's development. She is introduced when Ismā'īl recognizes the awakening of his own sexual desires—a woman whose occupation, or "fate" as the text characterizes it, is the commodification of passion and desire. Yet her commodified "fate" is mitigated by her presence in the mosque, by her devotion to Umm Hāshim. Ismā'īl again finds Naīma praying fervently in the mosque the evening before he departs for Europe and as he watches, "the young woman pressed her lips against the railing of the shrine. This was not a kiss of her trade but came from her heart."

When Ismāʿīl returns from England, he does not immediately encounter Naīma in the mosque or Square. His parents, Fātima, Sheikh Dardīrī, the people in the square—all of them fall under Ismāʿīl's distancing eye—all of them except for Naīma. On his first night at home, in a rage he shatters a vial of oil from the lamp of Umm Hāshim that his mother is putting in Fātima's eyes and, storming out of his parents' house, comes across another prostitute. But she is one described very differently from Naīma, though they both share the same "fate" or trade.

> A young woman passed in front of him with plucked and penciled in eyebrows and her eyes made up with *kohl*. She had pulled her *milaya* taut around her to accentuate her hips and reveal part of her clothes underneath and she wore a veil which revealed her face more than concealing it. And what was the sense of the brass tube attached to her nose? What an ugly and repulsive sight and how disgusting! (44)

It is only Naīma, of all the characters who surround Ismāʿīl, who escapes his critical gaze. He never has any direct contact with her; she is the embodiment of a desire that he will never pursue (their encounter might be one of the most radical possibilities that *Qindīl Umm Hāshim* could formulate). Ismāʿīl will marry his peasant cousin Fātima, curing her of her blindness with some never-identified combination of oil from the lamp of Umm Hāshim and Western science, and after "making a lady of her," teaching her "how to eat and drink, sit and dress." And yet, Naīma appears still a third time in this short novel, toward the end of the final chapter, when Ismāʿīl has rediscovered his identity as a good son of Egypt. He returns to the mosque and to the old mosque attendant, Sheikh Dardīrī, to ask for some oil from Umm Hāshim's lamp to cure Fātima's eyes. There at the mosque is Naīma again, having fulfilled her vow to Umm Hāshim to light fifty white candles if her prayers to escape her fate as a prostitute were answered.

The fictional artifice is distinctly foregrounded here. For Naīma is virtually an alter ego, a double, for Ismāʿīl himself.

If Naīma prostituted her body, Ismā'īl, "the educated young man, . . . cultured and intelligent," prostituted himself to a science and ideas that he could neither assimilate nor integrate. But as Ismā'īl is protected from the implications of his objectification by the privileged mantle of the storyteller and his familial relationship to the narrator, so Naīma must be and is granted a privileged position in the text as well. The implications of her objectification are fended off by her faith in and love for Umm Hāshim. The carefully symmetrical structure of *Qindīl Umm Hāshim* is perhaps the clearest indication of a meticulous textual attempt to stake out a territorial compromise. Haqqī's texts, particularily *Qindīl Umm Hāshim*, culturally recuperated as paradigms of literary style and utopic resolution, are perhaps more clearly understood as a desperately ideological gesture to represent some fictional response to the onslaught from without—foreign occupation and domination; from below—the potential for a radical social upheaval; and from within—the barely held off collective threat to Ismā'īl's differentiation as an individual subject.

The character of Ismā'īl, then, and the text itself, suggest what Jacques Berque expresses even more explicitly some thirty years later.

> Your own is never left to itself. To breathe is to hear. To be is to be together; an insistent invitation to think in unison. Prayer, music or harangue, the collective voice raised on all sides is animated by the very movement composing the urban landscapes that affirm the future ever more insistently. For this assertion, this action, perhaps tragic but certainly obsessive, arising from the distribution of space, the increase of volumes, and the immense swarming of human shapes, goes beyond a dull impulse. From these signs a discourse is fashioned; from these clamors a personality is constructed; from this stage setting arises a history, revised and corrected.[36]

It is against a very similar backdrop that the individual subject of Ismā'īl is posited. And it is in stark contrast to this milieu

[36] Berque, *Cultural Expression*, 15.

that *Qindīl Umm Hāshim*, and perhaps even Berque as well, posits the modern Western city.

> Ismāʿīl wondered: in all of Europe was there a square like that of Sayyida Zainab? In Europe there were huge beautiful buildings, refined art, isolated and lonely people, fighting without victory or reversal, stabbing each other in the back, and exploitation of every kind. A place for love and compassion existed only at the end of the day's work. People went to them as if they were a kind of recreation, like going to the movies or the theater. (51)

This is a rather too neat juxtaposition. Any visitor to, and certainly any resident of, Cairo recognizes that this opposition between Western and Arab, modern and traditional, and so forth is quite clearly present within the various districts of Cairo itself. Interestingly enough, Janet Abu-Lughod's analysis of the demographic and architectural development of Cairo—her reading of the text of Cairo's landscape—characterizes the district of Sayyida Zainab as precisely "a transitional buffer between past and present,"[37] between the "Eastern City" (the oriental City) and the "Western City" (the colonial, occidental City). What more appropriate setting for the conflicts embodied in the character of Ismāʿīl?

It is noteworthy though that Haqqī's fondness for the Sayyida Zainab district is not necessarily a shared one. In *al-ʾAnqa, al-tarīkh Hasan Miftah* (The phoenix, a history of Hasan Miftah), a novel written some ten years after *Qindīl Umm Hāshim* by the Egyptian novelist and critic, Louis ʾAwad, the character of Muna Rabi, unable to reconcile her

---

[37] Janet Abu-Lughod, *Cairo: 1001 Years of the City Victorious*, 172–73. The passage in full reads: "Just west of the Khalij begins the neomedieval stratum, a narrow *transitional belt* parallel to the Eastern City. While it was originally settled in premodern times, its development was so impermanent and spotty that it was easily transformed into a more modern type of urban quarter when the need arose. Its transformation was facilitated by the ease with which *the older buildings could be displaced or supplemented* by new additions dating from the last century. The *qism* of al-Muski lies almost entirely within this belt as do the easternmost portions of Abdin and Sayyida Zainab, their combined extent compromising a *transitional buffer between past and present*" (emphasis added).

theoretical support of the proletariat with her actions, chooses
to pray at the church of St. Therese in Cairo when her daughter dies, rather than at the mosque of Sayyida Zainab, because
"the filth of the quarter around the Muslim shrine disgusts
her." But, for *Qindīl Umm Hāshim* and for much of Haqqī's
other fiction, the center, the heart, of this district of transition
and confrontation is the mosque of Umm Hāshim. And the
lamp of Umm Hāshim remains the virtually imperturbable
heart of the mosque itself. The attempt to resolve the contradictions of Ismā'īl, of the square of Sayyida Zainab, or of
Egypt vis-à-vis the outside world and in terms of her own internal sociopolitical conflicts, cannot help, for this text, but be
emblematized in the flame of that lamp, flickering perhaps but
never entirely extinguished. But here, the postulation of the
mosque as the definitive center, both spiritual and social, not
only of the Sayyida Zainab square but also of a certain significant sector of Egyptian society as well, should not be considered as some faithful anthropological rendition of actual social or religious alignments. In this, *Qindīl Umm Hāshim*
participates in yet another overdetermined opposition. For the
café in Egyptian society is every bit as significant a center, a
gathering place, as the mosque.[38] The loaded valorization of
the mosque as *the* repository of spiritual and social meaning
contributes to an equally overdetermined opposition between
East and West, between science and rationalism on the one
hand and Islamic faith and spirituality on the other.

Nonetheless, if Ismā'īl is the human locus for the conflicting
influences in the text, the convergence for the nonhuman or
extrahuman forces is the lamp of Umm Hāshim. It is as interesting a comment on the text of *Qindīl Umm Hāshim* as it is
on the contemporary Egyptian cultural scene that the choice
of lamp oil to symbolize simple peasant faith or superstition
and the return of Ismā'īl to the mosque to obtain oil from the
lamp of Umm Hāshim for Fātima's eyes at the end of the text
caused some considerable consternation among Egyptian intellectuals. The text never specifies exactly what Ismā'īl does

---

[38] See Maxime Rodinson, *Marxism and the Muslim World*, 262.

with the lamp oil, only that he uses some combination of Eastern faith and Western science and technology and that Fātima's eyes are in fact cured. Twenty years after the publication
of *Qindīl Umm Hāshim*, the Egyptian critic 'Alī al-Rā'ī, in his
book *Dirāsāt fī al-riwāya al-Misriyya* (Studies in the Egyptian
novel), denies that Ismā'īl used the lamp oil at all in his treatment of Fātima's eyes.[39] This is, of course, only speculation on
his part, as there is nothing in the text to either support or
deny his allegation. But that it is considered an issue at all is
far more interesting than what Ismā'īl really did with the oil.
In 1967, the Egyptian novelist and short-story writer, Yūsuf
Idris, wrote what is considered a fictional rebuttal to Haqqī's
Qindīl Umm Hāshim—"*al-Nas*"—in which he describes a
peasant remedy that, unlike Haqqī's lamp oil, does have some
real scientific and medicinal value. The leaves from a tree in
the village are used as an eye balm. The remedy, challenged by
a group of educated young village men, is sent to the city for
chemical analysis and, upon examination, the leaves are
found, in fact, to be medicinal.

Haqqī's choice of the lamp of Umm Hāshim as a locus of
simple faith and devotion, of spiritual strength and authentic
identity, might seem to be a particularily unfortunate one
given that faith in the medicinal or magical power of the sacred lamp oil can be only that—faith, without a necessary basis in "verifiable" reality or science. A far better argument for
the efficacy of the native peasant tradition and faith might
have been made if, as in the story by Yūsuf Idris, the magic
potion was one that had the possibility of some actual medicinal and scientifically verifiable value.

And yet, to make this argument is quite possibly to overlook
the gesture that underlies the symbolization of the lamp and
its oil. For *Qindīl Umm Hāshim* does not articulate just any
folk belief or traditional cure. The confrontation, at least in
this text's formulation of it, is not between the effectiveness
and efficiency of one way of being over another, of what is

---

[39] 'Alī al-Rā'ī, *Dirāsāt fī al-riwāya al-Misriyya* (Studies in the Egyptian
novel), 173.

traditional, peasant, and thus somehow authentically Egyptian over what is modern, scientific, and foreign. The concern of *Qindīl Umm Hāshim* is only secondarily of verifiable results. The lamp is charged with a far more loaded meaning. It is a symbol of faith itself. Unlike Idris's folk cure, the lamp and its oil have a specifically Islamic signification. The veneration of Umm Hāshim as the protectoress of the weak and destitute, the mosque in which she is entombed, and by extension the lamp hanging over her shrine in the niche that marks her burial place, are specific markers for that body of belief that is Islam as a whole. The lamp and the oil of Umm Hāshim then are not just incidental or unfortunate symbols; they refer to an entire belief system in which the oil and the light of the lamp, and indeed the light itself, are "symbols coined by God."

There is usually a lamp hung over the middle of the mosque's *mihrab* or prayer niche. The *mihrab* is always built in the wall of the prayer hall (or *haram*) that is closest to, that faces, Mecca and the Ka'aba, the spiritual center of Islam. The Ka'aba in Mecca is the convergence of all axes of spiritual meaning. It is the spatial center of Islam, reinforced by the duty of the *hajj* or pilgrimage to Mecca, as the *Qurān* is the linguistic center. It can hardly be coincidental that the *manarah* or minaret from which the faithful are called to prayer is located on the wall exactly opposite of the *mihrab*, thus positioning the inviolate sanctity of the Ka'aba, marked by the *mihrab*, in diametric opposition to the secular world from which the muezzin summons the faithful to prayer. Roger Joseph, in his "Semiotics of the Islamic Mosque,"[40] characterizes the mosque as

a huge hinge between two conceptual worlds: the sacred world of Islam and the secular world of practical and often messy affairs. . . . not merely a gate between the secular world of peril and the sacred world of refuge. . . . it is also an environment in which the collective spirit asserts itself over an indeterminant

[40] Roger Joseph, "The Semiotics of the Islamic Mosque," *Arab Studies Quarterly* 3.3 (1981): 285–95.

world of uncertainty and danger. . . . The two tendencies of agonistic conflict and collective solidarity are coterminous in the semiotics of the mosque. (289)

In relation to the lamp, "presumably isomorphic to the distinction between spiritual light and spiritual darkness," that hangs over the *mihrab*, Joseph quotes the "Verse of Light" passage from the *Qurān* (XXIV):

> God is the light of the heavens and the earth. *The symbol of His light is a niche* [the *mihrab*] *wherein is a lamp*; the lamp is in a glass and this glass is as a radiant star. The light is nourished by a blessed olive tree, which is *neither of the east nor of the west*, whose oil would all but glow though fire touch it not. Light upon light, God guideth to his light whom he will and *God striketh symbols for man* and God knoweth all things. (291, emphasis added)

This lamp is the dominant source of spiritual light in the mosque. Although the light of the lamp of Umm Hāshim, the Prophet's granddaughter, is a secondary light to that primary and divinely inspired one referred to above, it is clearly related in kind, if lesser in degree. Thus, the verifiable efficacy of the oil as eye medication is not really the point at all. Unlike any number of other peasant remedies or superstitions—leaves, herbs, magical stones, or trees—the text suggests the lamp oil as the tangible stuff of faith itself. *Qindīl Umm Hāshim* deals in symbols; the lamp and its oil are a symbol (coined by god and represented by Haqqī?) of a spiritual faith that is not essentially concerned with pragmatics. This opposition, as so much else in this novel, is linked to the postulation of the dichotomy between East and West as one between knowledge or science and faith. The criticisms of Haqqī's choice of lamp oil comes in a much different context, after the officers' coup of 1952 and the rise to power of Abdul Nasser. If nothing else, Abdul Nasser supplied another vocabulary with which to respond to Western domination over Egypt, one not necessarily dependent on Islam. But, as suggested in the first part of this chapter, the range of possible responses to the hegemony of the West were markedly different during the interwar years. It is in this context that the gesture of *Qindīl Umm Hāshim* must be situated.

Clearly, *Qindīl Umm Hāshim* valorizes the Egyptian peasant tradition. In doing so, the text attempts a determination of value. Cloaked in the mantle of a storyteller and focused on a character whose roots are in the peasantry, *Qindīl Umm Hāshim*'s formulation of tradition is used to frame and articulate its formulation of the modern. That there is a carefully constructed resolution in the making is apparent from the opening of the work. After all, here is a modern novel that opens with a highly literary account of the first-person narrator's traditional peasant grandfather. But pressed by the exigencies of its form and its audience, *Qindīl Umm Hāshim* cannot possibly retreat into an entirely traditional refuge. Equally pressed by exigencies of time and place, the text also cannot suggest an unequivocal break with the past. The resolution of the contradictions embodied by Ismā'īl between tradition and modernization, spirituality and pragmatism, Western Europe and the Arab East, the peasantry and a national petite bourgeoisie, cannot lie in an outright rejection by Ismā'īl of the autochthonous tradition that the peasantry represents. Such a rejection would overvalue the modern, urban, educated, scientific, and the foreign. Such a rejection might entail an implicit acceptance, or even affirmation, of a secular, foreign, and particularily Western or European model. So Ismā'īl's traditional peasant origins are subjected to something of a homogenization process. He is divested of "undesirable" peasant elements that would render him too objectionable and is allowed to maintain those elements that can be safely subsumed to his education and change of status.

If, in the previous chapter, Papadiamandis's *The Murderess* was considered as the construction of a utopic refuge from foreign onslaught and a dubious modernization, that refuge was qualified as a distinctly negative utopia—one in which, virtually regardless of authorial intention, the refuge stands revealed as a prison in its own right, as a situation that might more justifiably be considered a pretext for radical social change. *Qindīl Umm Hāshim* goes at least one step further. It neither attempts to flee the modern, as Papadiamandis's *E Fonissa*, nor does it attempt to flee or ignore the traditional, as in *Kokoro* by the Japanese novelist Natsume Sōseki (see chap. 4). Yet, the utopic resolution of *Qindīl Umm Hāshim* is of such heavily loaded symbolic content that, in attempting to resolve all oppositions in the figure of Ismā'īl, to create Ismā'īl as the literally incorporating body—and it is in this context that Naīma as Ismā'īl's "double" becomes most suggestive— the figure of Ismā'īl becomes a peculiar (and commodified) vacuum at the text's center. In his ultimate all-incorporative meaningfulness, the figure of Ismā'īl borders on its opposite, on meaninglessness.

In *The Murderess*, Frangoyiannou, in thinking that she will relieve the poor peasants of her village of the burden of girl children by killing them, is described as having "exalted herself to higher matters" (44). She overreaches what was not in her domain to even consider. In a strikingly similar fashion, Ismā'īl, in the final sections of *Qindīl Umm Hāshim* is juxtaposed to the young, beautiful, and devoutly faithful prostitute Naīma, whose prayer to Umm Hāshim has been granted. Unlike Ismā'īl, Naīma has not rebelled, nor despaired in the grace of God. She maintains her humble belief. But Ismā'īl had "grown proud and rebelled, he struck out and attacked, and overreaching himself, he fell" (55). The characterization of Ismā'īl echoes that of Frangoyiannou almost exactly. Both the old grandmother and the educated young Egyptian step out of bounds. But if for the old Greek woman the consequences of that action are irrevocable and deadly, for Ismā'īl there is a way back to integration and plenitude. Perhaps this is one of the crucial differences between Frangoyiannou's situation and Ismā'īl's. There is no precedent of plenitude for the old woman. The past, the present, and the foreseeable future are for her just a dreary continuation of one another. And so Frangoyiannou murders. In that admittedly dubious way, she "rebels against and attacks" the misery, poverty, and oppression of her own life and of the lives of her fellow islanders. Ismā'īl does not kill. Situated though as a rather explicit parallel to

Naīma, he is also presumably a prostitute. He prostitutes a tradition, a past, and a possible present. There is no such possibility for Frangoyiannou; there is nothing for her to prostitute, either literally or metaphorically. Frangoyiannou's overreaching, her hubris, predicated on the absence rather than the presence of plenitude, places her beyond recuperation, beyond the reach of human or of divine forgiveness. But Ismā'īl is reinserted into both the divine and the human scheme of things. After an epiphanic moment in the mosque when Ismā'īl feels that the flame in the lamp of Umm Hāshim is an all-knowing eye smiling at him, he goes back to the square outside of the mosque and calls out to the people there, "Come to me, all of you! Some of you have harmed me, lied to me or cheated me, but it doesn't matter, for in my heart there is room for your filth, your ignorance, your debasement, for I am of you and you are of me. I am a son of this quarter; I am a son of this Square. Time has committed a crime against you and the greater that crime, the dearer you all are to me" (55–56).

So, Ismā'īl becomes the incorporative site of reconciliation. His corpulent, slightly disheveled, bleary-eyed, and smiling figure at the close of the novel embodies the impossible resolution of all contradiction. Ismā'īl, not unlike the light of Umm Hāshim's lamp, has been overwhelmingly transformed into a metaphor, if he was not already so constituted. After his death, people of the Sayyida Zainab district recall Ismā'īl with "kindness and gratitude" to his nephew. And they pray for the forgiveness of Ismā'īl's sins. What sins? The people in the district refuse to tell the narrator of Ismā'īl's sins. They, like Ismā'īl's narrating nephew, implicate themselves in creating symbols of resolution and compromise. And to question that process, to question the content of symbols, as we know from *Qindīl Umm Hāshim* itself, is to overreach oneself and fall.

The utopia of compromise that echoes throughout *Qindīl Umm Hāshim* is restricted neither to that literary work alone nor to the cultural realm as somehow separate from the sociopolitical. The cultural arena in the Arab world has frequently been the setting for political, social, and, not least of all, linguistic debate. The problems for Egypt in creating working definitions of nationalism, democracy, class, the individual, modernization, tradition, were set upon first of all in the realm of political and social praxis. For a literary text undoubtedly speaks the *word* every bit as much as it does the *world*. Much clever and dazzling literary theory has been produced to show this gap between the word and the world. So it might be useful here to recall Louis Althusser's definition of *ideology* as "the representation of the Imaginary relationship of individuals to their real conditions of existence." In spite of the contentiousness of many of Althusser's formulations, this passage serves as a pertinent antidote to any movement that seeks too totally to estrange the text from its context. As Fredric Jameson points out in *Fables of Aggression*, both ideology and the literary text, particularly the novel, share the engagement in narrative discourse that Althusser's definition indicates. And both ideology and the literary text attempt, like Tiresias, to grasp the waters of a history tantalizing, but just out of reach.

But if men and women create history in praxis, they create it in narratives and language as well, though not, as Marx reminds us, "just as they please." *Qindīl Umm Hāshim*'s attempt to create a literary integration of a language, a form, and the representation of a social reality rent by both internal contradictions and external domination is hardly extraneous to a society for which the issue is not over. Haqqī's fictional enunciation of the dilemmas facing his own and subsequent generations are expressed in the somewhat abstracted terms of a well-educated intellectual acutely aware of his alienation from both his own culture and that of the West. Perhaps then, Haqqī's utopia of a modern compromise is less "modern" than he himself might want to admit. But, the extent to which the formal and contextual dilemma of *Qindīl Umm Hāshim* is still a part of the contemporary Egyptian and Arab situation is suggested by the Lebanese writer, Fouad Ajami, in his *The Arab Predicament: Arab Political Thought and Practice Since 1967*. He concludes his interesting, if strangely static, account of political thought and action in the Arab world as illustrated by the situation of Egypt with what is here, given the focus of the following chapter, a particularly pertinent comparison of Egypt and the Arab world with Japan.

> At the root of the nativist view of the world is a utopia—a memory of a world that once was that can be adorned, worked over, and embellished to suit current needs. In the modern world, utopias can serve as correctives, as antidotes to cynicism, as sources of inspiration. But utopias can be pushed too far. Our imagined utopias turn out to be the source of much of our misery. We never quite approximate them, and we feel all the more diminished for failing to replicate the glories of our ancestors or the perfection of our plans.[41]

To this statement, one might add that, unlike either Ajami's conclusion or Haqqī's fiction, the choice is not solely or necessarily between "the glories of our ancestors"—the past, and "the perfection of our plans"—the future.

If *Qindīl Umm Hāshim* valorizes the authenticity of the Egyptian peasant tradition and oversimplifies a notion of the West as modern, rational, and individualistic, it also attempts with humorous perspicacity, in the margins of its story, in the wielding of its form, to burrow into the fields of history, to "represent the imaginary relationship" of the people who populate the square of Sayyida Zainab to their only too real conditions of existence. This focus need not obscure the extent to which Ismā'īl is equally a representation of an imaginary relationship of the Egyptian intellectual to the conditions of his existence. It is for its representation of the dilemma of the alienated intellectual, and even more, for the depiction of the people who push in on the peripheries of that alienated intellectual's life and of Haqqī's novel itself, that *Qindīl Umm Hāshim* is remarkable. Haqqī's much-praised eloquence and style are, in addition to the structure of his work, more interesting as commentary on the problems of an Arab writer's literary production than as ends in themselves, than as definitive solutions to those problems. As for the alternative to that in-

[41] Fouad Ajami, *The Arab Predicament: Arab Political Thought and Practice Since 1967*, 200.

soluble confrontation of traditional and past glories with the modern and the future, it is perhaps more fruitful, or at least an interesting alternative, to think of the dilemma facing Egypt, and not a little of the rest of the third world, as rather that between a heritage, a legacy, and revolution.

Ismā'īl is dead. The narrating nephew of *Qindīl Umm Hāshim* concludes his story with, "May Allah grant him peace." It is the others who populate *Qindīl Umm Hāshim* who have no peace. But then neither are they dead. For them, perhaps, the choice is not simply a compromise between the old and the new, or the East and the West but a reformation of legacies from the past and an urgent necessity for change in the present. If that is a literary possibility not available within the text of *Qindīl Umm Hāshim*, perhaps it is a literal possibility outside of the novel.

Chapter 4

OF NOISY TRAINS AND GRASS PILLOWS

The interpretation of our reality through patterns not
our own serves only to make us ever more unknown,
ever less free, ever more solitary.
—Gabriel García Marquez, Stockholm,
December 1982

THE WRITING AND LIFE of the Japanese novelist Natsume Sōseki (1867–1916) straddle a great many of the boundary lines
that are frequently traced in an outline of modern Japan. The
formulation of the conflict facing the non-Western world in its
confrontation with the West as that between the traditional
and the modern—or, in Yahyā Haqqī and Alexandros Papadiamandis, the authentic and the foreign—also informs the
works of Sōseki, who is undoubtedly one of the greatest writers of his own age and of modern Japanese literature as well.
Sōseki was born a year before the Meiji Restoration and had
an early education in the Chinese classics and a college degree
in English literature. A writer of modern novels and short stories, he was also a close personal and intellectual friend of Ma-
saoka Shiki, who was largely responsible for the twentieth-
century revival of the traditional haiku form. Celebrated for
the, presumably Western, lonely and alienated modern individualism of their narrative characters, Sōseki's texts are
equally, if not quite so famously, the terrain of modern Japanese characters who, no matter how hard they try, cannot escape the impingement of the community and its social obliga-
tions on that individualism.

Sōseki's texts have been read from numerous perspectives—
as the neurotic if brilliant products of his own precarious men-

tal state;[1] as the works of a master satirist, particularly in his early novels, closely linked to the writings of the late Edo narratives—*gesaku*, literally "playful writing";[2] from the rather more conventional perspective of thematic meaning;[3] or as the object of a quasi-Freudian analysis very much in the personal and impressionistic style of Japanese literary criticism.[4] The most perceptive treatments of Sōseki's work as literary texts rather than as philosophical treatises or as the pretext for critical impressionism or for an account of the critic's own relationship with Sōseki are undoubtedly those of Etō Jun in Japanese[5] and of Masao Miyoshi in English.[6]

Yet for all the critical attention he has received both inside and outside of Japan, with the exception of the critical readings of Miyoshi and Etō, Sōseki's work remains largely ignored as the construction of a discourse in response not only to his personal life but to a literary, cultural, and sociohistorical context in which the traditional role of the intellectual and artist was under assault—as was the role of tradition in general. Sōseki's valorization of individualism, for example, is well-known and frequently cited in both his fiction and nonfiction. He spent a lifetime elaborating the image, both personal and fictional, of the lonely and isolated artist/intellectual struggling to wrest meaning and form from the intransigent stuff of everyday life. But this highly ideological position can scarcely be taken only at face value. Setting aside for the moment the simplistic question of whether or not Sōseki was in fact lonely and isolated or, alternately, neurotic and disturbed, why the resolute assumption of this artistic fiction within his narratives? Lonely and isolated writers do not by definition

---

[1] H. H. Hibbett, "Soseki and the Psychological Novel," *Tradition and Modernization in Japanese Culture*, 305–47.

[2] Sumie Jones, "Natsume Soseki's *Botchan*: The Outer World through Edo Eyes," *Approaches to the Modern Japanese Novel*.

[3] V. H. Viglielmo, "Soseki's *Kokoro*: A Descent into the Heart of Man," *Approaches to the Modern Japanese Novel*.

[4] Yoshida Rokurō, *Sakka izzen no Sōseki* and Kitayama Takashi, *Natsume Sōseki no seishin bunseki*.

[5] Etō Jun, *Natsume Sōseki*.

[6] Masao Miyoshi, *Accomplices of Silence: The Modern Japanese Novel*.

have to write about lonely, isolated writers. Or perhaps more to the point—to what is the assumption of this stance a response? To what does the text stand in opposition? To what does it proffer itself as a utopic resolution? It is these questions that are posed to Sōseki's texts, and to *Kusamakura* in particular, in this chapter. And to pose these questions to Sōseki's texts is to pose them as well to his time—a period that spans the crucial transition of the Meiji era (1868–1912). For the dilemmas and resolutions of *Kusamakura* (Pillow of grass) or *Mon* (The gate) or *Kokoro* (The heart)[7] are most discernible when situated not only in a literary and cultural context but in the social and historical contexts of which the texts are a part.

Japan's seclusion during the Tokugawa period (1600–1868) found a culmination of sorts in the anti-Tokugawa or Bakufu slogan that is used to characterize much of the struggle, domestic and foreign, that broke out in Japan following the irruption of the West. That slogan—*sonnō jōi*, "Revere the Emperor; expel the barbarian"—was to remain a substantial underpinning of Japan's social and political framework for far longer than the eight or nine years that it took to overthrow the Tokugawa regime and initiate the construction of the Meiji state.

Much has been made of the amazingly rapid changes that took place in Japan following her initial confrontation with the West in 1860, and not without reason. Within the twenty years from the beginning of the Meiji era, Japan underwent certain striking political, economic, and social transformations. In keeping with the sentiment of *sonnō jōi*, she managed both to revere the Emperor, installing him as the virtually deified center of an oligarchic political structure, and, if not quite

---

[7] Natsume Sōseki, *Sōseki Zenshu* (Sōseki's collected works). All references to Sōseki's work are from this collection. The translations in the text are my own unless otherwise noted. *Kusamakura*, *Mon*, and *Kokoro* are available in translation as, respectively: *The Three-Cornered World*, trans. Alan Turney (New York: Perigree, 1965); *Mon*, trans. Francis Mathy (Tokyo: Charles E. Tuttle, 1972); *Kokoro*, trans. Edwin McClellan (Chicago: Henry Regnery, 1957).

to expel the barbarian, at least to keep him at bay. With the adoption of a modern legal code in the 1870s and of the Constitution in 1889, Japan successfully pressed for the abolition of the unequal treaties with the West that she had been forced to accept some thirty years earlier. And Japan's total and startling victory over the Chinese Empire a few years later in the Sino-Japanese War (1894–1895) served as an unequivocal declaration to the West of her no-longer-inferior position. Japan's entrance into the world capitalist system, regardless of the resulting character of her development,[8] was and still is an exception in the Far East and in the third world as a whole. L. S. Stavrianos, in his *Global Rift: The Third World Comes of Age*, cites precisely the singularity of "the Japanese exception" in a chapter of the same name: "By 1889, Japan had gained legal jurisdiction over all foreigners on her soil, and in doing so, she became the first Asian nation to break the chains of Western control."[9]

[8] See, for example, Jon Halliday, *A Political History of Japanese Capitalism*, 22, where he asserts that "two of the most remarkable distortions which mark Japanese capitalism—the process of the formation and accumulation of capital, and the specific form of Japanese imperialism which was distinguished by an acute lack of capital ('the highest stage of capitalism' without capital)." Studies of uneven development and of related theories of dependency, underdevelopment, and unequal exchange are many and of various perspectives but they afford valuable insights into "third," "second," and "first" world development. For the former (uneven development) see, for example, Marx's late writing on Russia—in English, Teodor Shanin, *Late Marx and the Russian Road* (New York: Monthly Review Press, 1983); in Japanese, Wada Haruki *Marukusu, Engerusu, to kakamei Roshia* (Marx, Engels, and revolutionary Russia) (Tokyo, 1975); or Lenin's *Imperialism*, Leon Trotsky's "Preface" to volume 1 of his *History of the Russian Revolution*. For the latter, see, for example, Samir Amin, *Unequal Development*; Emmanuel Arghiri, *Unequal Exchange: A Study of the Imperialism of Trade*; Andre Gunder Frank, *Capitalism and Underdevelopment in Latin America*; Immanuel Wallerstein, *The Modern World System*.

[9] L. S. Stavrianos, *The Global Rift: The Third World Comes of Age*, 358–59. This passage also suggests the contradictory role that Japan played in Asia. On the one hand, the example of her independence was an inspiration for many other Asian nations struggling for national independence from Western control. On the other, her aggressive and expansionist aims posed a very real and immediate threat of Japanese imperialist domination.

Internally, the threats of peasant uprisings, dissident samurai revolt, and dissatisfied daimyo counterrevolution were quelled. The peasant insurrections, which had contributed significantly to the overthrow of the Tokugawa shogunate, were systematically crushed with the help of a newly conscripted army and, in some cases, former Tokugawa officials. The samurai themselves were liberated by law in 1871 from what had been their official role as a military force and were then quickly inducted into the new "armies" of the modern Japanese state—government administration and government-sponsored business.[10] The daimyo were made governors of their former fiefs, to the great dissatisfaction of many of them, but awarded handsome financial recompense for their losses.[11] With these potential threats to the new regime neutralized, and with the emperor and his attendant oligarchy firmly enthroned, and enshrined, in Tokyo, and

with the class foundations of the new state well secured, the Tokyo officials proceeded to organize a bureaucratic machine that controlled firmly all key areas of power before the adoption of the Constitution in 1889 and the election of the first Diet in 1890. At the head of the new system was the imperial institution, which Hirobumi [Itō, a Choshu official and leader of the dominant government faction which shaped a great deal of the new political system] had viewed as the lynchpin of state ideology and bureaucratic authority; hence the support accorded to Shinto as the state cult, which exalted the Emperor as the descendant of the sun goddess, and the personification of national unity and patriotism.[12]

Concomitant with the delineation of this political framework was the construction of an educational system with similar goals and ideology. Itō Hirobumi himself selected the first minister of education, Arinori Mori.

It was within this conservative political context that Japan

---

[10] Stavrianos, *The Global Rift*, 357.
[11] Ibid., 358.
[12] Ibid., 357.

modernized her economy and increased her national productivity, with the vast majority of the resulting economic surplus awarded to the military and the ruling elite. Agricultural production was markedly increased and then used as the tax base for draconian land taxes. The capital from these taxes was used, in turn, to fund Japan's industrialization. Also centered in the countryside was the rapidly expanding and equally profitable textile industry, which for many years provided the bulk of Japan's exports. Because of the high rents that were extracted from the tenant farmers, making it more profitable to the landowners to keep them on the land than to drive them off, and because of the development of the textile industry in the rural areas, there was no large exodus of landless peasants from the countryside into the cities, as was the case in other third world countries.[13] With so much of the population of Japan actually living in the countryside, and with the countryside providing so much of the economic basis for Japan's modernization, it is an interesting ideological characteristic of early-twentieth-century Japan that the peasant or the rural resident does not figure largely in literary discourse. The peasant is, both literally and metaphorically, rather remarkably absent from the Japanese cultural text, in what seems a reversal of the situation in Greece and Egypt.

And unlike the construct of the Tokugawa period, in which the peasant, rhetorically if not in fact, was valorized as the backbone of the nation, second in the rigid class structure only to the samurai, there is little sense from the documents of the Meiji that the peasant was designated as anything like the ideological repository of authenticity or national pride or traditional culture. Both the Arabic and Greek novels of the early twentieth century focus to an inordinate extent on the life of the "authentic" and "traditional" countryside and peasant; Japanese novels, with few exceptions, more conspicuously ignore the peasant and his or her life, focusing instead on the nascent bourgeoisie of the cities. So it is not suprising that the

---

[13] Or, in fact, as was the case in Europe—with the land enclosures in Britain, for example.

nativist discourse that so strongly marked the fictions of both Alexandros Papadiamandis and Yahyā Haqqī is rather distinctively absent from the work of Natsume Sōseki. It is only in the contemporary novel, most especially in the fiction of Ōe Kenzaburo (discussed in chap. 7), that there is an attempt to locate in the Japanese peasantry what is postulated as a somehow more purely autochthonous identity.

By mid-Meiji, *sonnō jōi* was modified by another slogan—*bunmei kaika*—"civilization and enlightenment." It referred of course to that "civilization and enlightenment" that was considered a specific attribute of the West. W. G. Beasley, in his *Modern History of Japan*, summarizes the intent of *bunmei kaika* quite explicitly.

> Industrial civilization, which the West exemplified, was a stage of development to which all societies should aspire, including that of Japan. Hence all the manifestations of change we have been discussing—constitutions, conscript armies, factories, Western-style novels and art—were related phenomena. They were parts of a whole that embodied universal, not just Western values; to excel in them was to be civilized.[14]

Some sense of the content of these "civilized" changes is graphically illustrated in the juxtaposition of two well-known illustrations of the Japanese Imperial Court that Beasley includes in his history.[15] The first is set in 1868, the second in 1889. In just thirty years, the change in dress, architecture, and decor is of course truly striking. This is used as an illustration of Japan's modernization and Europeanization. It is a noteworthy detail that the barely visible traditional imperial garb worn by the emperor and his male nobles in the first illustration has been replaced, not by European-style court dress but by military uniforms. Modernization entailed a very specifically military character. But perhaps the most interesting aspect of these two paintings is not so much the outward changes as the social consistency. As striking as the changes in

---

[14] W. G. Beasley, *The Modern History of Japan*, 154.
[15] Beasley, *Modern History of Japan*, illus. no. 13 and 14, n.p.

appearance is the *retention* of a particular hierarchical order, with the emperor firmly established at the center. If anything, the emperor has assumed an even more openly dominant position in the later painting.

The position of the emperor in these two illustrations suggests Roland Barthes's brilliant and sometimes outrageously ingenious reading of modern Japan, particularly of the city of Tokyo that unfurls itself around the palace of the emperor.

> [Tokyo] offers this precious paradox: it does possess a center, but this center is empty. The entire city turns around a site both forbidden and indifferent, a residence concealed beneath foliage, protected by moats, inhabited by an emperor who is never seen, which is to say, literally, by no one knows who. . . . One of the two most powerful cities of modernity is thereby built around an opaque ring of walls, streams, roofs, and trees whose own center is no more than an evaporated notion, subsisting here, not in order to irradiate power, but to give to the entire urban movement the support of its central emptiness, forcing the traffic to make a perpetual detour.[16]

While the postulation of the empty center and, by implication, of the empty subject is certainly provocative, Barthes's formal reading of the text of modern Japan is at least equally a corrective prescription for the meaning- and subject-centered West. The formal posture of the emperor might very well be one of empty quiescence, but it was a posture that served an unquestionably useful purpose in the organization of the modern Japanese state and in the consolidation and maintenance of state power. Therefore, it is perhaps not quite the contradiction it might seem that in the second illustration the emperor is announcing the Meiji Constitution. The necessary correlative of Barthes's analysis is the qualification, but not negation, in Jon Halliday's *Political History of Japanese Capitalism*: "Though the formal institutions of bourgeois parliamentary democracy were introduced . . . the existence of the imperial institution placed the ultimate moral authority for all

[16] Roland Barthes, *The Empire of Signs*, 30–31.

the state's acts outside the bourgeois democratic arena. Emperorism was the foundation of Japanese authoritarianism."[17]

In addition to adopting the institutions of Western dress, decor, architecture, and parliamentary democracy, Meiji intellectuals, politicians, and social planners perceived quite accurately that there was a distinct relationship between the domestic achievements of the Western powers and their global acquisitions. These ideological links between Western liberalism and Western imperialism were not only apparent to the conservative shapers of Meiji Japanese policy. Frequently, even opposition demands and proposals for internal democratic reform depended on jingoistic foreign positions. The justification, for progressive liberals and conservatives alike, was that in order to protect herself from the expanding West, Japan had no alternative but to expand.

> This is like riding in a third-class train; at first there is adequate space but as more passengers enter, there is no place for them to sit. If while rubbing shoulders and supporting yourself with your arms you lose your place you can't recover the same position. . . . The logic of necessity requires people to plant both feet firmly and expand their elbows into any opening that may occur for, unless this is done, others will close the opening.[18]

Largely isolated from the outside world, particularly the Western world, for some two hundred years, Japan was flooded with new and foreign ideas in the Meiji period, if not with the foreign capital and consumer goods that were typical of the "opening up" of so many other third world countries in the nineteenth century. The rigid control that the new government maintained over foreign investments and imports played a crucial role in the ability of Japan to escape grossly dependent economic development. What the burgeoning Japanese state exerted less control over, at least for the first twenty years or so, was the influx of ideas: of bourgeois individualism and

---

[17] Halliday, *Political History of Japanese Capitalism*, 40.
[18] Nishi Aurane, a Meiji bureaucrat, quoted in Stavrianos, *The Global Rift*, 362.

parliamentarian democracy, of Darwin's theory of evolution and John Stuart Mill's *On Liberty*, of Samuel Smiles' *Self Help* and Thomas More's *Utopia*, Bulwer Lytton's *Ernest Maltravers* and Rousseau's *Social Contract*. All of these works were available in translation by 1880. The next decade saw the influx of the works of Turgenev, Dostoevsky, Tolstoy,[19] Victor Hugo, and Ibsen. Serialized in newspapers and periodicals, these translations were widely read and discussed, particularly among what had been the samurai and merchant classes. But the Japanese framework in which works such as these were situated is made quite clear in the autobiography of Fukuzawa Yukichi[20] (1835–1901), an educator, translator, and scholar who seems representative of a great deal of Meiji Japan. The patriotism/emperor worship (*chūkun*) and love of country (*aikoku*) equation that increasingly and decisively came to modify *sonnō jōi* and *bunmei kaika* as the official catch words of an age clearly inform Fukuzawa's statements: "After all, the purpose of my entire work has not only been to gather young men together and give them the benefit of foreign books but to open this 'closed' country of ours and bring it wholly into the light of Western civilization. For only thus may Japan become strong in the arts of both war and peace" (246–47). The ominous portent of Fukuzawa's closing phrase is made explicit later in his autobiography, as it was made increasingly explicit in the direction taken by the leaders of Meiji Japan: "One of the tangible results [of Japan's advancement] was to be seen a few years ago in our victorious war with China . . . unimpassioned thought will show this victory over China as nothing more than an event in the progress of our foreign relations" (335).

It is within this context of an increasingly authoritarian and

[19] The works of these three writers were available in Japanese translation largely through the efforts of Futabatei Shimei, probably Japan's first "modern" novelist. His *Ukigumo* (*Floating clouds*) (1887–1889) is remarkable for its successful linguistic compromise between the literary and the colloquial languages and for its creation of the modern and isolated fictional hero who struggles against what is posited as the hypocrisy of the society around him.

[20] Fukuzawa Yukichi, *Autobiography*.

imperialist nationalism that the work of Natsume Sōseki can be understood as a discourse of resistance, as a gesture of defiance, increasingly overcome by the narrowing boundaries of the modern Japanese state. In this sense, the isolation and alienation of Sōseki's characters from the presumably traditional ties that link members of Japanese society as they do members of the Japanese family can also be seen as an attempt to distance, to refuse, what was officially posited as the (ideo)logical extension of those social and familial ties—patriotic loyalty to the emperor (*chūkun*) as the father of the nation.[21]

Loyalty to the emperor had been an essential component of the samurai opposition to the shōgun in the late Tokugawa; the samurai had shifted their allegiance from the daimyo to the emperor. But the elite tradition imbuing the emperor with special significance was, clearly, not shared by the commoners. And so, from mid-Meiji on, educational and political leaders sought to focus popular attention on the imperial symbol. Traditional values, whether actual or only official, of familial loyalty and filial piety were extended to a larger loyalty to what is retrospectively called the "family state" (*kazoku kokka*)[22] with the emperor as the father of the national family.

> The Emperor was the family of the nation, it was argued, because the imperial family was the "national head family" (*kokumin sōka*) and the imperial family was the *kokumin sōka* because it derived from the topmost *kami* (spirits, deities) in the Shinto tradition. . . . The Confucian-type familistic ethic provided the real foundation for the society, and increasingly, from the late-Meiji period on, Japanese ideologists spoke of the nation

[21] For a somewhat different view of the ideology of Meiji Japan's emperor system, which proposes that the dominant "myth" of the Meiji Emperor casts him primarily as a modern, secular, and constitutional monarch, see Carol Gluck's *Japan's Modern Myths: Ideology in the Late Meiji Period*, esp. chap. 4. Atsuko Hirai's review article, "The State and Ideology in Meiji Japan" (*Journal of Asian Studies* 46.1 [1987]: 89–103), in addition to being an incisive commentary on *Japan's Modern Myths*, offers an interesting and informed overview of this issue in recent scholarship.

[22] Halliday *Political History of Japanese Capitalism*, 322, n. 10.

as an "extended family." The nation was not *like* a family, it really *was* a family. This national family, supported from below by the socio-ethical patterns of individual households, was then "sanctified from above by Shinto beliefs which imbued it with a quality of sacredness."[23]

From within the contracting national construct described above, the dominance in Sōseki's texts of characters, relationships, situations, language, and even narrative structures that transgress the borders of national (and nationalistic) definition belie textual characterizations of fleeting, haiku novels and poetic beauty that withdraws from the real world to a realm of some higher truth.

In Sōseki's novel, *Kokoro* (The heart), a young student abandons his dying father in the countryside in a futile attempt to rush back to Tokyo, to his mentor—*sensei* (teacher)—who is presumably already dead. This spiritual, familial, and geographic flight on the part of the student evokes a social chain of patriarchial symbols that lead from the father of a single family unit to the sacred person of what was, in late Meiji, postulated as the ultimate father of the nation, the emperor himself. Or, in *Mon* (The gate), the somber hero, Sōsuke, is unable to successfully participate in the material, commercial world[24] or to find traditional spiritual salvation at or beyond the gate of a Zen monastery, whence the title. In addition, Sōsuke has violated social and family mores by his marriage for love, as he fails those same mores by his inability to oversee the education and successful establishment of his younger brother. In a Japanese sociopolitical construct that privileged family loyalty and filial piety, and that, by mid-Meiji, had rather masterfully transmuted that loyalty and piety into loyalty and piety to the emperor and the nation, Sōsuke is indeed guilty of a major transgression. And if Sōsuke in *Mon* or the *sensei* and his young protege in *Kokoro* or the

---

[23] Ibid., 41.

[24] In a characteristic gesture of overdetermination that recurs in many of Sōseki's narratives, the landscape in *Mon* stands as a marker for, emphasizes, and makes textually inevitable and irresolvable Sōsuke's failures.

rambling artist/narrator of *Kusamakura* never quite manage
as characters within Sōseki's texts to assume a consciously
critical stance, Sōseki's texts themselves raise a darkly despairing and contradictory objection, not to modernization and the
foreign, not to nationalism and the leap from a feudal state to
a monoply capitalist one, but to the stultifying social and cultural effects of the specific direction that modernization, nationalism, foreign "importation," and capitalism took. Some
of the contradictory implications of such a position of resistance, of increasingly diminished defiance, are more apparent
on a closer analysis of Sōseki's novels.

The text as utopic gesture that was suggested in the consideration of the novels in the last two chapters, is a particularly
appropriate notion, though with a distinctly different reso-
nance, in the opening pages of Sōseki's *Kusamakura* (Pillow
of grass). Here assiduously creating the stance of the detached
artistic observer of life, Sōseki's first-person narrator muses on
the contradictions of existence.

> Climbing up a mountain path, I fell to thinking. . . . If reason
> prevails, you become rigid. If you pole [through a stream of]
> emotions, you're swept away [by the tide]. If you're willful, you
> become straitjacketed. The world of men is a pretty difficult
> place in which to live. . . . Stripping away the troublesome wor-
> ries from this difficult life, envision before you a pleasant world
> instead. This is what poetry, painting, music or sculpture is. . . .
> It is sufficient if you can see . . . this decadent and defiled every-
> day world purified and serene in the camera of your innermost
> thoughts. (387–88)

The text and art as a particular kind of utopia—transcendent, removed, elevated—could scarcely be more explicit. After almost two pages of these elevated meditations, the unnamed narrator stumbles on the rocky mountain path and
almost breaks his neck. Quite literally, and with no little
irony, tripped up in his philosophical speculations, the artist/
narrator is suddenly made aware of the dominating presence
of the natural world around him. It is this overwhelming and
powerful nature that gives rise, the narrator claims, to a work

of art. It is also in relation to this powerful and overwhelming nature that the narrator stands as peculiarly alien. Nature is here represented as distinctly foreign, beyond human control—at times frighteningly so. And thus perhaps it allows no human interaction other than passive observation. The narrator's characterization of his own mental state certainly suggests just such passivity: "Already I felt like a painted figure on a canvas" (410); or, "I wanted to stay there for a couple of weeks, quietly, like a plant growing from a root beneath the tatami" (426). This, then, is the basis for the narrating artist's attempt to escape the common world of men and women— although he is noticeably more reluctant to detach himself from one particular woman—and, like the representation of nature that he so carefully narrates, to look on "quietly," in "cold impartiality." This scarcely novel opposition—in either the Japanese or in the English traditions that *Kusamakura* explicitly cites—between the human world and an extrahuman natural world, gestures beyond itself, however, to what is perhaps a stance in the face of neither nature nor of society but of history itself. It is not Tokyo or human relationships alone from which our hero wants to escape. It is his own contingency in the face of a history that, like nature, appears impartial, overwhelming, and frighteningly beyond the control of any individual—even intellectuals, artists, or novelists. The bogeyman that insistently pokes his head up through the fabric of *Kusamakura* and the narrator's aesthetic utopia belongs "not to our world. . . . to a world far, far away. In that world, men are moving amidst the smell of gunsmoke. And floundering in crimson blood, they fall at random. In the sky overhead a terrible thunder sounds (546).

It is the presence of this "world far, far away" and its repercussions in the novel that scatter the narrator's grass pillow to the winds. But the overt confrontation between text and history, or text and train, is resolutely held off until the closing of the novel.

The intrusion of this train, carrying soldiers off to the war front in Russia, is not the only "secret" contained in the last pages of the text. It is in the closing pages of *Kusamakura* that the narrator finds the "missing element" that has confounded him throughout the text. Our artist has been perplexed by his inability to capture on canvas the face of Nami, the mysterious and beautiful daughter of the old man who owns the remote inn where the artist/narrator has taken refuge from the vile everyday world. Nami, the Chinese characters of whose name mean "what beauty" (although a homophone means, amusingly enough, "mediocre, average, ordinary"), manages to elude our narrating artist in more ways than one for virtually the entire novel. But as the train carrying both Nami's cousin and her estranged husband to fight in the Russo-Japanese War pulls out of the station, "compassion" flickers across her face. It is the manifestation of this "compassion" (*aware*)[25] that enables the narrator to complete the painting of Nami in his mind's eye. (And *only* in his mind's eye. Can it be a coincidence that our artist has been unable to paint a single picture during his retreat from the everyday world? A few sketches here and there, some poems, and the internal artistic endeavors that culminate in his mental "painting" of Nami are the sum total of his mountain oeuvre.)

Ironically though, it is precisely the train—that belching, noisy representative of the material world—that occasions the artistic climax of *Kusamakura*. This studied (and almost anticlimactic) gesture of closure in a novel that self-consciously lauds the arbitrary and nonlinear belies the presence that ends neither the novel nor the narrator's utopic retreat. It is the impinging presence of the train, and the history to which it gestures, that—rather than affording closure to the text, rather than marking the culmination of the narrator's artistic endeavors—calls both closure and culmination into question. It

[25] It seems hardly coincidental that this term—*aware*—is one loaded with classical literary associations. It is, for example, one of the distinguishing characteristics of the tenth-century romantic hero of Murasaki Shikibu's *Tale of the Genji*, Prince Genji. See Robert Brower and Earl Miner, *Japanese Court Poetry* (Stanford: Stanford University Press, 1961), for a discussion of the concept of *aware* in classical poetry and Peter N. Dale's *The Myth of Japanese Uniqueness*, especially 65–68, for a critique of the mystification of that term in cultural studies of Japan.

is the presence of history on the margins of this "poetic, haiku novel" that forms not an open-ended text but a curiously limited, even dead-ended, one. For the artful continuation of the narrating artist's story becomes more difficult with each successive page. In spite of the contention of the narrator that, in reading (or writing?) novels, "it doesn't matter whether you start from the beginning, from the end, or you pick out random passages here and there," *Kusamakura* does end, almost in relief. Though it is presumably Nami's compassion that "completes" the narrator's painting, and the novel as well, it is even more essentially the intrusion of the train on its way from the capital to the war front—"that unsympathetic and heartless contraption . . . so typical of modern civilization . . . [and] of the world of reality"—that ends *Kusamakura* and its narrator's musings. On the novel's most literal level, if it is an expression of compassion on Nami's face that allows the narrator to complete his mental painting of her, then it is the train, its destination and its passengers, that are the pretext for her expression.

The insistent assertion of the novel's artist/narrator is clearly, if ironically, that escape from the everyday world allows unencumbered artistic creation. But the novel itself belies that assertion, since the narrator is literally unable to create anything outside of his mind's eye (other than narrating the novel, of course). The freedom of *Kusamakura*'s narrator to "create" as he pleases is resolutely impinged upon, presumably by nature itself, in a narrative gesture that recalls the opening lines of Marx's *The Eighteenth Brumaire*.[26] Men and women make art but they do not make it just as they please or under circumstances of their own choosing. Like the making of history, the making of art is never free of what has already been and of what exists simultaneously in the present with the making. If Louis Napoleon's attempt to make history is marked by repetition, by the impingement of the past and the dead—all of which he seeks to ignore, the making of the narrator's art, and perhaps even of the novel *Kusamakura*, is im-

[26] See chap. 1, n.12.

pinged upon by the present, by history, by the social and political world of imperialist wars, belching trains, and actual
and potential death, all of which the narrator tries to escape.
His impinged-upon stance in the face of an overwhelming nature is, metaphorically at least, also his stance in the face of
history and a world that are equally overwhelming, over
which he has no absolute control. But then, ironically, neither
does he have absolute control over his world of artistic creation. He is repeatedly and consistently confronted with the
limitations and contingency of his own perspective. He arguably "makes" art but not—as at least we, if not he, recognize—just as he chooses.

It is here that the significance of Sōseki's ironic treatment of
his characters—a precious commodity in the modern Japanese
novel—is most apparent. Irony is there in the introduction of
his stumbling philosophical hero or the use of the train, the
growling monster of the modern world, to elicit the comple-
tion of our narrating artist's endeavors, and as an equally
ironic commentary on the very possibility of those endeavors.
Here too, the narrator's insistence on uncovering, like a good
detective, the real truth about, the real face of, both Nami and
nature cedes to an implicit artistic impotence at the literary
representation of the "real"—be it a face, a landscape, a story,
or a clearly defined relation to history and the past.

If nature is a loaded ideological marker in *Kusamakura*,
then the representation of the natural landscape must play a
significant role. Sōseki's literary representations of nature
have presumably been so evocative, so "immediate," that they
have actually occasioned a number of paintings. But the landscape of Sōseki's texts suggests much less the immediacy of
nature than it does an overdetermined construction of meaning *in* nature. The textual representation of the natural landscape, and even of the man-made aspects of the landscape,
serves as a petrification of the geographic and symbolic terrain
on and within which the narrative unfolds. So, in *Mon*, the
impotence, failure, and poverty of Sōsuke is graphically indi-
cated by his geographical juxtaposition to the prolificacy, success, and comfortable wealth of his neighbor. Sōsuke is situ-

ated in a dark, cramped house overshadowed by a sheer cliff
that rises to the sunny, expansive home of his "superior"
neighbor, Sakai. Although Sōsuke is near enough to see the
sunlight on the walls of Sakai's house and hear the other
man's children and dog playing in the yard, the steep wall of
earth—the natural landscape—separates the two families irrevocably. This "natural" geographic separation is then a
marker for the social, economic, and sexual (for Sōsuke and
his wife are physically unable to have children) difference between them. The only direct contact between the two households is precipitated by a clumsy thief who, hurrying to escape
from the wealthy man's home after an attempted burglary,
falls down the steep cliff into Sōsuke's tiny yard below. The
thief flees, leaving behind him Sakai's gold-lacquered letter
box, its contents scattered on Sōsuke's tiny veranda. And in
an ironic (and coprophiliac) gesture, one of the letters is crum-
pled and used to cover "the thief's calling card"—human
feces. It is the action of this defecating thief, a resident of neither Sōsuke's nor Sakai's strata, that transverses both literally
and metaphorically the mechanistic landscape. In order for
Sōsuke to climb up to Sakai's house, it is "necessary to walk
halfway down the street, then ascend the slope, and finally return halfway back again to arrive at Sakai's front door." Sōsuke and his wife are consigned to the bottom of the cliff. Direct ascent is impossible; direct descent is only possible the
way the thief accomplished it. And the impossibility of the col-
lapse of that natural landscape that separates the two men and
their families is insistently attested to by the neighborhood
grocer in the opening pages of the novel.

> The old greengrocer, who had lived in the neighborhood for
> some twenty years, had taken the trouble to explain at the
> kitchen door [one day] that the slope had in fact once been cov-
> ered with a bamboo grove but that when the bamboo was cut
> and cleared, the roots had not been dug up but were still imbed-
> ded in the slope. The soil was thus more solid than one might
> expect. The grocer had answered [Sōsuke's incredulous re-
> sponse] . . . that, nevertheless, the embankment was firm. He

had spoken forcefully, as if it were a matter of his own vindication, that, whatever happened, the embankment would not come tumbling down on them.[27]

Sōseki's fiction displays far more than just one instance in which the natural landscape is charged with unnatural significance. In *Kokoro*, the landscape is again made to speak of unbridgeable divisions, though in this text the divisions are rather more horizontal than vertical, as in *Mon*. At one end of the narrative's horizon is the country home of the young student who is a main character in the novel. In the country is the student's natural father, a wealthy and successful peasant. At the other end of the horizontal range is the capital of Tokyo and the student's symbolic father or mentor, the *sensei*. If the country represents the pursuit, and attainment in the case of the student's family, of financial success, the city stands for a world of intellectual pursuits and rather more questionable attainments. Situated above these two poles, in true Meiji fashion, as noted earlier in this chapter, is the ultimate figure of the symbolic father—the Meiji emperor. Here the vertical distance is passable only metaphorically and, even then, only in one direction, there being no thoroughfare to the imperial realm.

And so, in what seems a rather conspicuously noncoincidental maneuver, *Kokoro* situates its young student hero in a distinctly constricted and constricting landscape, however beautiful the details of that landscape might be. The novel opens at the seashore in Kamakura where both the student and the *sensei* are vacationing, though they have not yet met one another. The development of their relationship and the growing overshadowing of the younger man by the older (reminiscent of the literal overshadowing of Sōsuke in *Mon* by his successful neighbor) after their meeting and return to Tokyo makes up the first section of the novel—"*Sensei* and I"—and is narrated by the young student. The student's father falls seriously ill and, in the second section—"[My] Parents and I"—the young man returns to the countryside to care for the

---

[27] Sōseki, *Sōseki zanshu*, vol. 4, 628.

old man and to assume his familial responsibilities. Again narrated by the student, this section carefully elaborates that against which the life of the *sensei* in Tokyo, and by extension the future of the young student himself, is posited. Conspicuously loaded denominators of filial piety and familial loyalty are everywhere evident here, whether by their presence or by their absence, as the young man is absorbed into his family's preparations for the imminent death of the father. As the father lies dying, the imperial horizon is clouded by the death of the Emperor Meiji and, within days, by the dutiful double suicide of the hero of the Russo-Japanese War, General Nogi, and his wife. Toward the end of the second section, the student receives a long letter from the *sensei* in Tokyo, which concludes: "By the time this letter reaches you, I will no doubt already be dead." The young student leaves his dying father in the countryside and rushes to the station to catch the first train back to Tokyo. While on the train, he reads the *sensei*'s letter from beginning to end for the first time. Thus the third and final section of the novel—"*Sensei* and the Suicide Note"—is the letter itself, in which the *sensei* attempts to explain his life, his loneliness, and his guilty isolation to the young student. As he rushes away from his dying father, the young man violates the precepts of familial loyalty and devotion on which the ideology of social order and state power rests. His naive and rather thick-headed insistence that the *sensei* divulge his secrets—not unlike the artist/narrator of *Kusamakura*, who insistently pursues Nami's secrets—is rewarded by the suicide note that is the older man's letter.

Again the precepts of some extrafamilial or surrogately paternal relationship are violated. For to speak his secret means death for the *sensei*. With the list of the dead father figures in *Kokoro* at three, going on four, the young student is fixed in a spatial and temporal freeze-frame on the train, halfway between his dying natural father and his presumably already dead surrogate father. He is halfway, as well, between the material success of the countryside and the intellectual knowledge and despair of the city. Surrounded by death and the crumbling of the established order on three sides, the young student, or more accurately the text itself, never overtly constructs a fourth pole or alternative in this triangular opposition. Like the precipice that dominates Sōsuke's yard and home, the landscape of *Kokoro* is locked into a presumably unalterable natural setting. This then is the evocative landscape, the beautiful natural world, that marks Sōseki's works. Selected *details* of nature or of the landscape in Sōseki's texts might be framed in exquisite images of poetic beauty but the overall construct of nature is a rigid and not-quite-so-poetic textual schema that attempts to posit the naturalness and inevitability of the dilemmas and their solutions embodied in the text. Nature is not "immediate" in the works of this modern Japanese novelist, though there is undoubtedly a *pretext* of immediacy. Instead, the textual insistence on nature's immediacy calls attention precisely to the mediating forces at work on the text and on its representation of nature.

And so it comes as no surprise that the description of landscape in *Kusamakura* is hardly predicated on the immediate apprehension of an immediate and natural nature. Both nature, and what seems to be that other textual place marker for nature—the mysterious Nami—are persistently obscured and at a remove. This remove is both literal—mist, the rain, the dark night, the sleepy and dream-blurred vision of the narrator, steam from a hot bath, distance, falling cherry blossoms—and metaphoric—images from classical Japanese poetry, a Noh mask, a painting by Millais, lines from a poem by Wordsworth, the narrator's own pompous intellectualizing, folktales, and village gossip. Only presumably immediate, nature in Sōseki's text is always at a distance, always framed, and filtered. And unlike the presumptions of the English Romantics that *Kusamakura* quotes, there is no divine hand behind the "reality" of the natural world. But the absence of the divine or of fate does not make nature, for *Kusamakura*'s narrating artist, any less of an overwhelmingly dominant force. In the face of an imperturbably indifferent natural world and of a "contaminated" human world, art and nature are a utopic escape for Sōseki's narrating artist. This almost whimsical faith in the resolvent capabilities of nature and art is never again afforded a quite so insistent position in Sōseki's texts. For in the later novels, *Mon* and *Kokoro*, nature, the physical landscape, becomes not so much an opportunity for utopic escape as an almost mechanistically rigid symbol of the very fixed impossibility of "escape." So consideration of the gesture of escape in *Kusamakura* becomes a crucial departure point for the reading of virtually all of Sōseki's later works. What are then the dimensions of *Kusamakura*'s ironic escape that are so resolutely precluded from subsequent texts?

Kusamakura's unnamed artist/narrator sets off for a retreat in the mountains, an escape from the modern city of Tokyo, to contemplate life from afar, immersed in nature and his own thoughts of utopic creation. While this is not quite the same concept of utopic resolution that is suggested in earlier chapters, the aestheticist pose of Sōseki's narrator provides a convenient departure point for a consideration of *Kusamakura* as both individual and collective response to a specific historical moment. And, even solely within the context of Sōseki's fiction, a coherent treatment of the later novels is difficult without a consideration of this early work.

Kusamakura was written—incredibly, in only one week— and published in 1906. Sōseki had already established a reputation for himself with two slightly earlier satirical works— *Wagahai nekko de aru* (I am a cat) in 1905–1906 and *Botchan* (Little master) in 1906. And, although *Kusamakura* is not itself primarily a satirical work, it is difficult to miss the irony in much of this text. These works, like much of Sōseki's fiction, were serialized daily in the Tokyo newspaper, *Asahi Shimbun*. With the success of, and income from, the publication of these two works, Sōseki was able, in 1907, to resign, with few regrets, from his post in English literature at Tokyo University. From then until his premature death in 1916, Sōseki worked as staff novelist and literary editor for the *Asahi Shimbun* and devoted himself to the production of fiction. In the nine years that remained to him, he wrote at least as many novels, two more works of literary criticism on English literature,[28] and a great number of articles.

---

[28] *Eibungaku keishiki ron* [A study of form in English literature] had already been published in 1903.

Although *Kusamakura* is frequently treated as a case apart from the rest of Sōseki's fiction, it is in fact central to all of his work. The primary difference between the stance of the hero/narrator/artist of *Kusamakura* and the intellectual heroes of the later novels, such as *Mon* or *Kokoro*, is a certain loss of ironic innocence and optimism in the resolvent capabilities of art. The rupture of narrative voice, the discontinuity of narrative development, the impingement of a social reality that is posited as exterior and repressive on an individual character/protagonist/narrator that is himself (for they are invariably male) peculiarly dislocated—these characteristics mark *Kusamakura* no less than they do the later works. In fact, *Kusamakura* and *Botchan*, written and published in the same year, are test cases of sorts for the extension of Sōseki's narratives into the human realm.

Sōseki's first novel, *Wagahai nekko de aru* (I am a cat) was presumably narrated by a stray cat; the narrators of both of the subsequent works are conspicuously human. But the membership in the human species of the narrators of the two subsequent works assures neither their clear-cut identity as individual characters nor, particularly in the case of the artist of *Kusamakura*, the localization of a definitive point of view. Instead, *Kusamakura*'s narrator rather purposely flees a coherent and localized point of view. He is, if anything, the ironic deflation of the possibility of a bourgeois aestheticist hero. The opening passage of the novel cited earlier is less remarkable for what it reveals about Sōseki or his philosophy than for what, perhaps precisely through its ironic tone, it camouflages.

This is not to disregard Sōseki's critical commentaries and authorial positions on the problems of literature and culture. Nor is it to exclude a consideration of the effect on his fiction of his own critical participation in Japan of the late Meiji and early Taishō periods as one wrought with aesthetic and personal exigencies. Quite the contrary. But then neither is Sōseki's fiction the direct and unmediated presentation of his aesthetic positions. The award in Japanese fiction for equating the production of a life-style with the production of a literary work should perhaps go to the more insistent practitioners of the *watakushi shōsetsu*—or I-novels—such as Shiga Naoya, Dazai Osamu, or Nagai Kafū.[29] In contrast to these writers, Sōseki manages to exceed, to slip beyond, the boundaries of the authorial self as the delimiting factor of fiction.

Sōseki's title, *Kusamakura*—literally "pillow of grass"— immediately establishes, on one level, a link to classical Japanese literature, in that it is a classical epithet, or "pillow word" (*makura kotoba*), for a journey. And it is also a reference to a traditional genre of Japanese "travel journals," such as the poetry and prose of Saigyō or Bashō or Sōra. In fact, there is explicit citation in *Kusamakura*'s first chapter of Bashō, the seventeenth-century poet and writer, in the reference to a haiku written by him during his famous journey to the north of Japan.[30] Sōseki's narrator is determined to recognize, like Bashō, the sublimely poetic even in the most irritating and mundane aspects of his excursion. Landscape and people, plants and animals, are all just insignificant parts of the entirety of nature.

> I want to see human beings, as near as I possibly can, from the same vantage point as that from which [I see] skylarks or rape blossoms, the southern mountains or the bamboo groves, though their natures differ from one another. Bashō found a horse pissing by his bedside an elegant enough thing to write a haiku about. From this point on, I too will see [in the same manner as Bashō] the people I encounter . . . as depictions of incidental details of the entirety of Nature. (395–96)

[29] See the "Preface" to Miyoshi's *Accomplices of Silence*, esp. x–xvi. For an interesting and informative study of the *shishōsetsu*, see Edward Fowler, *The Rhetoric of Confession: Shishōsetsu in Early Twentieth Century Japanese Fiction*.

[30] Interestingly, the haiku to which *Kusamakura*'s narrator refers is found in the section of *Okuno hosomichi* that marks the beginning of the return journey southward, back to the world of men, for Bashō and his traveling companion Sōra. The haiku was presumably written during a three-day spell of wind and rain that forced the travelers to seek refuge in a "worthless/boring mountain retreat"—a distinct contrast to the narrator's assertions about his idyllic mountain retreat. A literal translation of Bashō's haiku to which the narrator refers is: "fleas lice / a horse [is] pissing / at [my] pillow."

Like the opening section of Bashō's *Okuno hosomichi* (Narrow road to the north), the opening of *Kusamakura* utilizes loaded and ornate language, seemingly contradictory clauses within the same sentence, a stance of artistic withdrawal from the everyday world of man into the "unmediated reality" of nature. Nature is characterized by *Kusamakura*'s narrator as possessing "perfect harmony and serenity," and "a virtue . . . an absolute impartiality . . . far beyond the corrupting reach of this world." Nature watches the messy affairs of the human realm with "cold indifference." Nature is enchanting, mystifying, seductive, delightful, all-encompassing, charming. If, as I have suggested, there is a parallel in *Kusamakura* between nature and history, this adjectival string of references to nature also suggests that from the narrator's perspective, there is a parallel between his view of nature and of the human object of his desire in *Kusamakura*. For the narrator has personified and feminized the "extra-human" natural world in the figure of Nami. She is of course "that beauty," the mysterious and compelling daughter of old Shioda who owns the hot springs resort to which the narrator retreats. She, too, possesses the string of qualities that the text identifies with nature. And *Kusamakura*'s artist stalks the mysterious and beautiful Nami just as he does the elusive beauty of nature, perpetually attempting to find the key that will make the raw stuff of nature and of humankind, or more specifically *woman*kind, a suitable pretext for the creation of a work of art. The irony of the narrating artist's energetic pursuit of raw materials for artistic production is, of course, that his perceptions and representations of both female and natural beauty are never without mediation, are never unfiltered or unobscured. The world, human and nonhuman, that surrounds Sōseki's narrator is enveloped in either natural or intellectual veils. For *Kusamakura*, then, the generative impulse of artistic praxis is marked by its own cryptic and enigmatic equivocation.

There is an interpretation of Sōseki's text that postulates the narrator's myopic inability to bring anything into focus as a testament to the poetic vision of Sōseki the author, notwithstanding the confusion of narrative levels that such a position incurs. *Kusamakura*, "fleeting" and "magical," "seems to be expressing a mood rather than a series of connected ideas."[31] Following this line of thinking, the consistent cloaking of the landscape, human and nonhuman, in a veil of one kind or another is poetically inevitable. "We do not want to see them more clearly, for to do so would mean a return to harsh reality."[32]

The extent to which such homage to a certain notion of classical Japanese literature as poetically evocative infiltrates discussions of Japanese culture is apparent in the consideration of a critic who is in many ways far indeed from the perspective of the Japanologist quoted above. Nonetheless, in a chapter in *Empire of Signs*, "So,"[33] which juxtaposes the Japanese haiku to the poetry of the European tradition, Roland Barthes exoticizes haiku as that which

> reproduces the designating gesture of the child pointing at whatever it is (the haiku shows no partiality for the subject), merely saying: *that!* with a movement so immediate (so stripped of any mediation: that of knowledge, of nomination, or even of any possession) that what is designated is the very inanity of any classification of the object: *nothing special*, says the haiku, in accordance with the spirit of Zen.

This is an especially interesting position in light of the fact that not only his commentators but Sōseki himself have characterized *Kusamakura* as a "haiku novel." If what Barthes suggests is true of haiku, what can be said of *Kusamakura*? Elsewhere in his textual reading of Japanese society and culture, Barthes points out that, renouncing metaphor and syllogism, commentary on the haiku becomes impossible. The only possible commentary is to repeat the haiku itself. This might be an accurate enough observation on the *intra*cultural reading of haiku in particular and on the critical predilection of perhaps

[31] Edwin McClellan, *Two Japanese Novelists: Soseki and Toson*, 22.
[32] McClellan, *Two Japanese Novelists*, 22.
[33] Barthes, *Empire of Signs*, 83.

too many Japanologists. But, haiku's *stance* of immediacy, of which Bashō and his poetry are certainly exponents, should not obscure its rigorously shaped and conventionalized *practice*. For it is a stance of immediacy that is effected by a most unimmediate insistence on the intertextual, on the mediation of poetic precedent, on the adherence to a highly codified and formalized poetic structure. The absent or barely discernible subject, nonlinearity, a most pronounced intertextuality are undoubtedly characteristic of certain aspects of Japanese culture. But to the great extent that these "characteristic" stances are also representations of men and women in relation to their environment, their society, and their work, they are just as susceptible to analysis as the sociocultural products and stances of any other society.[34] The "beautiful customs" of a "traditional" Japan, especially as they were resurrected and recast by the Meiji oligarchy, are not simply the unmediated legacy of the past.

In this context, it is difficult not to see *Kusamakura*'s ironic presentation of its bumbling artist as an implicit comment on the belabored Meiji reconstruction of "traditional" Japanese values, both cultural and social. Our narrating artist, too, however laboriously and self-consciously, attempts to affect the manipulation of a particular notion of traditional Japanese values by proposing some kind of synthetic combination of the "poetry of the East" with the "poetry of the West." So Bashō and Shelley or Wordsworth, and Noh and Shakespeare's plays, are worked into the text as a testimony to the transcendent interculturalism of the narrator, of Poetry and Nature, and, ironically, of the text itself. Space and time, geography and history, are forcibly conflated. But this conflation speaks of limitation and of difference every bit as much as it does of a potential overarching synthesis. In addition, the conflation of *Kusamakura* suggests the conflicting ideological underpinnings of "Eastern" and "Western," of "traditional" and "modern."

[34] Dale's *The Myth of Japanese Uniqueness* is an interesting and compelling ideological critique of the notion of Japan as inexplicably "other."

It can be and is argued that the Japanese language, and its literature, does allow nonlinearity, polysemic language/signs, and a loosely designated subject. But these characteristics are not quite some static cultural and linguistic marker for a timeless Japanese essence. And, even more to the point, the assumption of this literary stance was one thing for Bashō writing in the seventeenth century, and quite another for Sōseki, ironically evoking that stance in the midst of the recreation and imperialist expansion of the modern Japanese state. In the early twentieth century, the cultural promotion of a vaguely defined narrative subject serves to surreptitiously validate and camouflage a political structure that was "virtually impervious to popular influence and thus fundamentally irresponsible."[35] One of the distinctive characteristics of the emerging modern Japanese state is precisely that the political struggle of the Meiji Restoration of 1867–1868, subsequent to the forcible opening of Japan to and by the West, resulted not in the transference of power from one class to another but in the consolidation of political power by essentially the same ruling elite that dominated the late Tokugawa. For the emerging Japanese state, the manipulation of "tradition" was scarcely the innocent preservation of the past; it was an often openly ideological bid for power.

Thus, the attempt of *Kusamakura* as a text and of the narrating artist within that text to create some kind of idyllic compromise in the manipulation of tradition and modernism, of East and West, is most comprehensible within this larger context. And the attempt to create an idyllic artistic compromise cannot be divorced from the clearly ironic stance of the text toward that attempt. This irony is perhaps most apparent in the situation that is the pretext for the novel itself—the withdrawal of our narrating artist from the "cramped back street of that unstable and wretched city—the world of men" to "the pure and untainted world of poetry" high in the moun-

---

[35] Halliday, *Political History of Japanese Capitalism*, 40. Or, for a similar critique from another perspective, see Dale, *Myth of Japanese Uniqueness*, 56–99.

tains. Regardless of how seriously the narrator takes himself, or how seriously the reader chooses to take the narrator, the text resolutely insists on the incongruity and irony of his situation. So, as suggested earlier, it is scarcely a coincidence that it is a train on the way to the war front that ocassions compassion on the face of the enigmatic Nami. The "pure and untainted" poetry of nature and of Nami in the countryside is incomplete without what the narrator has supposedly forsaken—the modern city.

Kusamakura's narrative retreat to the past and to the "tradition" of the countryside of old Shioda's inn from what was arguably the primary stage for the modern, expanding Japanese state and its modern novel—the recreated capital city of Tokyo—is noteworthy. And it is precisely this narrative retreat from the un-"artistic" and un-"poetic" contradictions that the modern city represents that is one of the distinguishing features of *Kusamakura*'s idyllic compromise. *Kusamakura*'s retreat from the city is a retreat as well from the everyday, ordinary life of his characters—a retreat that Sōseki will not again really afford them. For the remainder of Sōseki's novels are marked by an almost desperate focus on the limited and limiting details of his characters' circumscribed daily lives.[36] What is presumably fanciful and lighthearted travel and narrative form in *Kusamakura* is replaced by the almost suffocating delimitation of *Mon* or *Kokoro* or *Sanshirō*.

Kusamakura, like Bashō's *Okuno hosomichi*, to which it refers, is precisely a journey away from the ordinary life of the average person.[37] But, even in *Kusamakura* (and perhaps even

---

[36] Even in his later works, however, Sōseki never approaches what could be called the "social realism" of writers like Sata Ineko or Hayashi Fumiko in their fictions of the lives of the urban working class and petite bourgeoisie. Sōseki's heroes are resolutely despairing and/or frustrated male intellectuals, distinguished from the mediocrity of their daily lives and environment by some irrevocable—and therefore, for the text, ultimately admirable—act or decision.

[37] The persistent avoidance of the everyday in this text is one that is shared by other works of modern Japanese fiction, a striking number of which are set on a journey to almost anywhere, but definitely away from the constraints of day-to-day life. Kawabata Yasunari's *Yukiguni* (Snow country) or *Sembazaru*

in *Okuno hosomichi*), contrary to the novel's claims, retreat is only feasible as a textual experiment in measuring the very impossibility of retreat. What is clear in *Kusamakura*, except perhaps to the narrator, is the impossibility of recreating the "traditional past," whether it be of Bashō's journey, of his poetic stance, or of anything else. The nonlinearity and sudden reversals of this "haiku novel" are not the utopic celebration of a "traditional" aesthetic stance but an ironic commentary on the manipulation of certain notions of tradition. For what the nonlinearity and the sudden reversals of the text reveal most clearly is the obscured vision, the almost desperate bewilderment, of the poetic eye in the face of a nature, an Other (Nami), and a history that are barely contained by the cultural and literary devices, "traditional" or otherwise. And the narrating subject, that poetic eye, unnamed and only partially represented though he might be, is scarcely an arbitrary social convention beyond which stands the "reality" of nature and of humankind's finite role in that nature. *Kusamakura*'s narrator/ subject functions instead as an indication of the ideologically loaded fictional construct of the individual subject and his or her point of view.

The impossible contradictions of the narrating subject and of his attempt at retreat and recreation are most evident in the scene that is central to both the structure and the content of the novel—the narrator's confrontation with Nami in the mineral baths. The bath scene is formally, and quite literally as the seventh of thirteen chapters, the pivotal center section of the novel. The chapters that precede and follow this confrontation are essentially an elaboration of, and an attempt to find a solution to, one of the questions that pervade the novel. That is—is there a content to meaning and the "real," how do we discern and/or construct it, and, most important for the

---

(A thousand cranes) or Kōbō Abe's *Sunna no onna* (Woman in the dunes) are obvious examples. Perhaps the possibility of an alternate narrative style is not to be found in the modern Japanese novel as readily as it is in the films of Ozu or Shimizu, with their meticulous focus on the details of the "minor" and everyday.

narrator (as it was, I suspect, for Sōseki), how do we represent it?

And so, the bath scene is preceded by the narrator's ruminations on perception and artistic production and followed by his pronouncements on the appreciation of art and art objects. Caught between the narrator's somewhat presumptuous prescription in these chapters, is his perception, appreciation, and what amounts to his theatrical production of the woman who is, with nature, the central art object of the novel—Nami. For the bath scene is a pivotal metaphor for the novel's meaning-making process, and for the contradictions of that process. In contrast to the lack of clarity that so frequently obscures the narrator's vision of Nature or Nami, this chapter opens with a methodical survey of the man-made physical surroundings of the hot springs.

> Removing my kimono in the three-mat room, I descended the four steps to the bath room, which was about eight mats. . . . the bath tank itself was about four feet deep. (464)

This is a rather pedantic opening for a chapter that is presumably the aesthetic wellspring of the novel. But that changes soon enough as, on entering the bath, the narrator recalls a poem by a Chinese poet; invokes the poetic mist, haze, and steam of a bath on a spring night; refers to a poem by Swinburne and to Millais's painting of Ophelia; composes his own eulogy on drowning; and detects the distant sounds of samisen music, which reminds him of his childhood and a young neighbor girl who practiced singing ballads as she played the samisen. Into this floating scene of reverie, distant desire, strains of samisen music, and misty spring haze steps a second person, the object of a more immediate desire. Luckily enough our narrator is blessed with no ordinary powers of observation. "Since I am an artist, I am gifted with exceptional perception about the structure of the human body" (469). It is a naked woman that the keen perception of the narrator makes out, standing at the second of those four steps that he was so careful to count in the opening of the chapter.

Almost immediately memory, desire, and sensation are re-

pressed as the narrating artist begins, predictably, to engage in
the obfuscation that is his hallmark. "Realising that [he] was
alone in the bath with a woman," the narrating artist describes
the woman's "slender figure topped with a floating cloud of
jet black hair." He then embarks on a page and a half of intellectualizations about the naked body and art. By the time the
frozen narrative is nudged forward a bit and the narrating artist actually begins again to see and describe the woman standing in front of him, she turns on her heel and, laughing, runs
from the room. The narrator is left almost empty-handed as
his "beautiful art object" deserts him, "tearing through the
veils of haze" as he himself has been unwilling or unable to
do. It is difficult not to read this scene as a comment on the
aestheticist attempt to capture beauty or truth or nature. The
inability of the artist to capture or define or describe, or even
to just *see*, the object of his artistic enterprise is not a coincidence here but a consistent characteristic. The "exceptional
perception" to which he lays claim as an artist might well be
more of an obstacle than anything else.

For what art does the narrating artist create? What is the
outcome of his attempt to assume Bashō's or Wordsworth's or
Keats's artistic perspective? As Nami pointedly reminds him,
he has been unable to paint anything since his retreat from the
city. *Kusamakura*'s artist seems more determined to *live* a poetic fiction than to write or paint one. But the narrator's visual
"silence" is the pretext that fends off narrative silence with the
novel itself. *Kusamakura* is, on the one hand, a story of an
artist who tries, as a detached observer of the world, to see
and narrate Nami, or nature, or history, and fails everywhere
except in his own head (and possibly even there). The fictional
retreat, the escape, of *Kusamakura* from the urban present,
from an impinging social and political history, is no retreat at
all. The train and the Russo-Japanese war invade the countryside. Even more, they occasion the hitherto absent quality—
compassion—that has rendered the narrator's perception of
Nami incomplete, less-than-human. It is that from which he
flees that completes the narrator's artistic "vision." His studied attempt to remain beyond the pale of human entangle-

ment, to escape from the contingencies of an (admittedly grim) historical moment, is doomed to failure from the opening of the novel. This outcome is clear in the text's ironic treatment of its narrating artist-cum-philosopher, from his first stumbling intellectualizations to his "keen" artistic perception in identifying a woman's naked body in the bath to his final observation of Nami's compassion (a compassion that might very well have been present all along though inaccessible to our slightly-less-than-perspicacious hero).

Equally ironic is the narrator's insistence on discovering Nami's "truth," her "secret" meaning. In fact, his dogged pursuit of her is rather like the activities of the Tokyo private detectives to whom the narrator refers so disdainfully throughout the text. For what reason might the narrating artist have been followed by a private detective in the big city? Is someone trying to locate the truth, the meaning, of the narrator's life as the narrator attempts to locate Nami or nature as some secret key to art? Is someone in the capital attempting to "catch" the narrator and insert him into their own narrative (whatever it might be) just as the narrator insists on catching Nami in his?

Kusamakura does in fact suggest itself as a detective story of sorts. But in a detective story, in order for there to be a final revelation about who-done-it, something has to have been done. There has to be a crime. The crime, though, is precisely what is missing in *Kusamakura*. Unlike the murder of young girl children by old Khadoula in Papadiamandis's *E Fonissa* or the violence to the mosque, his family, and himself wrought by Ismā'īl in Haqqī's *Qindīl Umm Hāshim, Kusamakura*'s artist doesn't seem to be the perpetrator of much more than a rather foolish pretentiousness and inability to see anything at all. Perhaps this is precisely our narrator's crime, or at least the irony of his fictional existence. And what is absent from the text in order to understand the implications of that crime is the context in which intellectual pretension and blindness are played out on the stage of a growing right-wing sociopolitical reality and a menacing imperialism. Perhaps the broader context in which the narrator's stance is, at least by implication, a criminal one is that history that the narrator seeks to escape, that history that intrudes in the conclusion of the novel with the train.

Contrary to the contentions of the narrator about the non-linearity of the foreign novel (and by extension of the novel that he himself narrates), about the reader's ability to begin and end anywhere in a text, the construction of a framework and the organization of content in a detective story has a definite, if artificial, beginning and end. There is a carefully plotted progression of clues gathered and pieced together to reveal the final revelatory "truth." To randomly read a detective story, to read the last chapter before the middle section, violates the significance of that truth. (And what truths are the object of the Tokyo detectives who, according to the narrator, devote their investigation to counting farts?) It might well be that the narrator's celebration of the random and the nonlinear is, like that of the detective story, or of classical Japanese poetry for that matter, not constructed nearly as randomly as it appears. To switch the first and third lines of a haiku is as unacceptable a violation of poetic form as to switch the first and third chapters of a detective story. The importance of the almost formulaic framework within which stories are told, observations made, value posited, cultural and social meaning located, can be camouflaged but not done away with. The formula is certainly not a static and eternal one but it is a formula. Or, more to the point, a text, any text, is a self-conscious fabrication of words or ideograms on a page and the fabrication of a structure within which content has meaning. You might read the last line of a haiku or the final chapter of a detective story or the middle section of *Kusamakura* first but the fact of the textual framework remains. Like the representation of nature in *Kusamakura*, and in much of Sōseki's fiction, what appears to be lyric randomness or unlimited evocation operates as a distinct textual boundary of its own.

Finally though, the narrator's "keen perception" culminates not only in the bath room confrontation with Nami but in an equally clouded and distorted confrontation with himself. In the opening of *Kusamakura*, we saw the narrator's pursuit of nature obscured first by his own intellectualization, then by

the conventions of Japanese art, then by the poetic stance of
the English romantic Wordsworth (whose poem Sōseki quotes
in English, an effect that maximizes its sheer difference in the
Japanese text), and finally by a sudden downpour of rain. In
the next chapter, the friendly gossip of the old woman at the
tea house, the shower of falling cherry blossoms, and the interjection of an old tale about the Maid of Nagara and of the
classical death poem attributed to her, irrevocably filter the
narrator's view of his natural surroundings, of the "enchanted
land" that is to be his retreat from the "common everyday
world." Then, arriving at his destination late at night, the narrator's perspective is again obscured by the dark night and his
own weariness. Drifting in and out of a dream-filled sleep, he
sees both the world of nature and of humankind (actually
womankind) through a series of lenses. Nature, like Nami, is
almost without exception mediated—by another poem, or another poet, by the image from a Noh mask or a figure from a
classical landscape. Consistently framed and filtered, it is seen
in relation to other texts and other gestures. It is always purposefully incomplete. So, after his late-night arrival, when the
narrator awakens to the midday light, the poems that he
scrawled across the page during the night have been edited,
annotated, by a not-so-mysterious hand. The ethereal figure
of beauty, the impelling object of his poetic discourse that he
could just barely make out the night before, blurred as she was
by his own sleepiness and the dark night mist, has risen in the
bright light of day to herself redress and emend the artist's
objectification of her. Surely there can be no more telling indictment of artistic contingency than this. If nature cannot rise
up and mock the artistic pretensions of the narrating artist,
Nami can and does. She provokes the narrator; she titillates
him and then mercilessly, or perhaps mercifully, cuts short his
presumptuous objectivity. And, in a way, so does the natural
world that surrounds the narrator, for all that he has taken
himself off to a natural mountain retreat to escape the everyday world of human intrigue and impurity. His poetic vision of
Nami's figure in the midnight darkness, his representation of
the "perfect harmony and serenity of nature" (448–49), is jux-

taposed to his encounter on the following afternoon with a garrulous, intoxicated barber and an impudent young priest. Their exchange is marked by gossip, jokes, and common, even simple-minded, banter. There are no ethereal spirits, ghostly women, or impendingly meaningful nature here. But even here in what the narrator sees as the reprehensibly mundane world, there is no direct and immediate vision of things, not even of his own face in the barbershop mirror. Like his encounter with so much else, the narrator's encounter with his own reflection is obscured and distorted.

> When I moved my head to the right, my face became all nose, and when I moved it to the left, my mouth became a slit which stretched from ear to ear. If I leaned back, I looked like the front view of a toad that had been utterly squashed. And if I leaned a little forward, [my body was foreshortened and] my head became like a swollen ball. As long as I was in front of the mirror, I would do nothing but change from one monster into another. . . . I came to the conclusion that the monstrosity before me was produced by a combination of the mirror's faulty construction and the fact that in places the silvering had peeled off the back. (440)[38]

Is it coincidental that *Kusamakura*'s problematic narrator casts a "problematic" reflection? Or that he blames that fractured reflection on the construction of the mirror? This passage epitomizes the contingency of the individual subject that

---

[38] This passage from *Kusamakura* suggests another from Sōseki's letters, although Sōseki was neither as presumptuous nor as self-assured as his artist/narrator is in this passage. Written during his two-year stay in England (1900–1902), it is a poignant comment on the distanced and estranged subject, at once surveyor and surveyed. "Everyone I see on the street is tall and attractive. . . . Sometimes I see an unusually short man, but as we pass one another in the street, he is still two inches taller than I. Then I see a dwarf approaching, a man with an unpleasant complexion—and he is my own reflection in the shop window. I don't know how many times I've laughed at my own ugly appearance right in front of myself. Sometimes I even watched my reflection that laughed as I laughed. And every time that happened I was struck by the appropriateness of the term 'yellow race' " (vol. 12, 36–37, quoted in Miyoshi, *Accomplices*, 57).

lurks around every corner in this novel of a "three-cornered world"—that which "remains after the corner we call common sense has been removed." But is it common sense, as the narrator of *Kusamakura* claims, that is absent from the world of the novel? Or is it history—that history that, however circumscribed by his narrative, is the ever-present and imminent threat to the narrating artist's search for "pure" and "untainted" nature or a complete representation of Nami. It is history that threatens to reveal his crime. It is not the Tokyo detectives who examine anuses and count farts that threaten the narrator and his narrative. It is the world of men and women, of desire, of political action, of a hegemonic and aggressive West, and an increasingly repressive and imperialist Japan. Perhaps this passage, as well, stands as one of the novel's ultimate metaphors for the "impact of the West," for the toll exacted by compromises between East and West, the traditional and the modern, as they were defined by Meiji Japan. The reformulation of the "traditional" in Japanese culture in the face of the Western onslaught is not, in *Kusamakura*, the unconcerned maneuvering of symbols playfully lifted from the past. It is a desperately defiant and bleak critical gesture toward a contradictory and overwhelming history from which there is no retreat, of which there is only the most provisional of textual resolutions.

It is here that Sōseki's text implies a recognition of the cultural limitations and differences of both "East" and "West" and of the implicit failure of bourgeois artistic solutions in the face of foreign or Japanese ruling-class hegemony. The textual presence or absence of common sense as the distinguishing characteristic of the narrator's "three-cornered, artistic world" is an example. For although, it is not, as the narrator suggests, the absence of common sense that defines the world of the text, it is difficult to overlook the ironic disdain of the text for just that common sense that, not "common" at all is more properly the ideological creation and perhaps the sole property of the bourgeoisie. And so, while the passage in which the narrator chastises Nami for expecting that novels should be read from beginning to end or that love leads to marriage, is not quite the innocent celebration of the play of empty signs that it purports to be, it is a wonderfully mocking comment on the bourgeois penchant for a certain kind of predictable order and practicality—a certain kind of common sense. Or, in addition to the ironic exposure of the limitations of bourgeois common sense, the text, equally ironically, reveals the limitations of the artistic stance of its pompous and pretentious narrator in his futile but persistent attempt to capture a true and pure art/nature/woman who consistently eludes him.

This kind of narrative irony is absent from Yahyā Haqqī's *Qindīl Umm Hāshim*; the narrative attempt there to create an Egyptian version of the coherent bourgeois hero is a deadly earnest endeavor. There is little intimation of the limitations of such an endeavor—in which Ismā'īl attempts to incorporate "East" and "West" in a gesture parallel to that of the narrating artist in *Kusamakura*—either from the perspective of the character Ismā'īl or from that of the narrating nephew of the text. Within the discourse of the Egyptian response to imperialism, the formulation of the politico-economic confrontation between Egypt and Britain as that between Eastern spirit and Western science and the subsequent attempt to resolve that confrontation in the same terms in which it was expressed was compromised from the beginning.

Narrative irony is largely absent as well from *E Fonissa*. But that novel, with its aversion to the West, to the modern capital of Athens, to the "Franks" as well as to the bourgeois urban Greeks, posits no compromise of the sort that Ismā'īl embodies. For *E Fonissa*, there is no redeeming value, literary or otherwise, in the bourgeois hero or heroine. *E Fonissa* is as critical of the foreign, the modern, the centralized state, as it is of the integrated narrative consciousness of an individual subject. What appears to be the irony of Papadiamandis's text arises from its equally critical representation of traditional Greek peasant life. *E Fonissa* refuses the ironic compromise of *Kusamakura* and the rather more earnest one of *Qindīl Umm Hāshim*. Instead, it remains within the essentially negative boundary of a distopia. And the textual "resolution" of its multiple contradictions is, can only be, the death of the old woman Frangoyiannou.

· · ·

> However, insofar as there is reference to a historic past,
> the peculiarity of 'invented' traditions is that the
> continuity with it is largely factitious.
> —Eric Hobsbawm, *The Invention of Tradition*

The relation to "tradition," to the "autochthonous," and to an oppositional non-Europeanism of the texts examined in the last three chapters is a profoundly ambivalent one. The reconstruction, after the rupture and "generative" fabrication of colonialism, of oppositions between "East" and "West," between Europe and "the rest," is a move (narrative or otherwise) fraught with contradictions. Something of these contradictions and ambivalences is suggested not only in a critical reading of the texts of Papadiamandis, Haqqī, and Sōseki but in the fact of the recuperation of those texts by their respective dominant cultures. Such recuperation would read Papadiamandis's *E Fonissa* as a nostalgic tribute to traditional Greek island life, Haqqī's *Qindīl Umm Hāshim* as a moving stylistic account and resolution of the confrontation between East and West, and Sōseki's *Kusamakura* as a fleeting and playful haiku novel that conjoins East and West. The valorized situations of these texts within the canons of their national cultures and the implications of that valorization in the constitution of national culture is a complex and interesting question to which I can only gesture here.[39] But, in moving from a consideration of these earlier novels to that of contemporary ones, it is worth considering that the national recuperation of these texts recreates and maintains a dominant cultural inter-

---

[39] But for an impressive critical account of this issue in the modern Greek context, see Vassilis Lambropoulos, *Literature as National Institution: Studies in the Politics of Modern Greek Criticism*.

pretation of them that, ironically perhaps, corresponds in more ways than one to a hegemonic Western reading.

In this context then, Papadiamandis's fiction can be cast as the faithful preserver of something very near that picturesque Greek way of life that is the selling point for tourist advertisements and popular (mis)conceptions of Greece. Without equal political and economic standing among her European and American neighbors to the West, Greece obtains a certain cultural standing as the folkish remnant of the "cradle of Western civilization." And *Qindīl Umm Hāshim*'s formulation of the Egyptian response to British imperialism as the opposition of Western science/mind to Eastern religion/spirit suggests that orientalist vision of the Arab Other—mysterious, impervious to reason and science, subject to violent and blind allegiances, backward, conservative—that Edward Said critiques so effectively in *Orientalism*. And even the narrative irony of Sōseki's text can be downplayed in the representation of *Kusamakura* as beautifully meaningless, a series of elusive haiku images, a play of linguistic symbols—a veritable Madame Butterfly of a novel.

To introduce this suggestion of the power of recuperation, of interpretive hegemonies, is not to dismiss or disqualify these texts as oppositional, both within their own cultural and social contexts and, by implication at least, in a larger global one. It is, however, to note the extent to which cultural resistance *resists* on the terrain of the dominant—the dominant of one's own culture and of an international scheme of things. In operating on that terrain, resistance is engaged not only in narratives of its own making but also in the dominant narrative(s). Questions of what we might call "narrative strategy," then, take on a more urgent significance. And the postulation of engaging exclusively in "authentic" narratives of our own making is not negated but qualified. This does not diminish the power of cultural resistance or opposition; it does not then shift critical or practical emphasis to engagement primarily with dominant narrative(s); it does suggest an alteration in the tenor of opposition, with the utopic (i.e., not as the impossible but only as the not-realized-as-yet) hope of not only reproducing the dominant narratives with a different cast of characters.

Nor is it to suggest that the dominant readings of these texts are "incorrect" or "false." That would be to postulate "correct" ones, a postulation that is as dubious as that of "false" readings. The readings of the preceding pages, then, are not offered as "correct" ones. Rather, they are an attempt at the resituation of these texts, ordained as predominantly aestheticist or ethnographically nostalgic, in relation to one of the dominant discourses of their time—the unequal confrontation—political, economic, and cultural—with the expanding West, that is, with imperialism and its latter-day variations. Removed from the contexts of that discourse and maintained as literary custodians of some definitive "native" essence, they are also (and ironically) removed from all but the most transcendent literary significance for their societies. Within the dominant definition of their national cultures, suitably sterilized and transfixed, they are lauded as "national treasures." But, for the people who live within those cultures, they are exiled from the possibility of a more immediate and literal meaning. They are divorced from the contexts in which literature or novels are more than just the intellectual or academic pastime of a few. Ultimately, that "loss" might be an inconsequential one. For there are certainly other ways of designating and knowing culture and literature—ways that do not necessarily privilege the chosen texts of a dominant class.

Still, the resituation of these (or any) texts within the literary, ideological, and historical contexts of which they are a part suggests, first of all, an understanding of literary texts as specifically *literary*, as one kind of cultural practice among others. And it problematizes those texts as some sort of essentialist national cultural repository. Such textual resituation proposes an examination of the roots of and impetus for the shaping and reshaping of national culture as a politico-cultural activity *of* women and men *for* women and men—an activity intimately concerned with, and engaged in the exercise of, political and cultural power.

For, cultures, national or otherwise, are not pristine and self-evident entities. Like language, perhaps, they are always there before us. But they are framed, shaped, and reshaped by people for specific ends. With this as a presupposition then, to resituate "national (textual) treasures" in the cultural and historical contexts from which they derived and in the contemporary contexts in which they are put to use is to resubmit them for social consideration. It is to question and reevaluate the significance and use value of cultural texts for the ordinary folks of that culture. If it was *of*, and perhaps even *against*, these ordinary folks that the early-twentieth-century novels examined above speak, it is *for* and *to* them that the contemporary texts examined in the following chapters attempt to address themselves.

So, the concern with the national that informs the fictions of Papadiamandis, Haqqī, and Sōseki becomes a concern with the international in Hatzis, Kanafānī, and Ōe. Literarily and literally, what was presumably the stability and "inviolability" of the bourgeois national subject is brought into question as that individual subject faces her counterparts within and without national boundaries. And the multinational character of late capitalism creates two primary thoroughfares between "third" and "first" worlds: market "participation" in "first"-world-dominated consumer society and the migrations of the "guest" worker. The figure of the already mobile peasant—central in *The Murderess* and *The Lamp of Umm Hāshim* and marginalized but significant in its absence in *Kusamakura*—is replaced by those of the migrant worker and migrant intellectual in Hatzis and Kanafānī or that of the already displaced and soon-to-be migrant intellectual in Ōe. The episodic format of the earlier novels is still present in the later texts. And the search for a viable language for the novel remains a contestable issue—in the carefully constructed linguistic "simplicity" of narrative language in Hatzis and Kanafānī and in the equally carefully constructed complexity of Ōe's language. The concern with religious faith that marks the narrative structure and characters of Papadiamandis's and Haqqī's fiction, or the aesthetic "faith" that distinguishes Sōseki's *Kusa-*

makura, figures far less significantly in the work of Hatzis or Kanafānī or Ōe. There is rather a crisis of a different "faith"— a crisis of an efficacious reason, of narrative representation, of coherent structural perspective. The urgent attempt at articulation of what was postulated as native tradition and foreign modernity, of Easts and Wests, takes on a different cast in light of the failures but also the successes of modernization.

Chapter 5

DOUBLING: THE (IMMIGRANT) WORKER AS (EXILED) WRITER

Sing through me, O Muse, of the man of many wiles
who
wandered far and wide after he sacked the sacred city of
Troy.
He learned the cities and the minds of many men
and many were the woes at sea that burdened his heart
as he struggled to win his own life and the return of his
comrades.

—Homer, *The Odyssey*

In *To Diplo Biblio* (The double book)[1] by Dimitris Hatzis, the clotted and almost tortured prose of the early-twentieth-century Greek novelist, Alexandros Papadiamandis, is forcibly refashioned into a narrative language of startling if contradictory simplicity. The vagaries of narrative voice; the uneasy linguistic wavering between demotic and *katharevousa*; the narrative imbedding of proverbial peasant wisdom, herbal remedies, and folktales; the intimations of a pre-Christian (or almost anti-Christian) animism; the presumption of loaded significance and authenticity in what is designated as Greek tradition—these characteristic narrative maneuvers of Papadiamandis's fiction are not rejected or abandoned in the work of Dimitris Hatzis; they are radically transformed. In Hatzis's fiction, the past, not least of all the literary past, is not a fixed entity waiting passively to be accepted or rejected in the pres-

---

[1] Dimitris Hatzis, *To Diplo Biblio* (The double book). All translations are my own unless otherwise noted. There are, at present, no English-language translations of Hatzis's work.

ent. The "use value" of the past is continually re-created in its relationship to the present. Whether it is designated as literary, social, or political, the past—history—is forcibly re-called, remembered, for both the critical function it serves and for the possibility of meaning and utopic direction it affords.

While firmly rooted in the modern Greek literary tradition of which Papadiamandis is a crucial member, Hatzis's fiction, and most particularly *To Diplo Biblio*, is an explicit attempt to confront the ideological construct that overshadows a great many of the works of that tradition—a nostalgia for the greatness of a classical past long since vanished, a morbid fascination with a contemporary reality (literary and socioeconomic) that denies the recreation of that past at every turn, the erection of a rhetorical refuge from the impingement of that reality in a search for linguistic purity and authenticity. For, although *To Diplo Biblio* is on one level the account of a Greek immigrant worker in Germany, it is also clearly an account of, and a handbook for the production of, modern fiction. That the contemporary world (*o simerinos kosmos*), and not least of all contemporary Greece, compel this manual, that they place new demands on the form and content of the novel is *To Diplo Biblio*'s implicit assumption. The novel reassesses the audience to whom its fiction is directed (the implied reader), the subject of that fiction (the story and its characters), the manner in which the narrative is constructed (narrative form), and the role of the writer in the society of which he is a part (the implied author).

From within the text, there are at least two writers at work on this most literal "double" book. The narrative interplay between these two authors attempts to redefine and broaden the more traditional function of narrative voice and of narrative subject. *To Diplo Biblio* presents at least two stories in one, two positions of work on the novel, a double attempt to delineate the novel and its function. It is the telling and retelling of a story, the telling and retelling of a narrative subject who is less a fixed identity than a place marker for a series of identities.

Rather than the direct narration of his own story to an

anonymous audience/reader, Costas, the immigrant worker of *To Diplo Biblio*, recounts his life to another Greek whom he meets in a Greek café in Stuttgart—a writer searching for "the roots of the *romeiko*."[2] This unnamed writer copies Costas's story into a notebook, which then becomes, presumably, the basis for the novel itself. The narrative pretext of *To Diplo Biblio* then is a dialogue between a factory worker and a writer, between the teller of a tale and the scribe who copies down the tale. But the writer in this instance is equally the narratee[3] of the tale told by Costas. And Costas is, in turn, an implied writer. There are still two further deflections in this rather ironic narrative role reversal. Costas is unaware of the facts or meaning of parts of his own past. The writer fills in those blank spaces in Costas's history, assuming the narration himself and telling Costas his story. But, finally, the writer disappears leaving his notebook—Costas's story—half-finished. It is Costas who transcribes what he is able to decode of the writer's notebook and finishes the novel.

> Outlines half-finished, comments, omissions, additions, in the Greek stories of this book—whatever the author didn't finish, wasn't able to finish . . . I copy it just as it was in the notebook, without disturbing anything of course—who am I to change anything? And there was more in the notebook, very confused,

---

[2] *Romios*, a noun referring to a person, *romiosini*, a noun referring to a characteristic, and *romeiko*, either adjective or noun, refer to the Greek people after the War of 1821 in which Greece was freed from Ottoman rule. Thus, it is by connotation the *modern* Greek in particular, and is often used implicitly to refer to one who struggles against tyranny, who is committed to freedom, who exemplifies the "new glory" of Greece. Perhaps ironically, the origin of the word is not Greek at all but, most likely, the classical Arabic term for Greeks—*roum*. The other term that Greeks use to designate themselves is *ellenes* or "hellenes."

[3] The narratee is, quite simply, the audience built into the narrative as a character, such as the person who listens and then presumably recounts Marlowe's tale in Conrad's *Heart of Darkness*. See Seymour Chatman's *Story and Discourse: Narrative Structure in Fiction and Film* for the elaboration of this useful notion, especially 150–51, where Chatman refers to the narratee as "a device by which the implied author informs the real reader how to perform as implied reader."

fragmented sentences, half words, erasures, meaningless scrib-
blings—I couldn't make them out. But I too have my own *"romeiko"* conclusions here—some few—to write in a word or two.
(190)

As Costas is unable to tell his own story without outside help,
so the writer is unable to "tell" his novel alone. There are at
least two immediately apparent implications in this "double"
format. The novel is acknowledged as an unabashedly fabricated construct and the possibility of its individual construction is called into question. For the writer, the connections
that provide the pretense of a seamless and realistic narrative
are missing. For Costas, those connections are denied by the
alienation and estrangement of his own experience. It is only
(the pretext of) collective authorship that makes the text possible. Like the narrating artist of Sōseki's *Kusamakura*, the
writer of *To Diplo Biblio* is unable to fix meaning, to represent the world, to reproduce the word. In fact, it is precisely
the attempt to capture, to articulate, the world or the "real"
that is its estrangement. It will be Costas, with his "small
brain," rather than the writer searching for truth who makes,
not some ultimate meaning, but only what "sense he can decipher of his story."

For *To Diplo Biblio*, there is no ready-made nexus, textual
or otherwise, from which a final meaning or truth or reality is
available. It is not available in the subject of Costas. The answer to the questions "Who is Costas?" or "Who can tell his
story?" or "What sense can be made of his story?" is one of
the obvious conundrums of the text. Costas speaks himself
and at least part of his story but he is also spoken by others—
the writer, Costas's sister and his father, his fellow worker,
Skouroyiannis. And Costas is also spoken by his situation, by
his environment. As his temporal, geographic, and human
contexts change, so does Costas and his story. As a character,
his ability to make sense of his environment is always partial
and provisional. And yet Costas's world is resolutely nonpsy-
chotic. If meaning or truth or reality are only provisionally
available in the text, in Costas's story and life, it is neither

tragic nor comic nor mad. About this, the stark and lucid simplicity of Hatzis's language, something of a scarce commodity in modern Greek literature, leaves little doubt.

The absence of psychosis, though, does not preclude the presence of contradiction. Costas is not a neatly contained and consistent entity. The provisionality and contradictions of his or the writer's attempt to create meaning are unavoidable. In the fourth chapter, "Kaspar Hauser in a Desolate Land," Costas describes his life in Germany as a foreigner, as an economic exile from his own country. And because he is an economic exile, because of the economic stagnation that compels him to leave in the first place, because there is no future for him in Greece, Costas concludes that he has no place in his country. He is Greek by birth, by ethnic and linguistic affiliation. He is a Greek because he has a Greek passport. Yet Greece is not his. He has no country. But this is clearly an untenable contradiction, not theoretically perhaps, but in terms of lived experience. So Costas attempts to resolve the contradiction, watching the trains that come and go at the central station outside of the factory. "And then I think that the larger world [*o megalos o kosmos*] could be my homeland—and there it is, I too finally have found my homeland. A new homeland. It's in this larger world" (65). But before the scene can close with resounding strains of "Workers of the world unite," Costas reconsiders.

> Later, I think again that, no, I have no such thing. All the trains that set out from here . . . have somewhere to go, a destination . . . *endstacion*, as they say in German. . . . And so, the larger world is a lie; it's only a lot of smaller worlds together. And I remain again without a country, without my own small world— I don't have one—and without nostalgia for the larger world— which doesn't exist. (65)

The provisionality of the narrative production of meaning is here forced to take account of itself. And the contradictions inherent in that production are performed within the space of a half a page.

The aporia that characterizes life in Greece for thousands of

Costases and Anastasias, Costas's sister, and that makes Costas's observations above unexceptional, is made clear in the sixth and eighth chapters of To Diplo Biblio. Not surprisingly, these two chapters are separated by the regrounding of the narrative in Costas's present in Germany, "The Pestles." The sixth chapter describes the return to Greece of Skouroyiannis, Costas's closest friend in Germany, who worked twenty years as a menial laborer in Stuttgart to be able to go back and live out his old age at home. But on his return, Skouroyiannis is increasingly isolated by a way of life that no longer includes him. His only companion is "the last bear of Pindos" of the chapter's title, which he sees, or imagines that he sees, talks to, and cares for in the mountains that surround his village. In The Seventh Man,[4] John Berger's attempt to illustrate the experiences and fractured present of the immigrant worker is a testament to the unexceptionality of Skouroyiannis's return.

> The final return is mythic. It gives meaning to what might otherwise be meaningless. It is larger than life. It is the stuff of longing and prayers. But it is also mythic in the sense that, as imagined, it never happens. There is no final return. Unchanging as the village is, he will never see it as he did before he left. He is seen differently and he sees differently. . . . His different experience is not applicable to the village as it is. It belongs elsewhere. . . . He has become a wage-earner. They have become the dependents of his wage. . . . An assured place for him no longer exists in his village. (216, 220–21)

The eighth chapter, "Anastasia of Molaos," describes the past and present of Costas's sister, Anastasia. With the same deflated dramatics characteristic of Costas's account of his life in Germany, Anastasia insists that her present is not hell, it is "at most, a shadow that falls from hell" (164). The fantasies of her girlhood, her almost hallucinatory communion with the birds, which creates what she calls her "double life," her rebellion, her desire for escape, are all brought to a swift end by a loveless if practical marriage. She leaves her village to live in

[4] John Berger, with Jean Mohr, The Seventh Man.

her husband's house, bear and raise their two children, and care for his embittered old mother. Anastasia, the daughter of a World War II partisan, nurses her mother-in-law, who still asks for a blood price for her oldest son, killed by the partisans. These are the small ironies that make up Anastasia's life. She is a participant in that system of dowries, marriages of necessity, and a life of servitude that the Khadoula of Papadiamandis's *E Fonissa* chronicled nearly seventy-five years earlier. And like the old murderess of the earlier text, Anastasia is a sign of the impossibility of things the way they are. Her past is an amplification of Costas's; her present is a reminder of what his future could have been. Like Costas, she meets the writer who, returning to Greece after the fall of the junta, falls in love with her, idealizes her, and inevitably misunderstands her. She tells him of her past and present, of her dead-ended future, and she tells him of himself. It is Anastasia who is the last person to talk to the writer before he disappears: "I see you. You are the most defeated of all. Among the lost lives that are ours, your life shatters into a thousand pieces. You didn't bring your book; it doesn't exist—raveling threads are all that's left" (180).

Perhaps, after all, Anastasia *is* the writer's Diotima, as he christens her. Like her classical namesake, a Pythagorian wise woman who purified the city of Athens in the plague of 429 B.C., Anastasia's memories of the past and clear-sighted perceptions of the present "clean the slate" for Costas and for the writer. She, as much as Costas, is witness to the impossibility and impotence of the writer's dreams. It is to her that the writer entrusts the "raveling threads" of his notebook. Surrounded by the dead bodies of the birds that were to be the way out of her situation, Anastasia's dead dreams are a sort of circumscribed libidinal counterpart to the writer's equally circumscribed intellectualizing search for truth. But if Anastasia's birds die, she at least survives. Two-thirds of the way through the novel though, the writer—unable to make sense of language, of his own world, of Costas's or of Anastasia's—disappears without a trace. If the writer as narratee is a textual paradigm for an extratextual counterpart, the implications of

the writer/narratee's impotence and disappearance are suggestively ironic.

The critical reception of Hatzis's novel would seem to verify
that irony. A narrative that suggests the limitations and provisionality of the textual meaning-making process implicate a
world outside of the text almost as much as they do the characters within the text or the narrative itself. So, *To Diplo Biblio* is criticized because it offers no solution to the lamentable
situation it presents;[5] because its depiction of Costas's men-
tality is a degradation of the Greek worker and his "Greekness"; because the use of language, images, and narrative form
violates the tenets of "progressive" social realism;[6] because
the text suggests the contradictory and conditional character
of the textual manufacture of truth (writing of an immigrant/
exile rather than a "real" Greek), meaning (the solution to
Costas's problems) or identity (Costas's Greekness or lack
thereof).

The tentative redefinition of the narrative subject in *To
Diplo Biblio* recalls and challenges the limitations posited by
Jacques Lacan's formulation of the Symbolic in its interaction
with the Imaginary and the Real.[7] For the Symbolic domain is
that which includes, but is not reducible to, the realm of language. If the child first becomes aware of herself as a separate
and apparently self-contained entity—as a subject—in recog-

---

[5] See, for example, Peter Pappas's review of Hatzis's novel in *Journal of the
Hellenic Diaspora* 4.4 (1978) especially 97–99 or that of Kostas Papageorgis
in *Anti* [Opposition] (11 Dec. 1976).

[6] See the edition of *Anti* devoted to Hatzis's work: B.183 (1981), especially
22–23.

[7] Jacques Lacan, *Ecrits*, especially sect. 1, "The Mirror Stage as Formative
of the Function of the I," and sect. 3: "The Function and Field of Speech and
Language in Psychoanalysis." Rather more to the point, but after this chapter
was written, in an interview on postmodernism (Anders Stephanson, "Re-
garding Postmodernism—A Conversation with Fredric Jameson," *Social Text*
17, [1987]: 29–54), Fredric Jameson incisively articulates that notion of the
subject that, I have suggested, is prefigured in Hatzis's novel: "Still, I always
insist on a third possibility beyond the old bourgeois ego and the schizophrenic subject of our organization society today: a *collective subject*, decentered but not schizophrenic" (45, emphasis in the original).

nizing a reflection, an image (whence the Imaginary), of herself in the mirror, this process of recognizing the self as Subject
is furthered when the child enters the realm of the Symbolic
with the acceptance of language. The self is first defined as
subject by an image cast by the outside world, by the child's
recognition of the outside world and the other—initially the
mirror—as precisely that which *is* outside and other. This essentially narcissistic dimension of the Subject is forcibly
broadened to include the sociofamilial framework, the network of social relationships, by the immersion in language, by
entry into the order of the Symbolic. In this scheme of things,
the Real, preimagistic and preverbal, is rendered unregainable
(but only quasi-utopic) by the workings of the Imaginary and
the Symbolic. What is suggestive for a discussion of literary
discourse is the formulation of the Symbolic Order. For if the
Imaginary is the domain of images and thus visual, the Symbolic is the domain of the verbal, of the linguistic. And language is a decidedly social phenomenon. As largely social discourses of the self, the Symbolic Order and language initiate a
cumulative process of the Subject's alienation. Language is,
then, precisely the estrangement of the real and of the subject.
Implicit in this process, is the privileging of language. Equally
implicit is "the subject" as the nonmonolithic, nontotalizing,
and fluid site of a number of constructed "meanings" or
"truths." But the successive estrangement or alienation of the
subject in an Imaginary and Symbolic order that precludes the
Real, that implicitly reveals the coherent subject as a fabrication, and that subjects the subject to a sense of his or her own
economic, political, sociocultural, and psychological contingency is perhaps nowhere quite so blatantly apparent as in
that configuration of racism, exploitation, and the multinational search for value that is colonialism or neocolonialism
and imperialism. Colonialism subjugates the local economy,
political and social organization, culture, and identity of the
colonized people—as collective and individual subject(s)—to
the expanding needs of the foreign metropolis. Frantz Fanon's
Wretched of the Earth chronicles the attempted destruction of
Algerian markets, agricultural patterns, bases of traditional

power, and of the Algerian people. This endeavour was essential to French colonialism in Algeria. Without it, the French could not have satisfied the very real economic and political needs that spurred the colonial expedition in the first place. In this configuration, racism plays a crucial ideological role, for it handily disallows the humanity and identity as equals of the colonized people. It makes of the African or Indian or Arab or Asian a less-than-human means to an imperial end, a replaceable part of the necessary machinery in the colonial or imperialist venture. But in dismantling the other as a one-time subject or even a potential subject, the groundwork is laid for that same dismantling process in reverse.[8] Colonialism and imperialism confront the colonized people with their own contingency in the face of a hegemonic foreign power, with alienation from their traditional economic, political, social, and personal definitions, but also with the blatant contradictions of bourgeois individualism and humanism in the colonial context. That the colonial endeavour would have repercussions for the colonizing subject was clear enough even thirty years ago. These repercussions were, in fact, the initial focus of Fanon's *Wretched of the Earth*. As a French-trained and -employed psychologist, Fanon's original task was to treat the problems of the French colonial administration in Algeria. The crises brought on by the brutality of their relationships with the Algerian people is almost as illustrative of the crisis of the individual subject in contact with the other as the theories of a very similar crisis some twenty years later. It is perhaps in the third world that the facile machinations, the ideological fabrication, of the individual subject was and is most starkly apparent. For it is there that the attendant supporting ideologies of democracy, progress, and civilization, were either altogether absent or else so contorted as to be nonfunctional.

If, though, the perception that the subject, language, and the

---

[8] The relationship(s) between European, British, and American modernism and its attendant ideologies and their simultaneous international context of imperialism seems an inquiry long avoided but well worth pursuing.

narrative act are compromised pervades *To Diplo Biblio*, there is a very clear sense in which the novel attempts precisely what Lacan's argument about language and its subject seem to preclude. Language for Lacan, like history for Marx, is always already there, always already begun. If the transparency of the subject, of the assumption of a decisive and unified entity, of the way in which the ideology of the subject is a product of language, does not preclude a change in that order (or orders), it certainly qualifies and limits change. The very fluidity of Lacan's notion of the subject as a linguistic matrix has as its counterpart a static notion of the boundaries and definitions of that subject and of language. A crucial narrative maneuver for all three of the contemporary novels here is the laying bare of the bourgeois subject as a figment of linguistic imagination. But in the texts of Hatzis, of Kanafānī, or of Ōe, the boundaries and definitions of language are pushed and pulled to force an opening for some new and still-impossible subject. Lacan's relegation of all subjects to the flux of a fixed and always already given language is modulated in the fictional attempt to forge an intentional difference. There is no sense in which this presumably newly forged and utopically transindividual escapes ideology. But if there is no end to ideology or to language, there *is* at least the implicit possibility of redefining the terms of ideology, of attempting to alter the "Symbolic order." Lacan's schema would seem to cordon off the realm of language from conscious, human intention in a grim commentary on the (im)possibility of either individual or collective action. As there is no return to some pristine origin of things, or of language, conscious human intervention in the dominant and effective order of things is, if not impossible, a loaded and restricted affair.

The narrative exposure of the fabrication of the bourgeois subject is an essential project of Hatzis's text. But the imminent (Lacanian or otherwise) impotence[9] of human intentionality in forging a new language or a new and presumably "de-

---

[9] This "impotence" is perhaps qualified by situation in its own historical context.

alienated" subject, is a conclusion explicitly contested by the three contemporary novels discussed here. Their decidedly literary and textual struggle with agency or intentionality is, however, grounded in the acknowledgment of the fabrication of the narrative subject and of narrative meaning, and the limitations of such literary fabrication.

Certainly, the fluctuation and confluence of narrative voice in Hatzis's text is an explicit attempt to foreground the narrative in its own fabrication. The text repeatedly calls attention to the necessity of linguistic manipulation to create its narrative voice and narrative subjects. The totalizing surface of the classic realist text is openly violated. But so is the self-referential and exclusive modernist text. There is no enclosure here within a self-conscious consciousness. The pretext of the narration of *To Diplo Biblio* is the necessity of successive positions of work on the text. The narration of Costas's story is possible only through what is presumably a (fictionally) collective endeavor. This pretext operates in three stages: (1) Costas tells his story to the author, who copies it into his notebook; (2) the author relates to Costas stories from his (Costas's) past and at the same time records them in his notebook; and (3) Costas finds the notebook, which the author has left behind, transcribes what he is able to decipher of it, and adds the last chapter—"Epilogue to the First Book and a Small Prologue for the Second."

This mode of production for the narration of the story is encountered progressively rather than omnisciently at the novel's beginning. It is a formal indication of the novel's operative mode, of the self-conscious exposure of the limitations and impossibilities of the more conventional narrative character and format. There is no point at which the novel offers a privileged knowledge beyond what is afforded to the novel's characters. We are as resolutely subjected to the absence of a unified and integrated narrative as the subjects of the narrative themselves. There is no clear vantage point from which the narrative pieces can be tidily put together and made sense of. The text narrates but also performs the disintegration of both the privileged individual subject and a privileged narrative realism. And, by implication, it suggests a prescriptive paradigm for the function of the novel in general or, minimally, of this novel in particular.

To Diplo Biblio also proposes itself as a record of the dialogue between the writer as subject and the written about as object. But in that wonderfully ironic reversal already noted, the written-about object, Costas, becomes a new writing subject. Or, at least, he exceeds the boundaries of the conventional subject/author as the origin of meaning, action, and knowledge. In a strategy reminiscent of the more attenuated tactic in Sōseki's *Kusamakura*, when Nami, the written-about object, emends the narrating artist's poems about her, the written-about object of *To Diplo Biblio* becomes the reader and finally the writer of the text. Costas is the critical reader of the text of his own life and of that text's author, which is not and then is himself. So Costas's mocking of the writer's illusions and inadequacies is double-edged.

> And what can you find in me, then, Mr. Author? And what kind of an author are you anyway to come to me for your novel? There are heroic acts and heroes, murders, diseases of the spirit, and unrest of the soul—why don't you write about those? The *romeiko* you ask to discover from me? From me?! The human being of today's world, you say? I'm a "hollow pumpkin" of a human being. And it seems to me that you're a "hollow pumpkin" of an author yourself. (29)

In this "double book," the means of telling the story is as important as the particulars of the story itself. The author and the text he attempts to produce are fraught with impotent contradictions. The state of the author's notebook when it is found by Costas is presaged by the plight of the author as Costas characterizes it halfway through the book.

> And then the author, our friend, who is writing this story too, arrives. And now his own weakness begins to reveal itself. He writes a story, he advances it and he doesn't know how to end it. Divided, allotted, fragmented, in the midst of forty-two villagers from Dobrinovo and forty-two modern countries, forty-

two good men like Skouroyiannis and forty thousand black faults of his own, he doesn't know how to find a solution. He had thousands, ready-made and appropriate, to choose like every respectable author knows how to do. . . . And he doesn't want them—not one of them suits him. (141–42)

Finally, it is not the author but Costas, the "hollow pumpkin" member of "today's world," and to a lesser extent his sister, Anastasia, who will finish the story. If the first book is about Costas, the second one will be by him. Costas appropriates what is to him the foreign territory of the novel as he appropriates the foreign territory of Stuttgart, Germany, and the factory where he works carrying boxes. To the extent that Costas operates in both places, there is a rather explicit opposition between two modes of production—the one of literature and the other, the more readily acknowledged economic one, of auto electrical parts.

To Diplo Biblio attempts to prefigure or predict—literally to outline or speak *before*—a proletarian literature that is imaginary, nonexistent, of the future. It is here that the utopian ideological thrust of Hatzis's novel is most apparent. For *To Diplo Biblio* is not "proletarian literature." There was no collaboration between a writer and a worker in the production of this text. Hatzis's novel is an individual fictional construct that tries to envision the *possibility* of collaborative, nonbourgeois literary production. One of the essential ironies of the text is precisely this extratextual one—that "today's world" does not (yet?) allow the possibility of the ideological construct that *To Diplo Biblio* posits. And so both of "the double books" are contradicted by their own impossibility, within the text and outside of it. In attempting to narrate the impossible, then, *To Diplo Biblio* offers, in its own construction, a rather explicit critique of certain literary and aesthetic modes of narrative production. For it violates the tenets of realism by an insistent focus on the self-conscious production of a literary text as it violates a particular definition of social realism in its refusal of the valorized organizing perspective of the "positive hero." It violates an older modernism too with its emphatic attempt to suggest some more resolutely postin-dividual and popular social consciousness.[10] Yet, the refusal or conscious violation of a position is inevitably its incorpo-ration on other levels. For at the same time, To Diplo Biblio implicitly engages in the highly ideological proposition of modernism that "if you alter the structure of artistic discourse in a decisive way, the realities to which it corresponds will find themselves thereby similarly modified."[11]

There clearly is an element of this position in Costas's resolution of his situation—the reformation of his own story, the rewriting of the past and its relation to the present. To Diplo Biblio also participates in the project of social realism that Georg Lukács has characterized as the necessary "por-trayal of contemporary man as he really is."[12] That is Costas's "romeiko uprooting." While it refuses and participates in these literary and aesthetic discourses, To Diplo Biblio at-tempts a reformation of its own. The novel's participation in the discourse of social realism insists on the portrayal of con-temporary fiction "as it really is." Nor, clearly, does the novel exclude the "universalist" assumptions of the modernist vi-sion. But it does attempt to redefine the dimensions and func-tion of that perspective. Perhaps it is Frederic Jameson's al-most hesitantly prescriptive conclusion to "The Ideology of the Text" that best suggests the literary and extraliterary con-cerns of To Diplo Biblio: "Writers who want to change their styles may well once again come to the conclusion that they must first change the world."[13] One might add that the gulf between the literary word and the world and thus between the attempt to change one or the other is more relentlessly present in modern, dominant West European, British, or American cultures. That separation never took hold so remorselessly in other "marginal" or marginalized cultures.

[10] This confrontation is, of course, famously argued in Georg Lukács, Real-ism in Our Time: Literature and the Class Struggle.

[11] Fredric Jameson, "The Ideology of the Text," Salmagundi (Fall 1976): 242.

[12] Lukács, Realism in Our Time.

[13] Jameson, "The Ideology of the Text."

But if this discussion of the formal literary concerns of *To Diplo Biblio* has emphasized the text as self-conscious literary production, it is firmly grounded in a production of another sort that the novel opens. From its loaded opening lines— "The factory, *our* factory, is a new one"—Costas's apprehension and appropriation of an alien and alienating world is evident. "The factory" is one of the classical sites of the alienation of the worker from himself, the activity, and the product of his work. It is also one of the traditional sites from which a call for individual and social reorganization and change is made. So "the factory" is appropriated as "our factory." The first-person plural possessive is here used in distinct opposition to the first-person singular, "my." Costas's appropriating maneuver is clearly a collective one, at least linguistically. This initial narrative statement by an alienated and marginalized subject—a Greek immigrant worker in Germany—attempts to postulate something beyond the individual subject and his isolated consciousness. Costas's initial acknowledgment and linguistic ordering of the outside world, and of himself in that world, presages the not yet possible—an *other*, different, and postindividual consciousness.

> *Aoutel*—which means auto electrical parts. *We* make the lights for automobiles. All the lights—that's *us*. . . . They go into their cardboard boxes with *our* firm name, the address and an advertisement that's written on every box. . . . *We, we* work on the fourth floor. *We*, the dispatchers, the forwarding department— *spendision*, they say in German. *We* send the lamps to wherever they are to go. *We* are right next to the larger room where they do all the packaging—a smaller room for *us*. . . . This I can describe somewhat better than the other sections of the factory since I know it from the inside. *We*'re six men—and the two of *us* [Greeks]—eight.[14]

The insistent and suggestive repetition of "us," "we," and "our" in this passage is striking. In its insistence on Costas's linguistically collective identification with an alienating and

[14] Hatzis, *To Diplo Biblio*, 1 (emphasis added).

exploitive situation, this passage suggests intentional struggle within Lacan's Symbolic order—in the use of language by a character within the narrative and in the use of language by the implied authors (and, of course, real author) of the text. The narrative here attempts to speak of a still-only-potential consciousness. It attempts to *predict*, which as Gramsci points out "only means seeing the present and the past clearly as movement."[15] The literary attempt is to wrest a redefined subject from the imperviousness of language to human intentionality. Language (and narrative) is here proposed not only as an arena for the modification and alienation of the subject; it is also a potential arena of struggle for the redefinition of some of the terms of that modification. As a formulation of words that attempts a formulation of the world, this passage performs a narrative/ideological battle to forcibly "predict" class consciousness on the written page with words. If we make our own history through action—though not, as Marx cautions, just as we like, not under circumstances of our own choosing—we equally, or alternatively, shape it through words. Certainly, *To Diplo Biblio* is an attempt at the latter.

Not only does Costas begin his story in a foreign factory, but we are told by him of his own place in the hierarchy of a capitalist industry, of precisely what and how the factory in which he works produces, of how much it produces, and of the place of the factory itself in a larger chain of production. Costas has measured and calculated his surroundings. Alienated menial "guest worker" that he might be, Costas is nonetheless lucidly situated in the present. He recounts or is told of the past always in relation to his narrative present. In *To Diplo Biblio* then, the evocation of the past is not a nostalgic yearning for or melancholy brooding on a plenitude left behind. Rather, the narrative of Costas's story undertakes the critical reassessment of the past; the recognition of the effects of the past on the present; the calculation of temporal, spatial,

---

[15] Antonio Gramsci, "Prediction and Perspective," *Selections from the Prison Notebooks*, 170.

and psychological distance from that past to the present; and the calculated engagement in the present historical moment.

The literary recounting and reassessment of the past in a literal context in which that past has been rather blatantly suppressed and denied is no pedantic exercise. Only in 1982—six years after *To Diplo Biblio* and some thirty-five years after Hatzis's first novel, *E Fotia* (The fire), which recounted the Greek resistance to Fascist occupation—was the role of the Greek World War II partisans officially acknowledged by the Greek government. Until that time, official history, and more than a little unofficial history, refused to recognize the Greek Resistance or recognized it only as the actions of gangs of thugs and criminals. The Greek Civil War (1947–1949), in so many ways the outcome of the direction that the Resistance took, could scarcely fare any better in the texts of official history. As for the unofficial history of the defeated participants in that war, the choice was either silence or the relative certainty of a rather methodical physical, political, and economic harassment. So then, "Requiem for One Small Tailor," the fourth chapter of *To Diplo Biblio*, in which Costas learns for the first time of his father's role in the Resistance and the Civil War, is not just an existential comment on a son's isolation from or lack of communication with his father. It is a critical commentary on a period of fear and suppression that followed the first exercise of the Truman Doctrine in the "successful preservation of democracy" in post–Civil War Greece. There are still some one hundred and fifty thousand refugees of the Civil War in exile. Hatzis, one of these refugees himself for twenty-six years, was allowed to return to Greece in 1975 as one of the early repatriates. The history of modern Greece for the entire period from the Metaxas's dictatorship in 1936 through the years of the Colonel's Junta (1967–1974) was, and to some extent still is, clouded with official misinformation, inaccessible documents, and a pervasive and not-quite-groundless fear of naming names.

The reclamation of history from this context of repression and denial is as crucial a concern in the work of Dimitris Hatzis as is the reclamation of modern Greek literature from a narrow cultural nationalism. While recognizing the defensive reflex[16] that underlies a good deal of the dominant definition of modern Greek literature—Papadiamandis, Sikelianos, Psycharis, Palamas, Kazantzakis—*To Diplo Biblio*, in fact virtually all of Hatzis's work, fiction and nonfiction alike, resolutely insists on the transnational dimension of "today's world." It is a world in which one of the most significant natural resources that Greece possesses, other than its classical ruins, is its migrant labor force. It is a world in which national boundaries—cultural, political, psychological—are frequently and necessarily crossed. The notion of an insular and self-contained Greek nation, however useful or appealing its invocation might be, is politically and economically untenable. The notion of such containment is undermined by some two million Greeks, of a total population of approximately ten million, who are forced to seek work and/or education outside of Greece. When almost one-fourth of a country's population lives outside its boundaries, when the amount of remittances to Greece by her emigrant workers equals one-fourth of her total merchandise exports,[17] when the rapid expansion of a consumer culture is based not on national growth or production but on the international commodity production of the industrialized and developed West European countries, then the search for "*romeiko* roots," for some pure and untainted national identity, is condemned to naïveté, to romantic idealization. And so Costas challenges the writer: "There it is, my *romeiko* story. My *romeiko* roots that you ask for. The *romeiko* uprooting if you ask me" (59). The opposition between

---

[16] That is, a national literature that seeks to locate and define an "authentic" national identity, usually in opposition to the hegemony and/or coercion of an encroaching outside power. The strategies and contradictions of this maneuver in general are discussed in chap. 1, of this maneuver in the modern Greek context in particular in chap. 2. For a standard, semiofficial account of the modern Greek literary canon, see Dimaras, *History of Modern Greek Literature* and, for an incisive critique of that account, see Lambropoulos, *Literature as National Institution*, chap. 1.

[17] These figures, for 1981, are from the UN Department of International Economic and Social Affairs and from the International Monetary Fund's *Balance of Payment Statistics*, vol. 33, 1982.

the writer's abstract literary search and Costas's literal narrative present is unmistakably evident in the instances in which the simple and direct conversational language of Costas's narration is interrupted by the writer's personal reflections, here on Anastasia.

> I see them in her eyes—greening fields of gentleness and stalks of grain, of despair, together scorched by the hot winds on the plain of Thessaly—all of the plain of Thessaly is in her eyes—the snow-covered peaks above glimmer at the height of summer . . . and I see in her eyes—the Virgins of the rocks, the wounded archangels on decaying icon stands from old churches. . . . And I hear them—bells from nocturnal litanies for the ships that are in danger on the open sea—women above on the look-out—yet one more ocean—black scarves. (56)

Even if these sporadic interjected passages were not distinguished by italic print, their difference from the rest of the text is unavoidable. For the language of the writer is ornate, sophisticated, studded with unexplained classical and historical allusions and images, laced with remorse, melancholy, and more than a little self-pity. It is in opposition to this burdensome self-referential language that *To Diplo Biblio* juxtaposes Costas's language—stark, spare, although with its own imagery to be sure. But the imagery of Costas's language is derived from his present and then related to the past rather than the reverse—the domination of the present by images from the past. It is the glass and aluminum of the Aoutel factory, the impossible consumer allure of Stuttgart's department store windows and billboards, that give rise to Costas's imagery. For "today's world" of *To Diplo Biblio* can no longer be narrated in terms of a faded past greatness. It is a world in which the ready solutions of the past are no longer workable. "Our ancient heritage doesn't help you in anything; the fantasy about 'tomorrow' is missing. Our spirit perches now, silent, in the dusk of the age" (203).

The oppositions that the text constructs in its juxtaposition of narrative voices and narrative languages is underscored by the temporal and spatial ordering of Costas's story. The successive chapters of the novel with their concatenation of pasts, presents, and implied futures accentuate the definition of the narrative as a matrix of times, languages, and identities that are essentially nonlinear, stratified, complex. If *Kusamakura*'s narrating artist was conspicuously facile in his assertion about being able to open and read a novel at any point, his comment is perhaps more accurate about the way we read the past, the way in which history is not merely a linear progression but a narrative of interrelationships, a network of figures, events, and conditions, both subjective and social.

The nine chapters of *To Diplo Biblio* then are episodic but interwoven with the writer's persistent attempt to discover and delineate the "roots of the *romeiko*"—the past, the dimensions of "*o simerinos kosmos*"—the present of "today's world," and, by implication, the possibilities for the present and future engendered by this reexamined past and present—the second and presumably unwritten half of "the double book." It is the architectonic organization of the novel that is the shape of and comment on its content. Some sense of this narrative fabrication can be suggested in a schematization of the novel's progression.

Costas begins the novel and the story of his life by describing that which most crucially affects him in the present—not his personal experiences in a foreign country or his childhood in his own country but what circumscribes both the personal and the national, what is *inter*national—or more properly, multinational—the factory. "And I know it too. And I think that that's for sure the way it is and, big and small, we all know it, the position we have in the system of production. *Integre* Savvithis, who's just come from France, calls it—another pseudo-philosopher, as if we didn't have enough of them here (19). It is from his "position in the system of production," from the Stuttgart Aoutel factory, that Costas recalls the past, his family, his childhood, Greece, poverty, and a probable future of grim survival. Filtered through his presence in the Aoutel auto-electric factory in Stuttgart, Costas sifts through and remembers his past. In the terms of the narrative, it is that present that makes his past available to him in just that way.

Chapter	Time/Place/Focus
1. "Aoutel—Auto Electric Parts"	Present/Germany, the factory/ Costas as menial laborer
2. "The Lumberyard of Volos"	Past/Greece, the lumberyard/ Costas as skilled worker
3. "Kaspar Hauser in a Desolate Land"	Present/Germany/Costas's social life outside of the factory
4. "Requiem for One Small Tailor"	Past/Greece/Costas's past as embodied by his father
5. "From 50/50 to Love"	Present/Germany/the female, German Other
6. "The Last Bear of Pindos"	Present (implied future)/Greece/ return of the immigrant worker
7. "The Pestles"	Present (implied future)/Germany/the German worker and his union
8. "Anastasia of Molaos"	Present (implied future)/Greece/ Costas's past (and alternative future) as embodied by his sister
9. "Epilogue for the First Book and a Small Prologue for the Second"	Present (implied future)/Germany/the second half of the "double book" and the story of many Costases

And then, it is and is not his past. The past that Costas re-counts to the writer could be the past of countless Costases like him. The conditions that circumscribe Costas's past are those that similarly affect the numerous pasts of migrant workers from Yugoslavia or Turkey or Korea or Portugal or India.[18] In spite of the furor among political and literary critics that the passage created,[19] perhaps Costas's assertion about his past is not so outrageous after all: "And so I tell you that I've been gone for four years and I've never felt the nostalgia for my homeland that they talk about. I don't know what it is. It seems that I don't have a homeland; I don't have a 'home' in my homeland" (63).

For a narrow cultural or political nationalism, this is a scan-dalous and even heretical statement. The homeland presum-ably is, or should be, the site of organic wholeness and well-being, the place in which mutilated meaning, the emigrant worker, is restored to its natural place. But it is the "natural" itself that is the problem, more blatantly perhaps in the situa-tion of the migrant worker but apparent nonetheless in the economic, political or sociocultural life of the "homeland" and its people. Certainly, for Greece, there was no "natural" state of grace before the imperialist advent of the West. There was the four-hundred-year rule of the Ottoman Empire. But the nine-year War of Independence and the political struggles that followed it were not the harbingers of independent devel-opment either. A precapitalist, quasi-feudal Greece became an underdeveloped, semicapitalist economy.[20]

It is the distorted or obstructed growth of that economy and the cultural and political disarticulation that that growth gives

[18] There is a growing body of literature on the essentially shared situations of migrant or "guest" workers in West Europe, the Gulf states, Japan, and other countries. See John Berger's *The Seventh Man* (footnote 4, above) or, for example, the issues of *MERIP* on migrant workers, especially nos. 123 (May 1984) and 124 (June 1984).

[19] See footnotes 4 and 5 above.

[20] See Nikos Mouzelis's *Modern Greece: Facets of Underdevelopment*, es-pecially pt. 1, "The Development of Greek Capitalism," for a penetrating dis-cussion of the nature and direction of Greece's capitalist growth and the na-ture of her relationship with the West.

rise to that compels Costas to leave Greece in the first place. In the novel's second chapter, the focus switches from the present of a factory in Germany to the past of a small, poorly run, and inefficient lumberyard in Greece. There is a parallel implied between levels of economic development and what the disparity between those levels means in personal terms—for Costas. The analogical compilation of the narrative takes shape quickly. In the following chapter, Costas narrates the isolation of his present in Germany, an isolation parallel to that of Kaspar Hauser, as the chapter's title suggests. The isolation in Greece and Germany of Costas/Kaspar is juxtaposed to the writer's narration of the similarly desolate isolation of Costas's father in Greece. The post–Civil War silence and almost merciful death of "one small tailor," betrayed and ostracized for his role in organizing the countryside during the occupation, suggests yet another parallel between that struggle in the past—originating in the Resistance and culminating in the Civil War—and a presumably analogous struggle in the present—that of the emigrant worker in a foreign and hegemonic country. If the achievements of the Resistance during the Occupation held some genuine potential for significant political and social change in Greece, a potential that was unequivocally eliminated by the conclusion of the Civil War, there is a utopic suggestion that the struggle of a Costas, or of many Costases, could hold a similar potential. But regardless of the tentative suggestions that *To Diplo Biblio* makes about the future, it does, in the person of Costas, make a number of relatively *un*tentative statements about the narrative present. It does this not only in the *details* of Costas's story but in the very structure of those details—in the spatial, temporal, and psychological juxtaposition of chapters, in the layering of narrative time and narrative voice and in the layered composition of the narrative subject—Costas.

Costas is granted a provisional and momentary reprieve from the "desolation of Kaspar Hauser" that dominates his life in Germany, as it does the lives of the other immigrant workers in Stuttgart or his father's life in Greece or the writer's life in transit, in the middle chapter of the text, "From

50/50 to Love." It is the story of Costas's love for a German worker, Erika—a love that Costas had considered impossible. What is possible is the "50/50" that Costas learns in Germany—

> as much as you give, you get in return. On Sunday when you're alone again, you think of it once more. Of the 50/50 that doesn't go any further than the moment that it lasts. And you think then of the woman, the good woman that you embraced, how she must be deprived too, poor and lonely like yourself. (79)

But Costas and Erika manage to exceed this "50/50," at least provisionally. They talk to each other of their pasts, of their dreams for the future, of their love that will help them overcome all the differences—of culture, of language, of dreams. But finally it is only an unstable resolution of their poverty, loneliness, alienation, and difference; it is an impossible love. "All in all, five months it endured. Is that its limit for others too? Or maybe that kind of love isn't for the poor—they confuse everything, too hungry for what we call 'real' life—they expect everything from love? Or maybe that's the way today's world is—we've unlearned how to love, we don't know what or who is at fault" (118).

Like the resolution of so much else in Costas's life, love is "bigger than a single person, and so unattainable for a single person, too." That "unattainability" (or more literally, "not-yet-accomplishedness") characterizes the subsequent chapters as well. Skouroyiannis's return to his village in Greece, Costas's recognition of his relationship to the native German workers, and Anastasia's grim present, are all marked by that quality of something "not-yet-accomplished" but undeniably necessary. Chapters 6, 7, and 8 are all set in a narrative present and narrated alternately by Costas and the writer. But their implicit direction is the future, the future in which the "not-yet-accomplished" is recognized as an essential necessity and begins-to-become-accomplished. Hatzis's text resembles Papadiamandis's narrative in this respect. For, in spite of what might initially appear to be *E Fonissa*'s valorization of peasant life and customs, the text equally indicts the oppressive circumstances of that life and, in doing so, indicates the necessity of change, even if a change that is only specified negatively.

Finally, the last chapter of the text—"An Epilogue for the First Book and a Small Prologue for the Second"—makes clear that it is toward the future that *To Diplo Biblio* points a cautious and very literary finger. It is the structural configurations of the novel that suggest, that predict or prefigure, the future. That prefiguration is present as well in the construction of a parallel between producing the narrative of an immigrant worker and the narrative of producing a novel. To alter the order in which the novel unfolds or the collective voice with which both stories—that of Costas and that of the making of a novel—are told would be then to drastically alter *To Diplo Biblio*.

To the closing page of the novel, the initial opposition between the production of a novel and the production of a life, between the writer's work and the worker's story, is maintained. The writer comments on Costas's past and present, on the possibilities for his future. Costas, in turn comments on the writer's fashioning of a novel. They speak to one another, about one another. And from this basic confrontation arises a complex configuration of analogies and oppositions—of present to past (and future), writer to written about, narrator to character, intellectual to worker, homeland to foreign "homeland." The foundation of the novel is cast on these oppositions. It is their interplay that will presumably create, or if we accept the pretext of the novel, has already created, the possibility of the "second book," the reformulation of the novel, the reformulation of "today's world."

The second book is to ground itself in the pages of the first. What began as a story about Costas by the writer will become a story about many Costases by Costas. The new novel, the new story of Costas, will be based on the lessons of the first book, as the writer reminds Costas, the lessons

of children defeated in their own time, in their own land, with their superstition or their remorse, their exaggerations, their perseverance or their escape—their sleeping bear, their murdered birds to cry over, and others with their irrational passion—a dictatorship so at least they'll find solace for their decline and their uselessness—they've all left, taking with them their age. . . . The other book, the second one, yours, it too starts out from there. (202)

So the stock tools of the writer are no longer effective and he must entrust the book to Costas (and Anastasia). And Costas, ignorant of parts of his own past, must turn to the writer to fill in the gaps in his story. The novelist is not, cannot be, an isolated and all-powerful creator. He is forced, at least in *To Diplo Biblio*, to reexamine and redefine his own role in the world of which he writes.

An outline of Dimitris Hatzis's life would suggest that this was not an incidental concern for the real author either. Born in the northern Greek town of Yiannina in 1916, Hatzis joined the young Greek Communist party by the time he was nineteen. His studies in Athens at the law school were cut short by the death of his father and he returned to Yiannina to manage the newspaper *E Epiros* and support his family. In the first days of the Metaxas dictatorship (1936–1941), Hatzis was arrested along with hundreds of other leftists and imprisoned. When he was released nearly five years later, Hatzis left Yiannina for Athens. There, during the first days of the Italian occupation, he formed an organization to reinfiltrate recently released political prisoners[21] back into the countryside and to organize and care for the thousands of refugees who thronged into Athens. This group and others like it became the backbone of the Resistance movement in Greece (EAM), which was formed shortly thereafter. Throughout the war, as a member of the Education Committee of the Communist party, Hatzis published broadsheets, pamphlets, and the newsletter, *From Liberated Greece*. He also wrote for and

---

[21] The Communists and leftists imprisoned and sent into internal exile at the takeover of Metaxas were turned over to the occupying Italian forces when Metaxas, with the rest of the Greek government, the royal family, and high-ranking military officers, left Greece for Egypt. Ironically, the Italians unwittingly freed the political prisoners who then thronged into Athens.

published EAM's newspaper, *Forward*. With the intervention of British and then American forces in postwar Greece, Hatzis returned to the mountains and continued producing pamphlets and broadsheets until the defeat of 1949. He went into exile with thousands of other participants in the Civil War.

It was during the Occupation that Hatzis began writing fiction,[22] publishing his first novel, *E Fotia* (The fire), which dealt with the day-to-day lives of the partisans, in 1946. Later, from exile in Hungary (1949–1957 and 1962–1967), Germany (1957–1962), and France (1968–1975), Hatzis wrote and published the remainder of his small oeuvre of fiction: *To Telos tis Mikris mas Polis* (The end of our small city, 1963), *Aniperaspistoi* (The defenseless, 1966), *Spoudes* (Studies, 1976), *To Diplo Biblio* (The double book, 1976), and *Thitia* (Service, 1977). He also wrote for a number of Greek newspapers and periodicals in both West and East Europe and, as a professor of modern and Byzantine Greek literature, wrote a number of long articles on literary criticism that have yet to be collected and published. Not unlike his last novel, *To Diplo Biblio*, Hatzis's journalistic and critical writings brought an invigorating analytical perspective to a discourse fraught with what could be called, after Nikos Mouzelis, Greek formalism.[23]

From exile, Hatzis was active in organizing other Greek immigrants, refugees, and exiles from the dictatorship of the Colonels (1967–1974) and students.[24] After his return to

[22] Before the war, under the influence of the poet Kostas Varnalis, Hatzis tried his hand at poetry, but he rather quickly abandoned the genre.

[23] On the pervasive "formalism" of modern Greek cultural and political life, see Mouzelis, *Modern Greece*, esp. pt. 3, chap. 8—"On Greek Formalism: Political and Cultural Aspects of Underdevelopment." In one of Hatzis's published critical works on modern Greek poetry—"Apo ton Solomo sti nea poiesi" ("From [Dionysus] Solomos to the new poetry")—in two parts in *Anti* 146 and 147 (February and March 1980), he addresses the problems that this "formalism" has created for modern Greek culture. His article is an exceptional analysis of modern Greek poetry in the light of its obsession with the opposition between a pseudopopulist demotic language and content and an equally artificial purist language and content. (See chap. 2 for a more detailed discussion of the language issue.)

[24] Between 1968 and 1970, Hatzis, in conjunction with other activists, es-

Greece in 1975, Hatzis wrote voluminously (for him) on contemporary political and cultural issues and became a central figure in the drive to establish a writers' union. In 1980, he began publishing a new political-cultural journal, *E Prisma* (Prism). He died prematurely in the summer of 1980.

Compelled by circumstance and Hatzis's own political commitment to the acknowledgment of a world larger than the national boundaries of any one country, the more properly international perspective of Hatzis's narratives is an implicit critique of a nationalism that, however genuinely defensive, does not account for the emigrants, refugees, and exiles of "today's world." The pages of Hatzis's fiction, like those of Kanafānī's *Rijāl fī al-shams* or Ōe's *Man'en gannen no futtōboru*, are peopled with fictional testimonials of seepage beyond narrow national boundaries and definitions. The parallels between Hatzis's fiction and the texts examined in the next two chapters indicate Hatzis's literary, political, or critical concerns not just as his alone but as shared by other writers from the "third world." And if their fictional "predictions" of the transnational or supranational are grounded in wrenching confrontations and grim exploitation in the narrative present, they are the source of yet-to-be-formulated narratives, literary and literal, that exceed the fixation of national and individual boundaries.

For *To Diplo Biblio* then, in what is clearly a loaded and symbolic gesture, the writer and the worker's critical reexamination of past and present and the future prefigured in this reexamination, is to be passed into the hands of countless Costases. Costas will write a story of and for a million menial laborers (*khamalides*)—foreigners in a strange land," the "uprooted," "today's people."

> For me. For those others, as he says. For hope. And what if it is and a little for Greece—why shouldn't it be? (203)

tablished the Union of Greek College Graduates of Western Europe. In 1973, he taught Greek literature and politics at the Summer School of Geneva and, in 1974, at the Free University of Paris.

Chapter 6

DESERTS OF MEMORY

Men make their own history, but they do not make it
just as they please; they do not make it under
circumstances chosen by themselves, but under
circumstances directly encountered, given, and
transmitted from the past.
—Karl Marx, *The Eighteenth Brumaire*

Today Palestine does not exist, except as a memory,
or—more importantly—as an idea, a political and
human experience, and an act of sustained
popular will.
—Edward Said, "The Idea of Palestine in the West"

"FOR ME. FOR THOSE OTHERS, as we said. For hope"—Costas's closing dedication in *To Diplo Biblio* can also stand as a metaphor for the work of the Palestinian novelist, Ghassān Kanafānī (1936–1972). *To Diplo Biblio*'s attempt to map out, to prefigure, some alternate terrain for the novel and for its cultural and social contexts is also apparent in Kanafānī's fiction. His novels and short stories as remarkable for their innovative language and structural narrative concerns as they are for their content. Kanafānī's fiction, too, attempts a reformulation of the relationship between literature and society, between the word and the world. But it is not only in the symbolic closing gesture of Hatzis's novel or in the "predictive" concern of their texts that Hatzis's and Kanafānī's work affords comparison.

The linguistic fabric of both Kanafānī's and Hatzis's narratives are distinguished by their construction of an understated and simple language that deliberately goes against the grain of cultural contexts marked by rhetorical virtuosity and complexity. Hatzis's *To Diplo Biblio* and Kanafānī's *Rijāl fī al-shams* (Men in the sun),[1] which is the focus of the present chapter, foreground their use, their manipulation, of language. The implications, literary and social, of this gesture in the work of Kanafānī and Hatzis is perhaps made most clear by the contrasting linguistic maneuver of the contemporary Japanese novelist whose work is examined in the following chapter.

The frequent indictment by Japanese critics that the language of Ōe Kenzaburo's texts "reeks of butter" (i.e., is foreign or not-really-Japanese) is a backhanded recognition of the fact that Ōe, unlike Kanafānī or Hatzis, is writing in and against a tradition of "poetic simplicity" and "understated meaning." Ōe's presumably convoluted grammar, complex imagery, and references to foreign texts and cultures is an equally deliberate attempt to break the hold of a linguistic tradition of (national) autoreferentiality, of an almost antiverbal fixation on "simple and direct" images, on haiku-like brevity and understatement. For the Greek and Arabic texts, though, in the face of a tradition of linguistic virtuosity, producing fiction that goes against their respective linguistic grain(s) results in the fabrication of a simple and understated, almost inherently ironic, language. For Ōe's texts, the linguistic emphasis and impetus is similar but its textual manifestation is a self-consciously difficult and complex language that refuses the pretext of the "traditional simplicity and lyricism" of the Japanese language.

All three of the contemporary writers examined in these last chapters attempt to fashion a language that will jar the hold of a manipulated tradition. All three are engaged, as well, in a

---

[1] Ghassān Kanafānī, *Rijāl fī al-shams* (Men in the sun). All translations are my own unless otherwise noted. For a translation, see Ghassān Kanafānī, *Men in the Sun*, trans. Hilary Kilpatrick (Washington, DC: Three Continents Press, 1978). See also Barbara Harlow's excellent translation of some of Kanafānī's short stories in Ghassan Kanafani, *Palestine's Children*, trans. Barbara Harlow (Washington, DC: Three Continents Press, 1984).

discourse that is self-consciously postulated as both literary and extraliterary. The attempt to fashion a language and fiction that will reach a broad audience, that will unsettle and stir its readers, and that will spark individual and social consideration and, implicitly, change of (textually) crucial issues is common to all three texts and authors. And all three recognize, from within and without their texts, that suggestion at the conclusion of Fredric Jameson's "The Ideology of the Text," of the mutually engendering imperative of changing the world and the word.[2]

Kanafānī, demonstrating that imperative to which Jameson refers, was engaged in both literal and literary change. Born in Acre, Palestine, in 1936, the son of a lawyer, Kanafānī lived in Jaffa until 1948. With the establishment of the state of Israel and the ensuing Arab-Israeli War, Kanafānī's family fled first to Lebanon and then to Damascus, Syria. He completed school in Syria and worked as a secondary school teacher in Damascus and then, in 1955, in Kuwait. There Kanafānī met one of the leading figures of the Arab Nationalist Movement, George Habash, and decided to leave Kuwait for Beirut to work as a journalist. Kanafānī's published work includes five novels (two of them unfinished), five collections of short stories, two plays, two studies of Palestinian literature, and a great many nonfiction articles and pamphlets. Of his completed fiction, the work that has had a striking effect on Arabic fiction and on Arabic intellectual thought in general is undoubtedly the novel, *Rijāl fī al-shams* (Men in the sun). A narrative of the attempt of three Palestinians to be smuggled into Kuwait to find work, it was written, for the most part, over a month-long period in Lebanon in 1962 when Kanafānī was forced into hiding because he had no official papers. From 1963 until after the June 1967 Arab-Israeli War, Kanafānī was editor in chief of the Nasserist daily, *al-Muharrir*. In 1967, he joined the staff of *al-Anwār* but two years later he left to become the editor in chief of *al-Hadaf*. *Al-Hadaf* is the official weekly of the Popular Front for the Liberation of Palestine

[2] See chap. 5, footnote 11.

(PFLP), an organization established in 1967 by George Habash as an outgrowth of the Arab Nationalist Movement. In addition to his role as editor of *al-Hadaf*, Kanafānī later became the official spokesperson for the PFLP. He continued to work in both capacities, and as a novelist, until his assassination in 1972.

The political and intellectual progression from Arab nationalism to Nasserism to some form of Marxism that is apparent in the movement of Kanafānī's career is noteworthy, for the direction of his political and cultural concerns were scarcely singular. The appeal of pan-Arab nationalism and of what was, to a great extent, its problematic if logical culmination in Nasserism[3] was felt throughout much of the Arab world in the 1950s and early 1960s. To the heirs of a generation that can be metaphorized by the ideological maneuver of compromise and synthesis that informs Yahyā Haqqī's *Qindīl Umm Hāshim*, pan-Arab unity and its frequent coefficient—pan-Islamism—seemed a promising alternative to the failures of both an Arab version of Western liberal humanism and modernization and of the responses of Arab states to challenges from within the Arab world.

With the establishment of the state of Israel in Palestine in

[3] Nasserism as a popular movement in the Arab world grew up around the charismatic figure of the Free Officers' Coup in Egypt in 1952, Gamil abd al-Nasser. From about 1954, with his consolidation of power in Egypt, until the Arab defeat in the 1967 Arab-Israeli War, a defeat for which Nasser was popularly held responsible, the figure of Nasser embodied, not just for Egypt but for a great deal of the Arab world, a combination of nationalism, "Arab socialism," and antiimperialism that promised a unified Arab response to the problems facing the Arab world. Maxime Rodinson's evaluation of Nasserism in 1959 proved to be almost prophetically incisive: "The cadres [of Egyptian Nasserism] are very exposed to compromise with the capitalist system. The authoritarian organization does not allow the masses to influence decisions. For the time being, it seems to be faithful to the proclaimed objectives of the anti-feudal and anti-imperialist revolution. Its socialist orientation is much more questionable. How far will its petit-bourgeois and popular bourgeois clientele follow it? In the event of a Kemal-type degeneration, will possible communist party take over in support of the working masses? That is possible, but it is not the only option." In Maxime Rodinson, "Arab Nationalism and Intellectual Life," *Marxism and the Muslim World*, 255.

1948, a radically new dimension was added to the makeup of the Arab world. It was the Palestinians themselves who felt this crisis most directly, but the surrounding countries of the Arab East were also undeniably affected. Increasingly, after 1948, in the rhetoric of the Arab states and in the popular conception of the Arab people, the dismemberment of Palestine and the transformation of over three quarters of a million people into exiles became a dominant issue. In popular conception and official rhetoric, the Palestinian situation was made a symbol of the struggle between the Arab world and the West, with Israel and Zionism as the West's junior partners. At the same time, as the Palestinians were dispersed to Gaza, Jordan, Lebanon, and Syria, they were forced to confront their own repression and ghettoization by the Arab regimes and also the poverty and oppression of the majority of native Jordanians, Lebanese, Egyptians, or Syrians. The loss of Palestine not only made apparent the new, postcolonial face of Western power in the Middle East, it also made apparent the collusion of the Arab ruling classes with that new power: "Finally, Dulles and Ike, Eden and MacMillan, Ben-Gurion and Moshe Dayan, were not a totally unmitigating evil; they gave us a rude awakening. . . . They forced us to re-examine the foundations of our society."[4]

By the end of the decade following the Second World War, the European colonial powers had withdrawn from much of the Arab East. The overt confrontation between the colonial powers and the colonized gave way to a domination, whether economic, political, or cultural, that was substantially more complex, more camouflaged, and more integrated. The end of colonial dependence brought, not independence in any real sense of the word, but a new kind of dependence that elicited the active support, or at least the acquiescence, of the Arab ruling classes. If in the anticolonial struggles for independence, the Arab people had been willing to accept the leadership of the traditional ruling class, in the postindependence struggle for the internal transformation of society, this was

[4] Leila Khaled, *My People Shall Live*.

not the case. The bankruptcy of the traditional rulers had become increasingly apparent. This was as true of their policies
toward the internal social and political change of their own
states as it was of their policies toward the Palestinian struggle. "Their announced aim was the salvation of Palestine and
they said that afterwards its destiny should be left to its people. This was said with words only. In their hearts, they all
wanted it for themselves; most of them were hurrying to pre-
vent their neighbors from being predominant."[5]

With the overthrow of Egypt's King Fārūq in 1952 by the
Free Officers' Coup, and the emergence two years later of
Nasser as the dominant figure, the assumption of power in
1954 of the Ba'ath party in Syria, and the increasing growth
and influence of the Arab Nationalist Movement (founded in
1953 by a group of predominantly Palestinian university students), a renewed political and intellectual response to the
postwar challenges confronting the Arab world began to take
form. If the underlying political and economic issues involved
in independent development for the Arab world were never
quite dealt with by the ANM (Arab Nationalist Movement),
by the Ba'ath, or by Nasser, initially at least, Nasser and the
ANM inspired an entire generation with hope for the future.
And both Nasser and the ANM, if not the Ba'ath, proclaimed
that the Palestinian issue was at the forefront of the struggle
for Arab unity and against Western imperialism and Zionism.
For the decade of the 1950s and most of the 1960s, the ANM
and Nasserism were intimately intertwined. Nasser was the
charismatic embodiment of a popular nationalist ideology of
Arab unity, antiimperialism, and independent development.
In this scheme of things, the resolution of the Palestinian
"problem" would be the result of the united effort of the existing Arab states. But it was not long before the limitations of
Nasser's appealing rhetoric became apparent. Though Nasser
himself hung on for three more years, the death blow for Nasserism as a popular movement, not only in Egypt but through-

[5] Musa Alāmi, "The Lesson of Palestine," *Middle East Journal* (October
1949): 385.

out the Arab world, came with the military defeat of the Egyptian-directed Arab forces in the Arab-Israeli War of 1967. Once again, as in 1948, the defeat of the Arab forces brought on a massive reexamination both of the existing Arab states and of their relationship to the Palestinian situation: "After the first catastrophe of 1948, the Palestinian Arabs, left fragmented and leaderless, naturally looked to the Arab states for salvation. After the second catastrophe they realized that salvation could only come through their own efforts."[6]

Some had come to this conclusion even before 1967. In 1959, in Kuwait, Yassir Arafat and eleven others formed the beginnings of an independent national liberation organization—*Fatah*. In 1960, the Arab Nationalist Movement, at the instigation of George Habash and Wadi Haddad, both Palestinians, formed a Palestine Division of its organization.[7] In 1964, the First Arab Summit Conference founded the Palestine Liberation Organization. The initial formation of the PLO, however, was as much a move to contain the Palestinian resistance as to organize it. The military arm of the PLO was placed under the control of the Arab armies and, in a further gesture of containment, the Arab states appointed Ahmad al-Shukeiri the leader of the new organization. After the 1967 debacle, with a growing challenge to the ANM's strategy of regional divisions by *Fatah* and by other resistance organizations among the refugee camps and cities, Habash and his comrades announced the formation of the Popular Front for the Liberation of Palestine. (Something of the direction the PFLP would take was inherent in the massive problems of converting a nationalist and anticommunist organization into a presumably Marxist one.) The defeat of 1967 also swept aside the appointed leadership of the PLO and all of the resistance organizations united under its umbrella, with *Fatah* and Ara-

---

[6] L. S. Stavrianos, *The Global Rift*, 776.

[7] The Arab Nationalist Movement (ANM) rested on a structure of regional divisions in each of the existing Arab states. Until the formation of a separate Palestinian Division, Palestinians, in accordance with the ANM's pan-Arab line, were to participate in the regional division of whichever country they found themselves in.

fat as its leaders. The stage was scarcely set for a victorious return to the secular and democratic state of Palestine. But the Palestinians, betrayed by their traditional leaders as early as the General Strike and Revolt of 1936–1939[8] as well as in the first Arab-Israeli War of 1948, and betrayed once more in 1967 by a new generation of leaders, managed to establish for themselves an organization that, at its best, could become exemplary in the Arab world for its democratic structure.

If the traditional position of preeminence, both cultural and political, in the Arab world had been occupied by Egypt, since the end of World War II that preeminence has been at least shared by the Palestinians. Since 1948, the Palestinian disaster has been, rhetorically at least, made the sign of the postindependence violation and dominance of the entire Arab world by the West. Unfortunately, some form of just resolution of that disaster was not granted quite so much significance, even rhetorically. But in spite of the uses to which their situation was put, scattered in a diaspora that extends from the Arab world to Latin America, the Palestinians became, in fact, the foundation of a new generation of migrant intellectuals, activists, and, not least of all, workers. They formed the vanguard of a somewhat older and wiser version of the late-nineteenth and early-twentieth-century *nahda* (see chap. 3). Their decisive participation in this latter-day "renaissance" has unalterably affected the political, as well as the cultural, complexion of contemporary Arab society.[9] It is for this reason that we turn from a consideration of the Arabic novel in early-twentieth-century Egypt to the contemporary Palestinian-Arabic novel in exile. The development of this national novel without a nation-state renews and redefines the questions of pan-Arabism, of the Arab world's relationship with the West, of the relationship among the existing Arab states, and, perhaps most crucially, of the relationship of the present Arab world

---

[8] See Kanafānī's analysis of this crucial period in *The 1936–39 Revolt in Palestine.*

[9] For an interesting examination of this relationship in modern Arab poetry, see Khalid A. Sulaiman, *Palestine and Modern Arab Poetry.*

to her past and future. The Arabic novel-in-exile can be seen as the counterpart of a genre increasingly exiled or stateless in other parts of the third world.[10]

While Egypt's cultural and intellectual production fell under the hand of Nasser's growing censorship and the stalemate of that country's unresolved internal problems, the issue of Palestine and the Palestinians themselves assumed a position of dominant intellectual, if not political, importance in the Arab world. This was no doubt equally the result of the fact that, in a generation or two, the Palestinians had become among the best educated of the Arab peoples. With the fulfillment of their nationalist aspirations consistently denied, they became the bearers of a new kind of "internationalism." Exiled citizens of no country, they became the (frequently second-class) citizens of many countries. Their "internationalism," though, demands quotation marks, for it is a distinct variation on that almost leisurely internationalism of the first world. It is an internationalism that is inexorably and contradictorily bound to nationalist aspirations. For it is an internationalism of necessity rather than of intellectual choice, of fact rather than of theoretical alignment.[11] It is this contradiction between internationalism and a denied nationalism that informs Kanafānī's *Rijāl fī al-shams*.

But it should not be so surprising that literal exile prompts literary internationalism. The internationalism of Costas, the migrant worker of *To Diplo Biblio*, is grounded in the de facto exile of a migrant worker; in a textual conjunction of the search for work and for meaning; in the recognition of one's otherness to the German citizen, to the emigrant Greek as well as the Greek citizen, and to one's self; in the inability to return

[10] Whether or not that internationalism is the (displaced?) intellectual and cultural outgrowth of a more properly political impasse is an interesting question. The implications of Barbara Harlow's discussion of "Narratives of Resistance" in her *Resistance Literature* are most suggestive.

[11] As is suggested in Harlow's chapter on narratives in her *Resistance Literature*. Three of the five novelists whose work she examines write from exile. The "exiled" fiction of Ghassān Kanafānī or Dimitris Hatzis has many more counterparts as well.

to the past, whether more immediate or distantly classical; or to return "home" to a narrowly defined nationalism. Thus arises the necessary postulation of an alternate subject that exceeds established boundaries—national, psychological, cultural. That text's most scandalous proposition, at least to its Greek readers, was that Costas no longer had a homeland. The myth of return was presented as just that—mythical and literary but scarcely literal. The narrative of the modern migrant worker from the periphery or semiperiphery is made to suggest the limitations of nationalism, the limitations of its failed and its realized promises. And those suggestions of the promises and limitations of nationalism are not altogether extraneous for another kind of migrant, for the exile, the refugee with no homeland, not even an alienated one. In a situation similar to, but even more exacerbated than that of Costas, the exiles and illegal aliens of Kanafānī's *Rijāl fī al-shams* are "at home" nowhere.

Kanafānī's text is a most literal, if only arguably "transcendental" illustration of the "homelessness" with which Lukács characterizes the modern novel.[12] Both the exiles in the novel and the text itself are confronted with the necessity of crossing over the boundaries of the countries through which they wander and over those other denied boundaries of Palestine. In addition, they are confronted with their situation *within* class boundaries which, before 1948, were only nascently present in Palestinian society: that is, the transition from peasant to often illegal migrant worker. But that boundary over which the text of *Rijāl fī al-shams* does not and cannot grant passage is that from the past to the present and future. It is the textual inability to clear this "border" that condemns the three Palestinian characters in the novel to death. The postulation of an alternative subjectivity, of a problematized (inter)nationalism, is only implicit in *Rijāl fī al-shams*. But the only textual alternative to such an implicit possibility is death.

When the novel first appeared, its conclusion, in which the three Palestinians suffocate in an empty water tank as they

---

[12] Georg Lukács, *Theory of the Novel*, 84–93 and 120–29.

wait for the truck driver who is smuggling them to be cleared
by the Kuwaiti border guards, provoked a storm of protest
among its Arab readers. Huddled inside the scorching metal
tank, the three die silently, without a cry of protest, and the
driver—who is also a Palestinian, but one with papers—abandons their dead bodies on a garbage dump outside of the city
of Kuwait after taking their money and watches. It was not
the death of the three exiles but their silence and the theft of
the men's possessions by the truck driver that was considered
unacceptable. Given the rhetoric generated by the Arab states
and the traditional Palestinian leaders about the Palestinian
situation, the conclusion of *Rijāl fī al-shams* seemed ignomin-
ious if not heretical. Images of the Palestinians' triumphant
return on the shoulders of their Arab brothers or at least of
resistance until death were preferable. The starkness and almost ironic understatement of Kanafānī's novel was a challenge to more than the formal and linguistic assumptions of
contemporary Arabic fiction. Some of the dimensions of that
other challenge are suggested by the fact that in 1972, when a
Syrian film, *al-Makhdusun* (The deceived), was made based
on *Rijāl fī al-shams*, the silence of the three dying men is eliminated. The film has the three Palestinians cry out and pound
on the walls of the truck's water tank, but their cries are
drowned out by the whirring air conditioners in the offices of
the Kuwaiti border guards. The film ends discreetly at that
point so that the issue of the driver's rifling of the dead men's
pockets does not arise.[13]

The usual justification for the "pessimism" of *Rijāl fī al-
shams* is typically that, written in late 1962, before the instigation of an official aboveground Palestinian resistance movement, the future for the Palestinians looked bleak. This novel
is presumably, then, an immediate reflection of that bleakness.
Concomitantly, the logic for the necessity of altering the end
of the novel in any later adaption is that, after the establish-

[13] The challenge that *Rijāl fī al-shams* continues to present to official Israeli
assumptions is no less loaded. An attempt in 1977 to produce a stage version
of Kanafānī's novel in Israel (in Nazareth) was banned by the Israeli authori-
ties.

ment of the PLO and its acceptance by the Palestinians as their sole legitimate representative, the conclusion of the novel is "glaringly incongruous."[14] Even the periodical that Kanafānī edited until his death, *al-Hadaf*, in a commemorative article on the tenth anniversary of his assassination, pays homage in passing to his fiction for its ability to faithfully represent the life of the Palestinians, but focuses much more on his nonfiction articles and on his analysis of the 1936–1939 Revolt. This reading of Kanafānī's fiction, while understandable, does no little injustice to what was precisely the attempt of *Rijāl fī al-shams* to do—to articulate a fictional resolution to an only-too-real problem—the construction and maintenance of some redefined collective and (meta)individual identity for a nation of exiles. *Rijāl fī al-shams* is, even more essentially, the utopian project of reconciling a past with a present in order to "predict" a future. The novel is itself an alternative reading of a historical situation that had become substantially encrusted with rhetoric about what-should-be. But with a precariously minimal analysis of what-is, what-should-be can become little more than a way to avoid the present.

In spite of the initial responses to the novel, *Rijāl fī al-shams* is not just a dismal exposé of the misery and circumscribed aspirations of three men's lives—actually four, if we include the Palestinian truck driver. The four Palestinians trapped in the separate chapters of *Rijāl fī al-shams* are trapped as well in a past that they can only partially understand, that they can, in fact, only partially recall. And for this narrative, there is no convenient textual equivalent to Costas's coffee-house writer. It is Kanafānī's later *Umm Sa'ad* (The mother of Sa'ad),[15] with its episodic series of conversations between a young Palestinian writer and intellectual and an old family friend from the refugee camp, the Umm Sa'ad of the title, that most nearly approaches the narrative format of *To Diplo Biblio*. But for the four "men in the sun," there is no one within the narrative

---

[14] See Hilary Kilpatrick, "Tradition and Innovation in the Fiction of Ghassan Kanafani," *Journal of Arabic Literature* 7 (1976): 53–64 and the "Introduction" to his translation of *Rijāl fī al-shams*.

[15] Ghassān Kanafānī, *Umm Sa'ad*.

to fill in the gaps between past and present. That task is rather clearly allotted to the implied readers of the text. Instead, the present of the four men is a continuous but delimited remembering of fragments of their personal pasts filtered through poverty, bitterness, long years in refugee camps, and the absence of any context in which to make sense of their memories. They are quite literally caught between the past and their hopes for the future. That this situation is not singular is suggested by Germaine Tillon's characterization of the Algerian people during their war of independence as "living on the frontiers of two worlds—in the middle of the ford—haunted by the past, fevered with dreams of the future. But it is with their hands empty and their bellies hollow that they are waiting between their phantoms and their fevers."[16]

The first three chapters of the novel present, in turn, the separate memories and hopes of the three illegal aliens—an old peasant, Abū Qais; a political activist, Assad; and a young high school boy, Marwān. In a stark and schematic gesture, the three are as structurally trapped and isolated in their individual chapters as they are in their individual memories of the past. The formal structure of the novel—its episodic format, its juxtaposition of chapters containing either isolated memories and dreams or the avoidance of impending disaster in the present—and the textual consequences of that structure are rather ominous portents of the narrative fate of the four Palestinians.

The narrative structure of *Rijāl fī al-shams* exerts an almost rigidly determining influence on its content, on the story of its characters. It constructs an opposition between individual subjects—their memories, fears, and dreams—and a narrative form that separates and, while not condemning them, decisively kills them. The textual insistence on the power of a structural force, here literally the structure of the novel itself, in distinguishing the content of that structure suggests itself as a textual metaphor for the position of the subject in the distinguishing structure of history. To that extent, the narrative

[16] Germaine Tillon, *Algeria: The Realities.*

form of *Rijāl fī al-shams* can be seen as an attempt to exert some kind of control over history, albeit a literary, textual control. The text's narrative framework exerts an analogous influence that structure/history exerts over the subject.

If narrative structure exiles the "men in the sun" spatially, it exiles them temporally as well. Time, the past, and history exert an ineluctable force over their lives. In their individual memories of the past, their present situations, and their hopes for the future, the men comprise a spectrum of sorts of (male) Palestinian society[17] as they evince the temporal conjunctures that influence their lives. The construction of a textual hierarchy is at work in the progressive introduction of the four men. It is no coincidence that the memories of a peasant open the novel. As the peasantry formed the greatest part of pre-1948 Palestinian society, they also constituted the majority of those displaced by the 1948 war. They were those who felt perhaps most immediately the appropriation of their land. Within Kanafānī's narrative, that is certainly true of Abū Qais. As the oldest of the men, he also has access, through personal memories, to life before the uprooting of 1948. Unlike the younger men, Abū Qais can potentially re-create, remember, Palestine. Within *Rijāl fī al-shams* though, Abū Qais's memories of the past in Palestine are fragmented, confused, and recalled only in isolation from the others. It is this failure of memory that decides his fate as it does the fate of the other three men.

The first lines of the novel establish what is the context for the entire text—displaced, exiled sensations, desires, and memories, the overshadowing of a repressed and impotent present by memories of a past that are of humiliation and defeat no less than they are of pleasure and fulfillment. In the opening chapter that bears his name, Abū Qais lies down on the damp ground and imagines that he can feel the "beating

---

[17] It is Kanafānī's novel *Umm Sa'ad* that deals most explicitly with women in Palestinian society. The central figure is the peasant woman of the title, whose story is recalled by the narrator, a writer who had been a neighbor of Umm Sa'ad's in a refugee camp. Interestingly, Umm Sa'ad recognizes the need for what is not available or apparent to the four refugees of *Rijāl fī al-shams*— collective action.

of the earth's heart as it tore its difficult path from the furthest depths of hell towards the approaching light." The old peasant's sensation of the the tired heartbeat of the earth elicits the memory of his neighbor mocking that fantasy. The earth has no life of its own, no heart; "it's the beating of your own heart that you hear when you lie on the ground." The memory of his neighbor's refusal summons still another memory—that of the earth's smell: "Whenever he breathed in the smell of the soil as he lay down [on the earth], he imagined that he was smelling the fragrance of his wife's hair as she came out of the bath after having washed it with cold water . . . the smell of a woman who had bathed with cold water and spread her hair to dry over her face while it was still damp" (11).

Abū Qais's sensations as he lies on the damp earth are linked to a delicate and lyrical chain of memories and images that become progressively more inclusive and personal, that approach but can never quite encompass that most elusive "memory" of history. If history bears witness to the old peasant's memories, for that history he is virtually an absence, a denied and repressed presence. It is precisely memory and its evocation that indict a present of denial at least as much as they "predict" some future of fulfillment. Abū Qais's sensual experience of the earth provokes a specific memory from the past—of his neighbor—and that specific memory leads to another—of desire and Abū Qais's wife. And the memory of past desire reminds him, brings him back to, the repression of desire, the impossibility of fulfillment, in the narrative present. The throbbing heart of the damp earth that spurred his memories is not that of his home, nor the dampness that of his wife's hair covering her face. He is on the banks of the Shatt al-Arab in Iraq, far away from his village, his home, and his wife. The denial of the old man's memories of the past and the denial or repression of present desire suggest an ever-broader memory of the past, an elusive memory of a history equally denied and/or repressed. In the tenuous chain of memory and desire from the past and of denial and repression in the present, it is the return to the present and denial that occasions different and distinctly less sensual memories. This time it is of the village schoolteacher, Istāz Selīm, drilling his young students about the source of the Shatt al-Arab—chiding them about their failure to remember; explaining to the village elders his refusal to lead Friday prayers; offering his services as a marksman in the event the village is attacked; and dying "just one night before [the battle in which] the wretched village fell." Again, denial surfaces. "The wretched village fell." Abū Qais's memory converges on a present of loss, of absence, of denial. And there Abū Qais's memory stops—at the boundaries of what at least implicitly exceeds the personal memories of one man. The loss of the "wretched village" is not only a personal loss, it is a collective one. But Abū Qais cannot move beyond the memory, the past, of his personal experience. He stops short of what John Berger, in *Ways of Seeing*, calls "the essential historical experience of our relation to the past: that is to say the experience of seeking to give meaning to our lives, of trying to understand the history of which we can become the active agents."[18]

It is precisely here on the borders of active agency in relation to the past that Abū Qais's memories, and his present, fail him. But his memories succeed in making most clear the absence, the denial, that characterize his present. Abū Qais's memories are a measure of his repressed present, his denied power. Structurally relegated to the confines of the chapter that bears his name, Abū Qais's memories and his present are equally confined. Like the forgetful student of Istāz Selīm, Abū Qais forgets. Those things that he forgets, though, are not the "facts" of the past—that the Shatt al-Arab is fed by the Tigris and the Euphrates. The old peasant has his viscerally "factual" memories of Palestine, of his wife and children, of ten olive trees. It is not the facts of the past that Abū Qais forgets, but the context for those facts. Abū Qais is textually foreclosed from situating his personal memories in the transpersonal history of which they are a part. And if the student's failure of memory invokes the scolding of the teacher, that failure, like the limitations of Abū Qais's memory, invokes the

18 Berger, *Ways of Seeing*, 33.

tragedy and dispossession of an entire people. Textually isolated, his relation to the past remains personal and quasi-pas-
sive. The meaningful appropriation of history is only an implicit narrative potentiality for Abū Qais and so he is returned
to his own bitter and impotent present. "He propped himself
up on the ground with his elbows, and began to watch the
great river again as though he'd never seen it before. . . . He
felt more foreign and insignificant than he'd ever felt before
[and] rubbing his hand over the stubble on his chin, he
brushed all the thoughts which had gathered like troops of
swarming ants from his head" (15–18).

At the chapter's conclusion, Abū Qais, frustrated and fearful after his meeting with the Iraqi who arranges the smuggling of illegal workers into Kuwait, returns to the banks of
the river and, throwing himself down on the damp earth, feels
"once again the beating of the earth's heart, as the smell of the
damp soil rose to his nostrils and flooded his veins." The chapter closes as it opens, with Abū Qais's chest pressed against
the throbbing heart of the earth. But the circular repetition of
this image is not just the rather mundane assertion of the Palestinian peasant's attachment to the soil. All peasants are proverbially "attached to the soil."[19] The circular composition of
images and memories, the closing repetition of Abū Qais's initial sensation of the throbbing earth, that characterize this
chapter intensify the fatal insularity of the proverbial peasant
closeness to the earth.

In spite of Abū Qais's "failure" of memory, the stance of
Rijāl fī al-shams toward the peasant and village life calls attention to itself. The ambivalence of *Qindīl Umm Hāshim*, that
text's alternately scathing indictment of peasant ignorance,
superstition, and conservatism and glowing romanticization
of peasant authenticity and "naturalness," is not to be found
here. The focus of the novel's opening chapter on a Palestinian
peasant is a direct challenge to the condemnation or ambiva-

---

[19] Although, as John Berger suggests in *A Seventh Man* and in *Pig Earth*, this
attachment is a distinctly qualified one. "Nature has to be bribed to yield
enough. Peasants everywhere know this" (24, *The Seventh Man*).

lent valorization of the peasant. Mediated by the dense complexity of the extratextual context, representation of the peasant in *Rijāl fī al-shams* is not an assertion of some essentialist "tradition" or "authenticity." Nor is Abū Qais a valorized symbol of nationalist resistance. As we saw to some extent in Haqqī, or even more clearly in Heikal, this position is ironically often underlaid by a profound distaste for the "authentic" or the "traditional" peasant and for rural village life. This ambiguous narrative perspective is also frequently that of a nonpeasant situated in what is typically considered the antithesis of the countryside—the modern city.[20] Is it possible that it is only from the city that the countryside takes on the dimension of preserving the past, of preserving what is "authentically" Egyptian, Palestinian, or, for that matter, French, German, or English?[21] The essentially conservative nature of this position is difficult to avoid. One of its logical conclusions is precisely that of *Qindīl Umm Hāshim*—the delegation of the no-longer-peasant intellectual or professional as caretaker of the less-than-civilized peasants/lumpen proletariat in that synthetic blaze embodied in Haqqī's Ismā'īl as the conjunction of the best of East and West.

In *Rijāl fī al-shams*, there is no such assertion of innate authenticity for the figure of Abū Qais. If he is to be read as a textual symbol of the peasant's attachment (and by extension, *right*) to his land, Abū Qais simultaneously suggests that symbol as a literally defused one. With his confusion of memory, desire, and history, the figure of Abū Qais is a lyrical and poignant reminder of the limitations of assumptions about "natural" attachment to the soil. For that "authentic" or "natural" and "traditional" attachment has insured nothing. On their own, Abū Qais's ties to the land, his memories and desire, are unable to effect a change either in his own personal situation or in the collective situation of the hundreds of

[20] But, for a fascinating exception, see the Egyptian Abd al-Rahman al-Sharqāwi's *al-Ard* (The earth), a novel of the peasant revolts in Egypt in the 1930s.

[21] Raymond Williams' *The Country and the City* is an excellent analysis of this opposition in English literature and culture.

thousands of uprooted peasants like him. *Rijāl fī al-shams* is distinguished by this recognition of the limitations of the peasant context, as well as by a narrative stance toward that context that is remarkably free of rancor, revulsion, or romanticization. That is not to say that Abū Qais is not a crucial and originary reference point for the narrative. The figure of Abū Qais himself literally provides the framing context for the remainder of the text. But he suggests the limitations of the peasant-as-symbol as much as he provides a framework and an originary source for the narrative, for the other stories of "men in the sun."

For there is an obvious contradiction in the situation of Abū Qais. What becomes of a peasant without land? If he is presumably a symbol of tradition and natural right to the land, what happens to the symbol when both tradition and natural rights are denied? The symbol begins to turn in on itself. It foregrounds itself in its very process of symbolization—in the attempt to articulate a meaning that escapes the readily apparent. Abū Qais is not a privileged bearer of tradition or authenticity. That tradition is textually, and extratextually, denied; it is no longer imminently or immediately available. Like his sensation of the weary heartbeats of the earth, like his memories of a Palestine that is so clearly beyond his reach, like his memories of desire for his wife, the visions and memories of Abū Qais border on the exaggerated intensity usually associated with dreams. In fact, *Rijāl fī al-shams* is pervaded by this sense of the ordinary-turned-garish, of the real and the symbolic as nightmare. It is here that one of the central contradictions of the text becomes apparent. That is the fabrication of a "realistic" fiction in a situation in which the conventions of narrative "realism" point up the unreal, in which the narrative of the surface of everyday life takes on the quality of a disturbing dream.

The displaced symbol, the rupture of the "real," that is the figure of Abū Qais is echoed and intensified in each of the succeeding chapters of the novel. The tangled memories of Abū Qais give way first to those of the one-time political activist, Assad, and then to those of the young high-school student,

Marwān. For each of the three men, and finally for the fourth Palestinian, Abūl Khaizurān, as well, the past is approachable only through a morass of memories and sensations that resist easy coherence. The four men are unable to cross the boundaries of their individual memories, fears, and hopes and thus they are unable to recognize the contours and boundaries of the past that might allow them to to make sense of and, most crucially for the novel, to affect change in the present.

Inexorably separated by the narrative framework of *Rijāl fī al-shams*, the men in the sun struggle instead for individual escape, for personal respite, from a dismal present. Abū Qais's memories and his present are bound by his vivid, if fragmented, memories and his proverbial "closeness" to the land. His present is the one that is most clearly dominated by the past and memory. Even Abū Qais's hopes for the future are predicated on the past, on a past that allowed some sense of fulfilled desire, dignity, and purpose. For Abū Qais, hope is somehow being able to approximate in the future what was lost in the past.

Assad belongs to the next generation of Palestinians,[22] those who grew up in exile. Unlike Abū Qais, his memory does not include a Palestine of ten olive trees, the throbbing heartbeat of the earth, or the fertile dampness of the soil and the just-washed hair of the peasant's wife. Assad's memories are of deception and betrayal, of the constraints of tradition and the desperation of poverty. It is hollow rhetoric and almost surreal images that bind Assad's past and present. If Abū Qais's vision of the future is defined by an attempt to recreate some part of the past, Assad's vision of the future is the more desolate one of simply escaping from an intolerable present. Assad's warning to Abūl Khaizurān to "leave the matter of honor for another time . . . it's better when a man doesn't

---

[22] Something of the significance of this difference between generations and its relation to history is suggested by the terms with which Palestinians refer to themselves. For example, Abū Qais and Abūl Khaizurān belong to what is called the "Palestine generation" (*jil filastin*)—those who knew Palestine before its partition. Assad and Marwān belong to "the generation of the [1948] disaster" (*jil al-nakba*)—"those who are born in exile."

swear on his honor" is a bitter comment not only on betrayal
and deception in Assad's past but on their likely recurrence in
his future as well. The money that Assad seeks in Kuwait is
not, as it is for Abū Qais, to buy an olive tree, to send his child
to school, or to lighten the burden on his wife. For Assad,
money is libidinally "soft and warm in his pocket." As he
grasps it, he feels it is "the keys to his entire future" (29). In
contrast to Abū Qais, Assad's vision of the future is one in
which money will free him from a present of denial and repression—from a forced marriage to his cousin, from harassment by the Jordanian police, from poverty.

If Abū Qais's memories are spurred by the smell and touch
of the earth, those of Assad and Marwān can have no such
source. They are the children of exile, of refugee camps and
UNRWA ration cards, of empty promises and empty claims
about avenging violated honor. The delicate and sensual chain
of associations that links the old peasant's fragmented memories with his present are supplanted by the hollow and rhetorical phrases that trigger Assad's memories. The transition
from Assad's present to a past of broken promises and betrayal is made by the fat Iraqi smuggler telling Assad to accept
his terms for being smuggled into Kuwait or to "turn around,
take three steps, and find yourself back on the road" or the
same man "swearing on his honor" that Assad won't be abandoned in the desert by his guide. The transitions are typically
stark and understated, almost imperceptible.

—I swear to you on my honor that you will reach Kuwait.

—You swear on your honor?

—I swear to you on my honor that I'll meet you just short of the
border [between Jordan and Iraq]. All that you have to do is to
make your way around that accursed place [an oil pipeline
pumping station about thirty miles short of the border] and you
will find me on the other side waiting for you there in the road.
(26–27)

The link between Assad's memory of a past betrayal by a
smuggler who "swore on his honor" and the present memory

of another smuggler who "swears on his honor" is so quick as to almost escape notice. This momentary imagistic conjuncture of memory and the present is repeated throughout the novel. As Assad recalls his struggle to circle around the pumping station in the Jordanian desert, a long run-on sentence attempts to lend linguistic shape to the memory of the scorching yellow slopes of the desert, Assad's headdress ablaze from the heat, "the horizon a conjuncture of straight orange lines" and "the earth a shimmering sheet of yellow metal."

> All of a sudden yellow sheets of paper began to fly about the room [of the Iraqi smuggler] and Assad bent to pick them up.
> —Thank you. Thank you. . . . This damned fan makes the papers fly about in front of me, but I can't breathe without it. Well, what have you decided? (27)

With the superimposition of the image of a desert that is a "shimmering sheet of yellow metal" onto the yellow sheets of paper flying about the smuggler's office, the sentence and the narrative slip back into the present. The boundaries between past and present are somewhere in between the two final clauses of the sentence, in between the shimmering yellow sheet metal of the desert and the scattered yellow paper sheets of the smuggler's notebook. They are blurred in the "run-on" memory of a half-page run-on sentence. It is precisely that blurring of past and present, the constant and tenuously linked movement back and forth between past memory and present denial, that marks all but the final chapter of the novel.

The construct of spatial and temporal boundaries in *Rijāl fī al-shams* dominates the third "man in the sun," Marwān—though, ironically perhaps, he is closer to childhood than manhood. The temporal scheme in which the blurring and fragmentation of the past and memory consume the present and finally the future are a little poignant in the case of Marwān, for his past is pathetically short. His memories are still contained within the circle of his family, of his mother and father and younger brothers and sisters. If, unlike Abū Qais, he has no memories of the past other than a life of exile and refugee camps, he is still too young to have known Assad's experiences of bitterness and despair. The preponderant temporal point of reference for Abū Qais is the past of life in Palestine; for Assad it is a hopeless and frustrated present of exile; for Marwān, though, it is the future. "The slender threads of hope," the "threads" of Marwan's future, are broken when, without enough money to pay for his passage to Kuwait, the fat Iraqi smuggler strikes Marwān and throws him out of the office. "The feeling that he had when he'd finished watching a movie and felt that life was grand and vast and that, in the future, he would be one of those people who spent every moment and hour of their lives in exciting fulfillment and variety. . . . the slender threads of hope that had woven grand dreams in his heart had been torn apart in the fat man's office" (36).

Abū Qais's lyrical and dream-like sensations of the earth are juxtaposed, in the following chapter, to the almost surreal nightmare of Assad's present. And here, in the chapter entitled "Marwān," the fantasy and the nightmare are both juxtaposed to the celluloid images of Marwān's impossible future. This movement from fantasy to nightmare to film traces is the outline of a text that is itself self-consciously cinematic in its manipulation of montage. It is the rapid succession of images that gesture beyond the specific content of those images to what is *not* included within that narrative succession. What is not included but what the composite of images gestures toward is the configuration of history itself. If it is history toward which the novel constantly gestures, it is a history that escapes the narrative's individual images and characters as it escapes the text itself. In a clearly contradictory maneuver, the text attempts to encompass the concrete details of the four men's lived experience and, by foregrounding its own schematization of that experience, to distance it, to gesture to that broader context—history—that frames the details of individual lives. It is this crucial distancing effect that is insistently repeated in *Rijāl fī al-shams*. And it is precisely this distance, this recognition of the situation beyond individual experience, that is unavailable to the characters within the text. As one isolated character follows the next, the narrative attempts to indicate something beyond the separate details of each character's life. It gestures beyond individual memory and experience to the broader schema of a common history. That common history is grounded in, but not definitively contained by, individual experience. It is a schema that clearly escapes the four men within the narrative. And it is ignorance of this historical schema that condemns them in the narrative schema. In this context, the foregrounding of the text's narrative structure is a suggestive and prescriptive comment on the myopic emphasis on individual experience. It is perhaps equally a bleak comment on the situation of the subject in history in which that history is experienced as a fearfully determining structure, almost impenetrable to change. The attempt to reconstruct the bourgeois subject as the individual nexus of meaning and action is fatal here. For this text, there can be no individual creation of meaning as there can be no individual escape.

But this is a novel of attempted escape. And so, as he leaves the smuggler's office, Marwān encounters his final chance to escape, the last man in the sun— Abūl Khaizurān—who offers to smuggle the young boy into Kuwait in the water tank of his employer's truck. The broken threads of Marwān's future, the bitter present of Assad, and the oneiric past of Abū Qais are forcibly conjoined in the fourth chapter—"The Bargain" that the three Palestinians strike with Abūl Khaizurān, the "bamboo man."[23]

Assad turned to Abūl Khaizurān.

—You understand? The others have made me responsible so let me tell you something: we all come from the same country; we

[23] A nickname, *khaizurān* means "reed" or "bamboo" and, in addition to referring to his tall, slender frame, also ironically suggests Abūl Khaizurān's impotence, the result of an injury when he stepped on a mine in the 1948 War. Even more ironically, it is in an attempt to hear the minute details of his fictional (and, of course, impossible) "affair" with a beautiful prostitute that the Kuwaiti border guards delay Abūl Khaizurān in their offices. It is this delay for an impossible and nonexistent story that costs the other three Palestinians their lives.

want to make a living and so do you; that's fine, but this deal
must be completely fair and honest. (50)

In spite of Assad's demand, the first narrative encounter of
all four Palestinians is an ironic evasion of "fairness" and
"honesty." Their "completely fair" deal is built on a web of
half-truths, deceptive omissions, and confused fears. "The
Bargain" and the final three chapters that follow it—"The
Road," "The Sun and the Shade," and "The Grave"—make
explicit a fatal process that was imminent in the very shape of
the earlier chapters. As the four men drive together across the
desert with the August sun rising threateningly in the sky, the
consequences of their unwillingness or inability to confront
the past and thus the present are unavoidably apparent. In
"The Sun and the Shade," the roaring engine of Abūl Khaizurān's truck enunciates the textual sequestering of the men from
one another. From an initial description of their *physical*
proximity the narrative moves, in the following paragraph, to
their psychological isolation, to the inability of the four men
to even speak to one another: "each of them [was] utterly lost
in the depths of his own thoughts . . . [as] the huge truck
plowed over the road carrying them, their dreams and their
families, their desires and their hopes, their misery and their
desperation, their sustenance and weaknesses, their past and
their future" (76).

With virtually the same phrase that characterized the heart
of the earth and the trajectory of Abū Qais as "plowing a road
from the utmost depths of hell toward the light" in the opening chapter, here the truck bearing the four men plows a road
toward the "light" of Kuwait—the "light" of death inside the
hot and dark water tank of the truck. Ironically perhaps, in
this passage the dreams and desires, the families and the
hopes, of the four men are plural but the past and future are
singular—a shared, one—even if it is a communality of which
the four men are ignorant. In an unequivocally damning structural manifestation of isolation and debility, the impossible
dreams of each man are separated and framed by virtually the
same phrase: "The truck continued on over the scorching

earth, its motor droning relentlessly. . . . The truck continued on over the scorching earth, its motor droning with a fiendish roar. . . . The truck continued on over the scorching earth, its motor droning with a roar. . . . The truck continued on over the scorching earth its motor droning like a huge mouth devouring the road" (77–78).

The narrative present, the four paragraphs in which each man restates the reasons (past) and hopes (future) for his flight to Kuwait, is resolutely fragmented by this insistent repetition of the movement of the advancing truck. In fact, the hurried advance of the truck suggests itself as a metaphor for the movement of the novel itself, advancing to a textually inevitable end, driven on by the movement of a history that "isn't made just as men please." It is a movement in which the four men are indubitably engaged; they are carried along in the truck. But it is a process over which they have precious little control, for which they are resolutely peripheralized, of which they are allowed little understanding. The very structure of the text persists in its emphasis on a fractured present, in which each man holds fast to his own private memories of the past and dreams for the future; on a shared past, a history, that the four are unable to apprehend; and on an indubitably shared future, the grave of the next chapter, to which they are textually consigned. The roaring truck transports them from their individual memories and ruptured past to their future—a garbage dump outside of Kuwait City. Like the past and future in the passage above, the men's grave is also linguistically singular and shared. The textual insistence on this communality—of past, of future, of death—is in clear opposition to the fragmented and isolated present of the four men. At the same time as it produces and compartmentalizes the details of its characters' individual lives in the narrative present, the very structure of the narrative insists on, attempts to accomplish by textual fiat, the shared history, the communality, of those same men. This is the crucial contradiction that marks *Rijāl fī al-shams*. The crux of this contradiction rests in the relationship between the individual subject—or, in this instance, the four Palestinians as separate and individual characters—and the

structure in which they are engaged—presumably that of history itself, certainly that of this novel in particular—that qualifies their positions as individual and autonomous subjects.

This contradiction is not only an aesthetic or literary one; it
is also and perhaps even more essentially a political one. It is
the problematic relationship of the individual to language, to
society, to the state, to social change, to history.[24] The ideological construct of the unified and autonomous bourgeois
subject that was the preferred self-image of the dominant early
English and European realist novel, as it was the ideology of
early industrial capitalism, is an attempt to resolve just that
problematic relationship. In that version of a solution, it is the
subject, rather than language, society, the state, or history,
that is the origin of meaning and action. More recently, in
structuralist and poststructuralist propositions about the interplay of subject and structure, language is designated as
dominant. For *Rijāl fī al-shams*,[25] there is little question of autonomous and unified subjects as the source of action and
meaning. Their textual construction is as impinged upon by
the structure of the text as the text itself is by the structure of
Palestinian experience and history outside of the text.

If Kanafānī's narrative does not quite absent meaning and
action, their presence is a distinctly qualified one. What *is* absent for the narrative subjects of this text is a recognition of
their own potential power. This might seem dubious in a text
that is so overwhelmingly concerned with the powerlessness
of its characters and their situation. And yet, the narrative gestures insistently towards the manufacture, the production, of
power. But it is a power that is unavailable as a reproduction
of the individual subject and of his individual history. It is a
rather distinctly *national* history and power that *Rijāl fī al-
shams* proposes.

But the creation of a nation in exile, of an (inter)national
identity in the diaspora, is as difficult as it is essential. It is a

---

[24] For a clear and incisive discussion of this problem, see Perry Anderson's
In the Tracks of Historical Materialism, especially 32–55.

[25] It could be argued that this creation of a unified and autonomous individual subject is problematic for a great deal of "third world" fiction.

distinctly qualified national identity, national meaning, and action, that is proposed as an alternative to the isolated desperation and powerlessness of the men in the sun. For by their individual attempts to escape from a powerless present rather than to collectively act in and on it, the narrative subjects of *Rijāl fī al-shams* begin and end as isolated and divided entities. The consequences of such isolation and division are the continuation of individual and national desperation and powerlessness until, in "The Grave," the four men are thrown onto a garbage dump.

Rijāl fī al-shams, then, postulates in its narrative structure and performs in the unfolding of its narrative content the necessity of a reappropriation of the past and the employment of the subsequent knowledge in the construction of a narrative of the future.[26] For Kanafānī's novel, without the reappropriation and understanding of a collective past that continues to shape a shared present, both of which must be commandeered in the creation of an alternative future, there will be no real future. The future is the unceremonious "grave" of the final chapter. And so *Rijāl fī al-shams* implicitly pre-dicts or prefigures the future in its demonstration of the limitations of individual memories and personal dreams that are an impetus for, but alone cannot "speak" or "figure," a future different from the present.

There is another and crucial demonstration of limitations that *Rijāl fī al-shams* performs. To the extent that Kanafānī's narrative pre-dicts a collective and national—a Palestinian—future, it is ironically one that is grounded in an almost metanational necessity. For, there is an unavoidable contradiction in tracing the national body in the diaspora. The diaspora body, diaspora nationalism, is bound to be distinctly qualified by necessarily multiple and international perspectives. So the immigrant worker of *To Diplo Biblio* is forced to acknowl-

---

[26] To the extent that the text makes this attempt, *Rijāl fī al-shams*, like Hatzis's *To Diplo Biblio* or Ōe Kenzaburo's *Man'en gannen no futtobōro*, share an implicit belief in the efficacy of literature and culture to effect a change in individual and social consciousness—if not inevitably in individual or social praxis.

edge the narrow and even arbitrary definition of contemporary nationalism—contemporary "Greekness." The diaspora
national body cannot be essentialist, unified, monolithic. It
necessarily exceeds any one spatial designation. In its exile,
dislocation, and marginality, it has at least potential access to
a perspective that exceeds an attempted reproduction of bourgeois nationalism. It is that radical potentiality, that prefigu-
rative power that both *To Diplo Biblio* and *Rijāl fī al-shams*
suggest in their narrative performances.

But the ironies and contradictions of (inter)nationalism are
perhaps nowhere more apparent than in the forced internationalism of a nation of exiles—the Palestinian refugees of *Rijāl fī al-shams*.[27] Hatzis's Costas in *To Diplo Biblio* has the
advantage of a certain luxury—qualified though it may be—
in recognizing his own postnationalism. He has known the political and social fact of nationhood and citizenship, regardless
of their specific content. It is precisely this political and social
experience to which the four Palestinians of *Rijāl fī al-shams*
do not have access. But still, with and without the presupposition of nationhood, both *Rijāl fī al-shams* and *To Diplo Biblio* suggest the limitations of a narrowly defined nationalism.

In the course of the four men's "trajectory towards the
light," in the boundaries over which they are compelled to
pass, and in the implicit assertion of the necessity of what is so
conspicuously absent from the novel—a collective Palestinian
nation/subject, the assertion of national exclusivity, of invio-
lable national boundaries, of hostility toward other nations
and people is conspicuously absent. There is no indictment of
the countries in which or the national peoples among whom
the four Palestinians find themselves—not of Iraq, to which
the four men have gone in the beginning of the novel, not of
Kuwait, where they die, and not of Israel, whose creation cast

---

[27] There is yet another sense in which the irony of such an "internationalism" is made apparent. It is typified by the recuperation of one of the slogans
of the 1968 Paris uprisings—"Down with borders"—by none other than the
IBM World Trading Corporation, which uses the slogan to illustrate the "internationalism" of the world economy in general and of their (more properly
multinational) corporation in particular.

them into exile in the first place. The "fat Iraqi smuggler" is not indicted because he is Iraqi but because of his exploitative peddling of illegal workers. Nor are the Kuwaiti border guards condemned for their lascivious curiosity that detains Abūl Khaizurān and causes the death of the three Palestinians in the water tank of Khaizurān's truck. The Kuwaiti's delight in Abūl Khaizurān's fictitious sexual affairs is "the result of his long, tormenting deprivation." And, perhaps most startling for a Western audience, given the dismal prejudices about Palestinians here, there is no condemnation of the Israelis because they are Israelis or Jews but rather because their attempted resolution of the problems of Jewish nationhood and identity was based on the oppression and/or expulsion of another people—the Palestinians. Rather than chauvinistic condemnation of any ethnic group or nation, the condemnation of *Rijāl fī al-shams* is reserved for a state of affairs in which exploitation, deprivation, and isolation produce victims of circumstance rather than what Berger calls "active agents of history." That state of affairs was instituted and is maintained in the interests of particular groups, perhaps, and of particular classes, but not necessarily in the interests of the people of particular nations. Thus, the radical suggestion of *Rijāl fī al-shams* is not merely its assertion of political and social nationhood for Palestinians. It is what is at least the implicit dimensions of that nationhood as an international or metanational phenomenon. This novel, as much of Kanafānī's other fictional and nonfictional prose, asserts the at least potential fluidity and permeability of national, ethnic, linguistic, and perhaps even state boundaries. This is the most radical suggestion of Kanafānī's text as it is of Hatzis's *To Diplo Biblio*. The nation-state is not eliminated or denied, but, in a radically utopic gesture, it is redefined and resituated in a broader international or global context.

Such a realignment and redefinition of nationalism is figured in the realignment and redefinition of the narrative subject. For, in spite of the problematic relationship of structure, or nation (or novel), and subject, it is in the delineation and manipulation of its narrative subjects that *Rijāl fī al-shams* suggests a structural realignment and redefinition of a narrow nationalism. The decentered bourgeois subject "discovered" in the last twenty or so years by critics and theorists of the West was perhaps already there, one of the casualties of colonialism, in the texts of the "third" world. "For the majority of Third World peoples, the experienced alternative to the past is a limbo—of alienation from the soil, of living in shanty-towns, of migration into foreign lands, and, at best, of permanent expectancy."[28]

If the past is fractured by the intrusion of foreign capital, colonization, the creation of the state of Israel, the underdevelopment of metropolis-linked markets, states, societies, and cultures, the present is fragmented by the persistence and reproduction of that fractured past. It is present in the absence of resolution of just that fractured past, in the absence of the knowledge, the power, and the organization to create viable alternatives to a fractured past and fragmented present. But it is this absence that engenders the possibility of creating a new subject that is neither the bourgeois subject of the West nor the idealized traditional and quasi-authentic one of the third world past. If *To Diplo Biblio* attempts to formulate that new subject in the "double" person of Costas and his polyphonic history, *Rijāl fī al-shams* makes a similar gesture to that necessary formulation, but in the consequences of its narrative for its implied readers rather than for any character within the text.

And, in spite of a number of obvious differences, this impetus and its literary and extraliterary situation are familiar to the work of the contemporary Japanese writer whose works are examined in the following chapter—Ōe Kenzaburo. For modern Japan occupies a curious median position in relation to the third world and the countries of the West. If the mid-nineteenth century saw Japan in a social and economic position comparable to Egypt, in the late twentieth century there is a vast gap between the two countries. Japan has technolog-

---

[28] Eqbal Ahmad, "From Potato Sack to Potato Mash: The Contemporary Crisis of the Third World," *Arab Studies Quarterly* 2.3 (1980): 223–24.

ically and economically leapt far ahead of the third world. But—and here the question can be extended to include Europe, England, and America as well—ahead to what? As will be apparent in the novel—*Man'en gannen no futtōboro*—examined in the next chapter, this question is a major preoccupation of the texts of Ōe Kenzaburo.

Chapter 7

HUNTING WHALES AND ELEPHANTS, (RE)PRODUCING NARRATIVES

A people or a class which is cut off from its own past is
far less free to choose and to act as a people or class
than one that has been able to situate itself in history.
—John Berger, *Ways of Seeing*

In awe of the fierce sea
where whales are hunted down
we clutched the steering oar
holding the plunging ship on its course
and though here and there
we saw scattered island coasts
to rush upon for safety
we sought refuge on rugged Samine
the island of the beautiful name.
Erecting a shelter, we saw you
pillowed on the trembling beach
on the wave beaten rocks
as if the coast were laid out for your bedding.
On such a rugged place
you have laid yourself down to rest.
—Hitomaro (7th century Japan),
"On Seeing the Body
of a Man Lying Among the Stones
on the Island of
Samine in Sanuki Province"

NOTHING MIGHT SEEM FARTHER from the dominant notion of
the Japanese cultural tradition than the texts of Ōe Kenzaburo
(b. 1935). Certainly, to many of his Japanese critics, Ōe's fic-

tion, and even his use of the Japanese language, are an affront of sorts to the "traditional" sensibility. That traditional sensibility, reformulated and assiduously maintained in contemporary Japan, prescribes lyric simplicity, brevity, and poetic vagueness and imagism as that which is culturally distinctive. And so, critical commentary on Ōe's work insists that his prose is foreign influenced and not really Japanese or that it purposefully violates the "elegance and simplicity" of the Japanese language. Yet, as any reader of Ōe's texts in the original could confirm, Ōe does write in what is undeniably Japanese; the language of his fiction is not a Japanese approximation of Chinese or English or French. And if his language is "difficult" or "awkward" or "violent," it is so in a remarkably familiar, if antithetical, fashion to the "difficulty" or "artful elegance" or "lyric simplicity" of "traditional" Japanese culture and texts. Ōe's fiction and language are the inversion of that tradition, its negative image, so to speak. They push a recuperated Japanese cultural "tradition" to its opposite extreme. But as negative inversion, they are scarcely foreign violations of the Japanese tradition. Or, if they are violations, they are violations performed precisely on the terrain mapped out as "Japanese."

What is presumably the "foreignness" of Ōe's fiction does not necessarily derive from other literatures or cultures at all. Ōe's texts are read as foreign as much because of their critical distance from the myth of traditional Japanese culture as from some perfidious non-Japanese influence. *Man'en gannen no futtobōru* (Football in the first year of Man'en, 1967)[1] derives as much from the deliberately aestheticizing distance of an Ōshima Nagisa film as it does from a novel by Samuel Beckett or a play by Arnold Wesker or Jean-Paul Sartre. But that distancing, that sense of discourse as a ritual performance, is as striking in a Noh performance or in highly conventionalized classical poetry. A text like *Man'en gannen no*

---

[1] Ōe Kenzaburo, *Man'en gannen no futtobōru*. All translations are my own unless otherwise noted. For a translation, see Ōe Kenzaburo, *The Silent Cry*, trans. John Bester (New York: Kodansha International, 1974).

futtobōru is "foreign" to the Japanese context not for its literary practices per se but for the attention it calls to the ideology of its own practices and the practices of the culture of
which it is a part. Ōe's texts do assume a deliberately oppositional stance to routine Japanese linguistic and cultural practices, but they are not quite cultural pariahs. In fact, in spite
of the conventional isolated reading of Ōe's texts both inside
and outside of Japan, they stand in all their complexity and
intensity when they are situated within the context of the Japanese tradition rather than when they are isolated from it.
Ōe's fiction is not outside of the Japanese tradition at all. And
if Ōe's narratives are a profoundly negative image of that tradition, it is not negative in terms of its bleakness or pessimism,
though a text such as *Man'en gannen no futtobōro* might very
well appear bleak and pessimistic. It is rather the simplicity or
lyric imagism or vague subjectivity of a *waka*,[2] for example,
pushed to the opposite extreme. It is a negative critique of a
culturally recuperated tradition that, sometimes rather explicitly, has served fiercely ideological purposes.[3]

In *Man'en gannen no futtobōru*, "traditional" simplicity
becomes purposeful complexity, "lyrical" imagism that of a
dank, obsessive bleakness, and the poetic vagueness and un-
defined subjectivity of the Japanese language becomes a linguistic sign of a modern subject divorced from the collective
identity of the past and unable to fabricate either a collective

---

[2] *Waka*, or *tanka*, is the poetic form par excellence of classical Japanese
court poetry. It is composed of only 31 syllables in 5 lines with the distribution of syllables fixed as 5, 7, 5, 7, 7. Linked to this poetic form and to the
courtly way of life that it embodied was an elaborate if conventionalized aesthetic that was, with significant modification over time, maintained throughout the classical period and, following the Meiji Restoration of 1861, resurrected for modern Japan.

[3] The uses to which the Japanese "cultural tradition" was put from the early
1930s (if not earlier) through the end of World War II is one rather obvious
example of the explicitly ideological purposes of the cultural recuperation of
"tradition." Another, in the mid-nineteenth century, was the official reformulation of Japanese "tradition" and the uses to which that reformulated
tradition was put at the creation of the Meiji state. (See the discussion of this
period in chap. 4.)

or individual identity in the present. The deterioration of the contemporary subject is demonstrated in action in the person of Nedokoro Mitsusaburo. Blind in one eye, he fancies himself something of a modern-day variation on Tiresias. And, virtually asexual since the birth of his severely retarded son, Mitsusaburo is given to hiding out in empty septic tanks, imagining himself a rat, and longing for a visceral feeling of "hope" that will let him know unequivocally that he is alive. But Mitsusaburo's predilections for rodent behavior and damp holes are not the primary focus of Ōe's novel. It is rather what is the impetus for such predilections—Mitsusaburo's impossible attempt to escape from history and desire. But even this attempt is textually qualified and contained. The metaphor of the family dominates the narrative delineation of history in *Man'en gannen no futtobōru*. Rather than being threateningly general, beyond individual influence, history is genealogy, the history of a family.

As the oldest living male of the family, Mitsusaburo is heir to the Nedokoro family's name and legacy, or perhaps more accurately, to his own ignorance of his family's name and legacy. The birth of a retarded and deformed son, his wife's subsequent alcoholism, his best friend's suicide by hanging, his wandering younger brother's return to Japan from America— these things send Mitsusaburo burrowing into himself and into the past—and literally into the earth—for some key to the present in which he finds himself. The first chapter finds him in the city and witness to his best friend's bizarre suicide; in the second chapter, Mitsusaburo, returning to his family home in the mountain village of Ōkubo (literally, "the big hollow"), is witness to his family's role in history, to his own "roots." (The Chinese characters for *Nedokoro* are literally "root place.") And in the violent course of the novel, Mitsusaburo is compelled to recognize his own unwilling role in history as well as his attempt to absent himself from history. But the ultimate symbol of the subject who is absented from history has to be Mitsusaburo's son, "that hideous, utterly abject thing existing on a wooden cot" in an institution somewhere. Mitsusaburo himself is as fascinated as he is repelled by such pas-

sivity. His son's (non)existence is a hyperbole of Mitsusaburo's own life: "[I] . . . had sought meaning in a placid way of
life, . . . continuing to live in vagueness and uneasiness, refusing to confront that something which led to an inner compelling demand for an abrupt and discontinuous leap" (393).

But, in spite of himself, Mitsusaburo is compelled to come
to terms with a past and a present that press in all around him.
In his native village, Mitsusaburo is forced to confront the
past by the histrionic determination of his younger brother,
Takashi, to reenact their great-uncle's role in an 1860 peasant
uprising. Passive, withdrawn, and insulated from the outside
world by his ample body, blind eye, and uneasy awkwardness,
Mitsusaburo's regressive hiding places fall under attack by the
violence and bizarreness of the world from which he thought
to remove himself, not to mention the bizarreness of his own
personal world. His brother Takashi, something of a repressed
alter ego for Mitsusaburo, organizes the village youth into the
somewhat incongruous football team of the title and begins
the construction of a present that is nestled in his memories
and dreams of the past. In spite of Mitsusaburo's resistance,
Takashi draws his older brother into the attempt to remember
the past.

And it is Mitsusaburo's attempt to recollect the past, to situate himself in history, in order to create meaning and action
in the present that signals the implicit attempt of *Man'en gannen no futtobōro* to resituate Japanese tradition in something
of its own historical context. Ōe's novel belies the legacy of a
"traditional" and "beautiful Japan" that is so carefully maintained in and outside of contemporary Japan. In fact, the
thrust of *Man'en gannen no futtobōro* is precisely the attempt
to reconstruct or remember a past that is almost hopelessly
overlaid with dreams, unfulfilled desires, and a most fragmented memory. For this text, there can be no cultural creation of meaning in the present that is not situated in a recollection of the past. And the necessarily critical function of such
recollection is an implicit underpinning of *Man'en gannen no
futtobōru* in its attempt to create meaning in the narrative
present.

It is to this end, then, that the opening of *Man'en gannen no futtobōro* resembles nothing quite so much as a kind of negative image of the traditional aesthetic. The dominant definition of that traditional aesthetic is ususally characterized by allusive language, lyric imagism, and restrained and elegant simplicity. Oe's fiction, with its complex language bristling with Chinese ideograms, its startlingly unconventional images, its confusion of narrative time, place, and subject and its purposeful structural denseness inverts the traditional aesthetic. *Man'en gannen no futtobōru* is implicitly a negative critique of what is considered the Japanese cultural tradition; it stands that aesthetic tradition on its head. But the inversion is possible only in the context of that notion of tradition against which the inversion pits itself. The novel's opening is an allusive and loaded reference to absence, to a confusion of desire, repression, and despair. In as lumpy a language and rhythm as classical diction is measured and flowing, the novel's opening passage is, more than anything else, the (anti)poetic invocation of nothing, but not necessarily of nothingness. The linguistic gesture of this passage is reminiscent of that of a famous haiku that repeats the place name "Matsushima" over and over again, presumably for the evocative allusion of the very word itself. But, on the face of things, such a haiku is strikingly short on meaning. So the opening of *Man'en gannen no futtobōru* links a repetitive succession of bleak and contradictory words and images whose meaning is subordinated to the materiality of the language on the page.

> Searching for a feeling of passionate "hope" as I awaken in the predawn darkness, I grope among the lingering sensations of bitter and painful dreams in my consciousness. I grope in unsettled expectation for the certain recovery in the depths of my body of a feeling of passionate "hope"—like the feeling of being alive when gulping down whiskey burns your insides—but still there is perpetually nothing. (7)

What is this passage "about"? Somebody, presumably a man, awakens before daybreak, looking for, and not finding, a libidinal something—a "hope" (*kitai*). The implicit auto-erotic impetus and impotent contraction of this opening passage might seem unavoidably antithetical to the "traditional" Japanese sensibility—if not to the sensibility of certain modern Japanese novels.[4] And, on the one hand, both the impetus and the bleak impotence are just that—the antithesis of what is commonly articulated as the traditional Japanese aesthetic. But in its very oppositeness, these lines suggest not only the impotence of its own self-referential desire. They are a negative evocation of precisely the aesthetic tradition so valorized in contemporary Japanese culture. For in another context this passage could be read, or could have been written, as one every bit as poetically evocative and lyrically meaningful as any haiku or classical tanka—"predawn darkness," "tormented dreams," "nervous expectation," "infinite nothing." If this were a classical lyric, the lonely lover could have awakened in the predawn darkness from tormented dreams about his or her companion for whom she or he had waited in nervous expectation the night before, and yet the only visitor to our lonely lover was an infinite nothing. A rather clumsy approximation of a poem, perhaps, but not altogether implausible in terms of classical Japanese court poetry.[5] What is distinctive

[4] The contemporary fiction of Kurahashi Yumiko or Kaiko Takeshi would seem to share this forceful violation of a "traditional" aestheticism. A certain negative aesthetic of violence marks more than a few modern Japanese texts. Even in the presumably high poetic works of Kawabata Yasunari or Tanizaki Jun'ichiro (the latter almost more widely read outside of Japan), a great deal of the starkest violence lies just beneath the lyric surface of the text. In modern Japanese film, the work of Ōshima Nagisa is a striking parallel in this respect to the fiction of Kurahashi, Kaiko, or Oe. Roland Barthes has suggested in his *Empire of Signs* that there is a sense in which violence in the Japanese text, film, theater (if not society) can be read differently, as the form of another "language" without quite the same content that it has for a Western audience. Be that as it may, to the extent that such literary or cinematic works are appropriated by, or even composed for, an international rather than only Japanese audience, they participate in the "poeticization" of violence. An interesting comparison could be between the fiction of violence and self-mutilation in these Japanese texts and the fiction of Ghassān Kanafānī, Dimitris Hatzis's stories of the Greek Civil War, or the novel of colonial and postcolonial violence, *Mawsim al-hijra ilī al-shamāl* (Season of migration to the north, 1967) by the Sudanese novelist, Tayeb Saleh.

[5] Some of the more famous classical poets to write in this vein are, to name just a few, Ariwara Narihira, Saigyo, Izumi Shikibu, Komachi, or Lady Sagami.

about the opening passage of Ōe's novel though is that the evocative phrases evoke neither an absent lover, nor even some abstract and equally absent "meaning of life." If anything, this passage seems to evoke, and itself borders on, linguistic impotence. It is as much about nothing as the repetition, in a well-known haiku, of the place name Matsushima. Matsushima, however, is a culturally acceptable "meaninglessness." The opening of *Man'en gannen no futtobōro* is not quite so acceptable.[6] It forces attention on the very process of positing, or absenting, meaning. This endeavor is one in which even the novel's title participates. For, "football in the first year of Man'en," though apparently comprehensible, is a somewhat convoluted way of saying "football in the year 1860." But then, dutifully translated, with the linguistic riddle of *man'en gannen* eliminated, the immediate response to "football in the year 1860" would almost have to be—what football? Who played football in Japan in 1860? Deciphered, the title itself suggests the concern with the confusion of history that informs this text. And so, autoeroticism and impotence are of more than narrowly sexual significance. They are signs of a search for another kind of elusive climax, for what is perhaps some more properly historical gratification or "pleasure."

The confusion and thwarted meaning (and thwarted pleasure) of the opening sentences of *Man'en gannen no futtobōru* are not confined to the linguistic realm of the narrative alone. The existential presence of a narrative subject is more than a little dubious as well. It is only in the short sentence that follows the compilation of the "evocatively meaningless" phrases cited above that there is any textual evidence of distinguishable narrative existence: "[I] close fingers that have lost their strength." At least, with this sentence, there is ascertainable life in a discernible and animate narrator—the "I" who

---

[6] This kind of "meaninglessness" is perhaps more culturally acceptable in Japan in (modernist) West European or British and American literature—as in the much-translated work of Samuel Beckett, Jean Genet, or Eugene Ionesco, for example. In Western literature, the "poetic repetition" of a place name is far less the cultural norm.

has fingers. The title of the first chapter is, after all, "Guided by a Dead Man." And if the chapter goes on to describe the bizarre suicide of the narrator's best friend—the "dead man" who presumably "guides" or "leads" the narrator to some inarticulable understanding—the implied reader is also "guided" by the almost "dead man," who is the narrator, into the maze of memory, history, desire, and grotesque clues that make up this novel. Like the inarticulable understanding presumably available to the narrator as witness to his friend's suicide, there is some implied narrative "truth" presumably available from the jumble of memories and dreams, ritualized present, and recalled history to which the narrator (and the implied reader) is witness. But like the truth of the dead man's suicide, which persistently haunts the narrator and the narrative, narrative truth is inarticulable. Like the pursuit of (auto)erotic pleasure or linguistic meaning in the novel's opening lines, it is always only implicitly available, only provisionally containable.

> Writers perhaps . . . tell something that is no doubt close to the truth and continue living without being beaten to death or going mad. [But] their kind deceive others with their framework of fiction. And in imposing a fictional framework, the writer's work is essentially weakened by the fact [that it is fiction,] that they can say anything no matter how frightening, dangerous, or shameless. . . . The real thing, the truth, doesn't exist anywhere written or printed. The most you can expect regarding what's called the truth is the writer who performs the pretext of a leap into total darkness. (230)

As a negative inversion (and attempted subversion) of the Japanese tradition, *Man'en gannen no futtoboro* attempts precisely that "leap into total darkness," to gesture toward one of the dangerous, shameful, and frightening things that presumably escape Japanese fiction—the movement of history. That the relationship between history, "truth," and culture or fiction is one of the dominant concerns of Ōe's novel is made even more apparent in another reference to (f)actual history and the mediating role of art: "It wasn't a memory of the actual raid on the Korean settlement; it was the experience in the world of nembutsu dance, the revival of the facts transformed in the collective sentiments of the people of the valley" (183).

For this text, history lives not only in "actual" events but in a cultural—and here, in what is rather clearly a wish-fulfilling gesture—a collective transformation of the "facts." Memory, then, is at least twice removed from the world of real men and women, from their ideas and their actions; history is an almost libidinal desire for meaning, for consummation, for "[re]experiencing the past as intensely as possible." It is this interdependence between memory, desire, and art and their relationship to history that obsesses both the narrative and its narrator. Perhaps it is for this reason that Nedokoro Mitsusaburo, the narrator of *Man'en gannen no futtobōru*, fancies himself a rat or a fetus or a coelenterate and is textually relegated to the dark recesses that such creatures inhabit. From what does Mitsusaburo seek escape or refuge? His burrowing is at least partially an attempt to escape the demands of, to repress, desire—and a peculiarly displaced history. For it is history that stalks the pages, and the narrator, of Ōe's *Man'en gannen no futtobōro* as it did the *Kusamakura* or *Mon* or *Kokoro* of Natsume Sōseki.[7] If anything, it is the peculiar and sometimes grotesque attempt of the former text to come to terms with the past and its implications for the present that make *Man'en gannen no futtobōro* "foreign" to the dominant Japanese aesthetic. But, then, Ōe's fiction has its own precedent of sorts precisely in the work of Natsume Sōseki.

History, for *Man'en gannen no futtobōru* as for Sōseki's texts, is not a monolithic construct or an assiduously linear progression. Instead, there is an implicit sense of history as the object of a repressed desire for climactic meaning—or perhaps even of history as desire itself. But between desire and its object is a temporal labyrinth, rife with half-understood clues, fragmented messages, vague memories, and conflicting official reports, in which the remnants of the past, or of many pasts,

---

[7] See chap. 4.

coexist with a multitude of presents. And that labyrinth of time is as much history as it is the barrier to history. If history is somehow implicated in this maze of time and of desire, whether it is the voracious Minotaur or the source of climactic meaning is not clear. Perhaps, for Ōe's text at least, history is both the Minotaur devouring not-so-virginal and not-so-young boys and girls and the source of climactic, if clearly fabricated, meaning.

The attempt to encompass this contradictory sense of history within the text is most apparent (but by no means only so) in the explicit narrative references to major historical junctures. There are at least three distinguishable histories that converge in the textual present of what is Nedokoro Mitsusaburo's version of a family chronicle. There is the present of the first-person narration itself, presumably sometime after the recent narrative past of Japan's anti-Security Treaty demonstrations of 1959–1960. There is the past of 1945 after Japan's defeat in the war, when an entire social and political order were called into question. And there is an even more distant past in which once again a social, political, and, this time, economic order were challenged in the peasant riots of 1860, riots that contributed to the overthrow of the Tokugawa regime and the eventual establishment of the "new" Meiji state. But the relationship between these narrative times is as problematic for the narrative itself as it is for the narrator, Mitsusaburo. For the narrative, for Mitsusaburo, and most especially for his younger brother Takashi, all of the various pasts exist, in something of a coterminous fashion, in the narrative present of *Man'en gannen no futtobōru*. They crowd in on and characterize the boundaries and direction of the narrative.

But in spite of what appears to be the temporal confusion of both narrative and narrator, there are a number of elements that bind these narrative times together. They are all centered around various members of the Nedokoro family, and so there is a sense in which some kind of "familial" meaning and continuity should be available. For example, the manner in which earlier members of the Nedokoro family played out their roles in history is made a definitive influence on the characters and lives of later members of the family. In a related fashion, Ya-hyā Haqqī's *Qindīl Umm Hāshim* makes implicit assumptions of familial value and meaning. The narrator of Haqqī's fiction is the nephew of the novel's main character, Ismā'īl. Presumably, in the understanding and retelling of his uncle's story of crisis and resolution, Ismā'īl's nephew shares a privileged relationship to value and meaning in the narrative. The narrative valorization of "traditional" Egyptian values of family, faith, and continuity from the past are underscored by the very ties of kinship that link the narrator to his uncle. In Oe's text, something of a similar relationship is at least implicit. At least presumably, familial ties and significance and continuity—scarcely insignificant assumptions in themselves—predominate. The most apparent mystery in *Man'en gannen no futto-bōru* (other than who played football at all in 1860 Japan) is the role of an earlier generation of Nedokoro family members in history. The actions of and relations between Mitsusaburo and Takashi's great-grandfather and his younger brother are made of pressing if not quite clear importance to the narrative present and its characters. Here familial affiliation subsumes that of nation or class, or even race. The problematic relationship of the individual subject to the larger structure—of state or class, etc.—is confined to and is perhaps textually emblematized in the relations within the family. Yet the textual positing of value, significance, and meaning within the confines of a family is undermined by the definitive characteristics of that family's relationships—incest, violence, self-imposed isolation, madness, and retardation. At the same time, however, the bizarreness and grotesqueness that lie beneath the surface of the Nedokoro family's relationships and history is equally the source of a reformed morality or ethics for the narrative present. It is the grotesque suicide of Mitsusaburo's best friend that marks the first chapter of the novel and the violent suicide of his younger brother that brings to a close the mystery of the past and what is almost a replay of that mystery in the narrative present, although perhaps as farce. Both deaths speak an inarticulable "truth" for the narrator. A similar truth can be "heard" or "read" in the self-imposed isolation of Mitsusaburo's great-uncle in the cellar of the family storehouse after his role in the disastrous peasant uprising of 1860.

> . . . that "something" within my friend that had made him paint his head crimson and kill himself, naked, with a cucumber stuck up his anus. . . . (391)
> . . . that made Takashi stand facing the muzzle of a gun that in an instant turned the naked upper half of his body into a pomegranate. . . . (392)
> . . . that made that tall, ashen-faced and stoop-shouldered man . . . voluntarily imprison himself in the cellar of the storehouse to the end of his days. (382)

What is that "truth" contained in the deciphered narrative of at least three deaths? Mitsusaburo's great-uncle, locked underground for the rest of his life, was as dead to the world as Takashi or as Mitsusaburo's best friend. For Mitsusaburo, it is some climactic meaning, both individual and historical. In death, the three "ascertaining their own hell, in crying out the 'truth' had surmounted it . . . ascertaining (their) own identity, had achieved self-coherence" (391–92).

It is death and death-in-life that provide the impetus for and the conclusion of the narrative. If the deaths described above offer some kind of "truth" to the narrator, the birth of a severely retarded son (death-in-life) elicits in Mitsusaburo's own existence, and in his relationship with his wife, Natsumi, a rupture that leads them to the Nedokoro family home in the mountain village of Ōkubo and to a (family) history that has marked the past of his childhood as it plagues his present. The absolute passivity of the retarded Nedokoro heir is an unavoidable if extreme sign for the situation of his father, Mitsusaburo. If Mitsusaburo fears his own death and any definitive action in life, he equally fears and is obsessed by the near deathlike life of his retarded son.

> The baby looked up at me as always with wide-open eyes but it was impossible to understand whether he was hungry or thirsty or felt some other discomfort. Like a marine plant in the water of dusk, lying with eyes open and blank, he simply and placidly

existed. He demanded nothing and expressed absolutely no emotion. He didn't even cry. At times one even doubted that he was alive at all. (22)

In fact, the narrative origin of virtually all of Ōe's fiction,[8] is the birth, and stubbornly continued life, of a severely retarded son. In Ōe's novel *Kojintekina taiken* (A personal matter), the father of a severely retarded newborn son attempts but fails to kill his "vegetable monster" child by watering its milk in the hospital. The child insistently clings to life, and the father, incapable of a more direct attack on his son, takes the child home with him, accepting him as a "life-sustaining" burden. In his college dictionary, inscribed with the word "hope," he intends to look up "forbearance." In the short story, "*Warera no kyōki o ikinobiru michi no oshieyo*" (Teach us to outgrow our madness)[9] the corpulent father of a similarly retarded son "enjoys thinking of himself as a passive victim quietly enduring a heavy and troublesome bondage imposed by his son." Before the birth of his child, the father (like "Bird," the father in *Kojintekina taiken*) was a "painfully thin Japanese"; with the birth of his retarded son, he quickly becomes "continentally fat." In addition to the interesting if implicit comment on national identity, the retarded child is in both instances virtually the germinal pretext for the narrative itself. So, too, in *Man'en gannen no futtobōru*, the birth of the placid and expressionless "marine life" that is his son, jolts Mitsusaburo into a crisis that eventually spurs an examination of his present situation and of his childhood past. Like the grotesque deaths referred to earlier, his son's severe retardation becomes the pretext for the "redemption" of Mitsusaburo's life.

It is in contrast to, and yet because of, this kind of vegetable

---

[8] See, for example, Ōe's account of the genesis of his fiction in his "Hyōgen-seikatsu ni tsuite no hyōgen—waga moratoriamu 1" ("Expressing the expressive life—my moratorium 1").

[9] See John Nathan's excellent translation of this and other short stories by Ōe in the collection of the same name: Ōe Kenzaburo, *Teach Us to Outgrow Our Madness*, trans. John Nathan (New York: Grove, 1977).

existence that the narrative posits the life of "great-grandfather's brother"—the leader of a bloody and futile peasant uprising in 1860—who, after eleven years of self-imposed penance hidden underground in the cellar of the family
storehouse, returns, an older and wiser leader, to head another, and this time successful, peasant revolt in 1871. After
this return to the world of the living, the pale-faced, stoop-
shouldered man returns to the cellar for the remainder of his
life, having cultivated, from the time of his disappearance after
the first uprising, the myth of his escape from the village across
the forest to the West. In a later variation on the same event,
Mitsusaburo's older brother, referred to only as "S," returns
from Japan's defeat in World War II to organize and take part
in a raid on what had been during the war a Korean slave-
labor camp just outside of the village. The first raid was to
avenge the village farmers for the fact that, in the wake of
postwar land reforms, a group of Koreans discovered stashes
of illegally concealed rice belonging to the Japanese farmers in
the valley and sold them on the black market in the nearest
town. In that raid, a Korean was killed, presumably by acci-
dent. And so, as in the repeat of the peasant revolt, there is a
second raid on the Korean settlement in which "S" is beaten
to death to atone for the excesses of the earlier raid. After his
modern-day staging of a revolt against, and raid on, the local
branch of a large supermarket chain, owned ironically enough
by a former resident of the Korean labor camp, Takashi's suicide scarcely comes as a surprise. The narrative has unequivocally established a historical, familial precedent for such sacrificial atonement. And like the earlier incidents, Takashi's
organization of the young village men has a concrete enough
social and economic basis. Demoralized by unemployment
and a moribund village economy, and, for the small local
shops, by the devastating success of the Korean supermarket
magnate, the young men are only too willing to be organized
into a football team some one hundred years after "football in
the first year of *man'en*." They, and the majority of the village,
are no less willing to vent their anger and resentment on a
racial minority whose second-class status in Japan is still well-

known. Takashi and his team of young men initiate and oversee the organized looting of the Korean's supermarket, draw-
ing the entire valley population into a "newfound collectivity," into what is, for Mitsusaburo, a hitherto unknown ability
to "interact so freely and tolerantly toward one another not
even in [his childhood memories of] village festivals" (275).
But like the revolt that is the generative impulse of carnival,[10]
the subversive power of Takashi's uprising rather quickly sub-
sides. Takashi attempts to forestall the deceleration of the revolt by claiming to have raped and killed a young village girl.
He thus provides the village with a justifiable reason for condemning him and for expiating their own role in the uprising
at the same time. The almost hysterical histrionics of Takashi's gesture do not preclude the accuracy of his implicit conclusions about the outcome of the revolt: "The valley is grad-
ually growing tired of the uprising and of their own complicity
in it. So no doubt it will probably occur to some one of them
that if they make me responsible for the entire evil of the uprising and then beat me to death, they can compensate for everything" (339).

But just in case the villagers are not willing to take matters
into their own hands and instead decide to let him stand trial
like an ordinary criminal, Takashi "sacrifices" himself with a
shotgun given to him by one of the village farmers to ward off
the gang of the Korean supermarket king. In so doing, Takashi
becomes a part of the legend of the valley as his great-uncle
and older brother had done before him. He creates a place for
himself in (a rather attenuated) history, as Mitsusaburo has
not or cannot. The "Emperor of Supermarkets" returns to the
valley after Takashi's suicide, reclaims his supermarket and
his economic hold over the valley, and asserts his claim to the
Nedokoro family storehouse, which had been sold to him by
Takashi. And the Korean, now textually distinguished by a
name—Paek Sun-gi—dismantles the old building to move it to
a nearby city to house his newest supermarket outlet. (This

[10] M. M. Bakhtin's *Rabelais and His World*, is an impressive and now well-
known analysis of the social, political, and cultural workings of carnival.

suggests an ironically bleak allegory of modern consumer culture's reformulation of the past for the present. The past—the storehouse—is dismantled and reassembled, or recuperated for the present, to house another outlet of a supermarket chain.)

The text privileges a family history that is itself emblematic of a broader and less easily contained history. Mitsusaburo's attempt to piece together, in *bricoleur*-like fashion, the fragmented pieces of his family's, and thus his own, past offers itself as a paradigm of the attempt to recollect, to situate oneself in, a history that is of class, race, gender, and nation as much as it is of familial genealogy. The diaries, memories, dreams, eye-witness accounts, and historical "research" that constitute Mitsusaburo's knowledge of the past are a kind of narrative synecdoche for the textual knowledge of history in general. It is through the assembly and integration of these various texts that Mitsusaburo "knows" and assumes a place in history, both in family's and, by implication, in some broader, if textually delimited, history. But Mitsusaburo's experience of history is an ironically literary one. He assembles and translates the scattered "texts" of history to reach some (anti)climactic understanding. The texts are as numerous as they are contradictory: Mitsusaburo's own dreams, his mother's memories, the research of a local schoolteacher cum historian, the account of the village priest, the oldest Nedokoro brother's diary, the five letters from great-grandfather's younger brother and official reports and pamphlets given to Mitsusaburo by the local priest, a folklorist's article on the meaning of the local nembutsu dance, Mitusaburo's memories, Takashi's memories mixed with dreams, and, of course, Takashi's actions themselves. In an astute fictional variation on a good deal of contemporary critical theory, history, for *Man'en gannen no futtoboru*, is a text that we read and rewrite as much as it is a series of events and actions. And it is unequivocally to Mitsusaburo, the translator, that the textual task of rereading (translating) and writing history falls.

In contrast to Mitsusaburo's "readerly" participation in the texts of history, Takashi assumes his place in and toward history through his literal participation in the life of the village and the valley beyond the village. If Mitsusaburo pieces together history in his reading of it, Takashi attempts to recollect history through a series of events and actions, both those of the past, which he remembers, and those of the present, in which he participates. He attempts to (re)organize the young men of the village; he initiates and administers the looting of the Korean's supermarket; he recreates, through his suicide, the sacrificial penance of his ancestors. Because of his actions, Takashi's spirit is granted a permanent place in the village's newly revived Bon festival's nembutsu procession. So too, his great-grandfather's younger brother and his own older brother, "S," have been and are represented in the festival procession.

It is an interesting comment on the narrative countryside and its residents that the revival of traditional culture is presumably the result of, and a utopic comment on, the reentry of the Nedokoro brothers into their native village. There is certainly a utopic impulse in the narrative production of such effectiveness. The specter of prolonged political effort that bears little immediately visible fruit lies just beneath the surface here. Also just beneath the textual surface is the urban perspective on the countryside and its people as stagnant and "corrupted," unable to respond effectively to the threat that endangers their social and economic integrity. Bereft of meaning and value, the very inability of the peasants of Ōkubo to fabricate meaning or value, even to recognize their own dire situation, is a contagious malady that menaces the urban resident and landscape as well. In spite of the fact that the city exists only at the peripheries of the novel, the return of the Nedokoro brothers to, and their engagement in, their family's village and its people places the urban subject, and by implication the urban environment itself, in the midst of contradictions that plague Ōkubo village and the surrounding valley. And Takashi, and most especially Mitsusaburo, are as much repulsed by or disdainful of the countryside as heroically enamored of it. They are as much the unwilling witnesses of forces beyond their control as the rational subjects confronting the less-than-rational countryside.

It is here, perhaps, that the text most explicitly suggests a sense of history as that voracious Minotaur guarding the palace of meaning on the far side of the labyrinth. Contrary to what it might appear, for *Man'en gannen no futtobōru* it is not really the proliferation of textual violence and death that make of history a ravenous monster. It is rather the absence of historical meaning that threatens to devour narrative and narrator. Thus the frequent criticism of Ōe's fiction for its manipulated deus-ex-machina conclusions seems to somehow miss the point. It is precisely those laboriously constructed textual "resolutions" that suggest most strongly the impetus of the text that precedes them. *Man'en gannen no futtobōru* concludes with Takashi's "meaningful" suicide and Mitsusaburo's "meaningful" and almost silly decision to go off to Africa to build his "little thatched hut" and immerse himself in his job as translator in the "humanitarian" effort to find elephants for a zoo somewhere. But Mitsusaburo's attempt at the meaningful closure of his "fiction" is much the same attempt to ward off superfluity in the face of history as what inspired great-grandfather's younger brother or "S" or Takashi. (As perhaps it inspired even the pompous fascism of the oldest Nedokoro brother, killed in the Japanese invasion and occupation of the Philippines.) The Nedokoro family history, Mitsusaburo's own story, and the history that subsumes them all does not really begin and end anywhere. If historical or fictional beginnings are arbitrary, conclusions are manufactured. Whether their manufacture is made more or less textually obvious is only one narrative characteristic among others. The clearly fabricated meaning that concludes this novel, as it does much of Ōe's work, is not a violation of the text that precedes the conclusion; it makes very clear the concerns that underlie the text. That is not just the delineation of the modern dilemma (however and for whomever it might be defined) but the clearly provisional assertion of value and meaning given the precedent of the text itself. It is the perhaps inevitably doomed textual attempt to create meaning through a meaningful subjectivity and the attempt to simultaneously be critically self-conscious of the fabrication of meaning. In Ōe's fiction, the contradictions of this meaningful (im)possibility are made most evident precisely in the arbitrary and manipulated narrative conclusion.

If meaning is provisionally and contradictorily fabricated in the text, so is the impetus for meaning. The specter that haunts and compels the fabrication of provisional meaning is the passivity, the absence, of the narrative subject that is epitomized in Mitsusaburo's severely brain damaged child. But like the safer containment of history within the boundaries of a family history, the narrative implications of the absent subject are contained by Mitsusaburo's newfound commitment to action as a subject in Africa—his definitive emergence from the burrowing subterranean hideouts of his past. In what is ironically reminiscent of the colonialist endeavor, the continent of Africa is the "primitive" stage on which our impotent, autoerotically burrowing narrator will presumably act out meaning and manhood. And, in a further gesture of recuperation, the absent subject himself is to be recuperated for society and family from the institution where he had been installed, although, significantly enough, not by Mitsusaburo but by his wife, Natsumi. Mitsusaburo, Natsumi, and their retarded child, and Natsumi and Takashi's unborn child, fabricate a new, if nonetheless arbitrary, beginning. In a similar fashion, Takashi, obsessed with (recreating) history and the past, fabricates his quite literal conclusion. He sacrifices his young followers and his own life in the attempted creation of a synthetic understanding of history (and meaning) that consistently eludes him in life. For Takashi at least (and peculiarly for the text itself, I suspect), it is the dead who are able to integrate themselves into history. Mitsusaburo's rather laboriously produced (self)insertion into history and desire is at least facilitated by, if not culminated in, death. But perhaps most significantly, in spite of arbitrary beginnings and fabricated conclusions, the Nedokoro family line and family history, which is so privileged in this text, is forcibly made to continue. The end of history, like the end of the subject, is staved off precisely by the dubious conclusions and closure of the text.

Familial continuity is not the only link between the various pieces of this text's construction of history. There is another relationship that the narrative events of 1860 and 1871, 1945, 1959–1960, and the narrative present share. That is the confrontation with the West. The repercussions of this confrontation are not as textually explicit as those of the confrontation with a family history. But they are no less critical. The crisis between the "revolutionary" forces that wanted to overthrow the proforeign shōgunate and restore the power of the emperor and the supporters of the shōgunate was exacerbated, if not instituted, by the forceful intrusion of the West.

The disastrous 1860 peasant uprising led by "great-grandfather's younger brother" was one of a multitude of revolts that contributed substantially to the demise of the shōgunate and what the peasants must have hoped would be the end as well of the shōgunate's increasingly stringent economic policies. But, if the peasants were quite willing to take part in the overthrow of an oppressive government that had long been in internal crisis, the resolution of that crisis was not quite what they had in mind. Frequently, the same peasants whose participation in popular uprisings had led to the downfall of the shōgunate were methodically eliminated by the "new" government and its officials. And, in fact, the peasant rebels of *Man'en gannen no futtobōru* are all beheaded just outside of the Nedokoro storehouse, with the exception of "great-grandfather's younger brother" of course. The Tokugawa shōgunate was overthrown in 1867–1868 and a series of reforms instituted that insured the almost absolute power of the emperor and of the oligarchy that surrounded him. The second narrative uprising, in which "great-grandfather's younger brother," took part was occasioned by one of the reforms established by the new, and itself pro-Western government—the abolishment of clans, their replacement by prefectures, and the installation of new government officials. Unlike the unsuccessful first narrative revolt, the second resulted in the suicide of the newly appointed chief councillor and in the restoration to local power of pre-Restoration officials. In 1860, the peasant revolt was in opposition to the pro-Western sentiments of the shō-gunate; in 1871 it was the Prussian-style reforms of the new government that incurred their angry rebellion. So in 1945 and the raid on the Korean settlement that Takashi and Mit-susaburo's older brother "S" led, it was the consequences of land reforms mandated by the American Occupation forces that sparked the racist attack.

The narrative's peasant revolts of 1860, 1871, and 1945 in-dicate a conservative nationalist sentiment that dominates the narrative countryside. In contrast, the more recent narrative past of the 1959–1960 riots against the renewal of the security treaty between the United States and Japan is conspicuously urban and worker- and student-dominated. It is Takashi who takes part in the narrative reference to what were, in fact, widespread popular protests against the continuation of the security treaty in general and against the presence of American nuclear-equipped bases on Japanese soil and against the re-militarization of Japan that was being carried out under cover of the treaty in particular. Like the earlier incidents, this layer of narrative history is also a reaction to the Japanese response to the irruption of the West. The urban uprising in which Ta-kashi, and coincidentally Mitsusaburo's best friend, whose suicide dominates the opening chapter of the novel, take part presumably affords some kind of parallel to the earlier narra-tive revolts. It was, in fact at least, conspicuously antiimperi-alist, opposing both the continued American domination of Japan's military development and the use of Japanese soil for the containment of other countries in the region. The security treaty demonstrations, which included the successful occupa-tion of the Diet grounds—"the taking back of the Diet for the people"—were also opposed to the American encouragement of Japan's conservatism and imperialism, economic or politi-cal, in Asia. What would seem to have been a very different kind of revolt from the earlier and essentially conservative peasant rebellions is here textually linked to the latter. The link, other than the textual juxtaposition of the incidents and their shared resistance to the impingement of the West, is, of course, that of a family history. Here the familial link is not quite the innocuously symbolic one it might have initially appeared. Because of the historical leadership of the Nedokoro family in what is presumably a series of uprisings, the events of 1959–1960 are narratively linked to the precedent events of 1945, 1860, and 1871. The parallels between these events, even strictly within the boundaries of the novel, are less those of political and social similarity than of familial "tradition" and "continuity."

The implication of linking this "series" of quasi-historical narrative events is rather like that sentiment that awarded narrative privilege to family history in the first place. In the face of an uncontainable yet overwhelming history, *Man'en gannen no futtobōru* does not proffer, as did Natsume Sōseki's *Kusamakura*, the pretext of a "playful, haiku novel" that acknowledges the absence of meaning and centrality. Instead, *Man'en gannen no futtobōru*, in a desperately solemn gesture, tries to manufacture that meaning and centrality by narrative fiat. History is transmuted into genealogy and the "integrated subject" is some synthetic cross between the self-destructive histrionics of Takashi and his part of the family tree and the vegetable passivity of Mitsusaburo and his retarded son.

If the genre of the modern novel initially functioned as a cohort of Western cultural hegemony, it is here that the consequences of that hegemony manifest themselves. Japanese literature scarcely needed the example of the West to arrive at the literary recognition of the absent or distanced subject or temporal nonlinearity or the linguistic fabrication of meaning. These elements were a significant part of Japan's redefinition of its own cultural heritage. And they do, to varying degrees, mark the classical tradition and, to a lesser extent, perhaps, Edo culture as well. But regardless of what was surely the historical modification and alteration of these cultural qualities, they were vigorously resurrected and maintained in the society and culture of modern Japan as precisely what was culturally and socially distinctive and unique.

The modern Western novel was perceived as a challenge of sorts to this cultural schema. It was a genre that, certainly in the widely translated romantic and realist texts,[11] postulated an identifiable meaning in the individual bourgeois subject, in the details of everyday life, in what was presumably the immanently rational progression of events. But the coming into being of the bourgeois Japanese subject and of his or her rational progression was obstructed by the dominance of a political and economic, not to mention sociocultural, system that was precisely the positing of meaning and value elsewhere. That "elsewhere" was beyond the boundaries of Japan, in spite of the economic "miracle" that placed her in the same league, at least economically, with the major world powers.[12] (In fact, to a much greater extent, the center(s) of meaning and value are outside the boundaries of third world countries in the power structures and institutions of the International Monetary Fund or the World Bank or any of various corporations.) In an at least metaphorically similar fashion, meaning and value for an individual subject derive less from a strictly national definition of the individual (whatever that might be) than from a collection of imported hegemonic and national ideas of what the individual is or should be. But the hegemony of such structures of thought is never total and complete. They exist, if in a position of dominance, in interaction with counterhegemonic or oppositional notions of individual and social construction. And, as Antonio Gramsci among others has pointed out, these structures of thought operate in conjunction with economic and political forces, not in privileged isolation.[13]

This is not to suggest a simple opposition of the indigenous delineation of the subject to a foreign and hegemonic defini-

[11] See chap. 4. The sheer quantity (and the frequently impressive quality) of translations into Japanese remains exceptional.

[12] But for critical qualifications of this "miracle," see, among others: Herbert Bix, "Japan's New Vulnerability," *Monthly Review* (December 1982); Paul Sweezy, "Japan in Perspective," *Monthly Review* (February 1980); Jon Halliday, *A Political History of Japanese Capitalism*; or, *The Selling of Japan*, spec. issue of *The Nation* 234.6 (1982).

[13] In *Selections from the Prison Notebooks*, especially 12–13, 55–60, and 416–18.

tion. *Man'en gannen no futtobōru* makes that rather clear in its confrontation of various synchronic moments in history and the subjects of those moments with the attempt at a diachronic perspective by still another subject or subjects—Mitsusaburo and Takashi. The project of recreating the subjectivity of the textual past is as doomed to failure as the project of recreating the meaning of the past. As was apparent as well in the discussion of the fiction of Dimitris Hatzis and Ghassān Kanafānī, if those moments in a textual history are essentially linked to the confrontation with the West—a multifaceted confrontation to be sure—they are equally linked to internal confrontations, pressures, and contradictions—for *Man'en gannen no futtobōru*, those of the family and genealogy, for example. For this text as for those other contemporary novels, the "indigenous" and the "foreign," whether in terms of the subject or of the forces of a given historical moment, escape a simple binary opposition.

The absence of a simply delineated opposition is apparent in the stance of the text itself; *Man'en gannen no futtobōru* simultaneously operates in opposition to and in conjunction with the foreign and the indigenous. The text offers itself as resistance, as opposition, to the meaning- and subject-centered narrative in its textual conjunction of history (or histories), in its fixation on the absented subject (the severely retarded son as narrative impetus, for example), or in its refusal of individually defined action and meaning. But in the privileging of an overdetermined family history and in the implicit designation of extrafamilial history and of the fulfillment of desire as a dangerous threat to narrative autonomy, the text itself attempts to peripheralize both history and desire. And so *Man'en gannen no futtobōru* is in complicity with the contradictory ideology of the genre in which it exercises this resistance. For Ōe's narrative engages in an ambiguous attempt to create, in conclusion, a meaningful and integrated subject, to recuperate the absent son from the institution as it recuperates Mitsusaburo from his septic tank holes and covert of autoeroticism. This is one of the central contradictions of *Man'en gannen no futtobōru*. In the concluding chapter, Mitsusaburo as fragmented subjectivity is made to come into his own as a quasi-integrated (and quasi-Western?) subject. Gone is his certainty, generated by the "sameness" and "continuity" of the natural environment of his family home, that Mitsusaburo the child and Mitsusaburo the adult are two utterly separate and unconnected I's, that "the present adult 'I' had lost all true identity," that "nothing within me or without me, offered any hope of recovery of that continuity." Presumably Mitsusaburo will begin a "new life" at the end of the novel, having learned the "silent truth" that the suicides of his friend and younger brother, the murder of his older brother and the isolation of his great-grandfather's younger brother have to offer. So too the novel comes into its own in a way, precisely through the machinations of its attempt at closure.

It is in the forced conclusion of the novel that we are equally forced to recognize not just some evocative chain of symbols about the anguish and fear of modern life or the suggestively allegorical story of emerging from the underground of absence, silence, and quasi death into the light of action and identity. Instead the text suggests, in perhaps its most truly oppositional stance, the virtual impossibility of the attempt to construct a subject in history that is at the same time aware of its own subjectivity. For Mitsusaburo is most conscious of his own subjectivity precisely when he has burrowed into a hole somewhere, precisely when he has absented himself from history and desire. It is here too that the implicit significance of Mitsusaburo's retarded offspring becomes apparent—as the fulfillment of desire that results in catastrophe, specifically in the "absented subject" that is the retarded child. There is a similar implication in the textual treatment of family history and the role of the familial subject in history—for the fulfillment of their historical role as subjects leads equally to catastrophe, to the even more literal absenting of the subject whether in death or in self-inflicted imprisonment. Ironically, of course, the subject absented from the world by death or isolation is, for the narrative at least, decisively inserted into history as a subject. Nor is the attempt to create some metasubject, grounded in a past collectivity and aware of his own

role in history, much more successful. The textual conse-
quence of that attempt is the bloody pomegranate-like mass
that used to be Takashi.

Thus, the conclusions to Ōe's texts are not the violation of
what was hitherto some narrative integrity and infinite possibility. The obviously manufactured textual closure is the assertion of precisely the impossibility of integrity; the impossibility of manufacturing narrative authenticity, value, or
meaning that is anything more than the most provisional and
fabricated of fictional constructions. Perhaps, after all, the
conclusion to *Man'en gannen no futtobōru* is not a bid for the
integration and recuperation of the subject. For, in a distinctly
distanced and almost antitraditional manner, it suggests what
is perhaps one of the dominant stances of the classical Japanese cultural tradition—the assertion of an only provisionally
differentiated subject, of the provisional appearance of a linguistically fabricated meaning, both of which are always imminently capable of eliding, of slipping, into an undifferen-
tiated and "nonmeaningful" silence or ritual or (Natsume
Sōseki's) "nonhuman" realm.

Ultimately, whether or not the conclusion to *Man'en gannen no futtobōru* (or *Kojintekina taihen*) is intentionally
ironic scarcely matters. As it scarcely matters whether Ōe's
fiction exempts narrative meaning or assiduously fabricates it.
In spite of the utopic promise that textual contradictions will
be resolved in the *next* text,[14] *Man'en gannen no futtobōru*, as
Ōe's earlier and subsequent fiction, distinguishes itself precisely for its balancing act between the absenting of meaning
and the narrative subject and the studied fabrication of both
of them—meaning and subject. Both attempts suggest the ar-
bitrariness and contingency of the finished product. Perhaps it
is this curious vacillation in Ōe's fiction between what is absented and what is fabricated that makes texts like *Man'en
gannen no futtobōru* capable of being at least marginally culturally acceptable. If the text wavers between effacing and
manufacturing meaning and the integrated subject, it wavers

---

[14] In a personal conversation with the author.

as well between an attempt to be encompassed within and recuperated into the dominant order of things—like Mitsusaburo and his son, reclaimed for the world—and an attempt—rather more distinctly nonfictional and autobiographical for Ōe—to challenge the existing order.[15] History, for *Man'en gannen no futtobōru*, even family history, might demand a resolution of sorts, the situation of the present in the past, to reiterate John Berger's phrase. But that resituation, for this text, does not quite so clearly suggest the need for some kind of new transpersonal or metaindividual subject as it does for Kanafānī's *Rijāl fī al-shams* or Hatzis's *To Diplo Biblio*. Instead, *Man'en gannen no futtobōru* makes a much more grim and threatening gesture—the (re)creation of the images that characterized the imperialist endeavor. That is the search for value—or for meaning or manhood or action—in the "primitive," "natural," and ever-so-exploitable arena of the "dark continent(s)" of the world. In Ōe's novel, that search for value takes as its object the capture of wild beasts in a "primitive" Africa. The wild animals as signs of "primitive" value are to be recuperated and contained in one of the collector's cabinets of the "modern," "advanced" world—the metropolitan zoo. The savage, the primitive, the "natural"—untamed meaning—is put in a cage somewhere in a modern city and thereby helps to define the city, the "modern," and the "advanced." Ironically, of course, as a Japanese, Mitsusaburo is himself on the geographic and cultural, if not economic, edge of one of those ultimately exploitable and "backward" continents. But, in his role as translator between the first and the third world, he will go to an even "darker" continent where he can perhaps enjoy the distinction of his somewhat lighter color. This resolution of internal contradictions (for imperialism, the confines

---

[15] See Ōe's essays and articles opposing nuclear buildup, the remilitarization of Japan, the legal and social discrimination against Koreans and other minorities in Japan, or in support of national liberation movements, the peace movement, the democratization of the Japanese educational system, or third world writers in his *Collected Works*. Perhaps, autobiography—Ōe's personal and political involvement—comments on, and even intervenes in, the contradictions and sense of futility that his fiction cannot efface.

of a national capitalism, and national markets) by a move beyond national boundaries is a familiar literal or literary one.
That Takashi fancies such an endeavor—though he refers specifically to capturing elephants for a zoo after the world is de-
stroyed in a nuclear war—as a "truly humanitarian" one
hardly covers the rough edges of *Man'en gannen no futtobōru*'s resolution of its narrative dilemmas. One would certainly
hope that this is an ironic conclusion.

It is perhaps in this international or global context that the
textual eruption of foreign words and phrases and of translated passages from, or references to, foreign texts and authors
makes the most sense. Certainly, the appropriation and use in
the modern Japanese literary text of foreign words and the
reference to foreign texts, paintings, authors, and political or
social figures is familiar. The work of Natsume Sōseki is
marked by an apparently similar use of foreign words and references. But for Oe's text, the interjection of a reference to an
English novel or of a translated passage from Jean-Paul Sartre
or of foreign words and phrases, whether written in Roman
script or approximated in *katakana* (a Japanese alphabet used
largely for just such loan words) is not a textual tour de force
in the synthesis of international culture. Nor does such linguistic eruption afford what might well have been, for early-
twentieth-century Japan, the critical force of a foreign, untra-
ditional, and unpredictable mode of expression. Neither do
the foreign interjections in *Man'en gannen no futtobōru* function quite as the narrator, or here Takashi, imagines when
they occur during a Japanese conversation in America: "The
Americans nearby grew tense at the single English word 'penis' inlaid in their otherwise incomprehensible Japanese conversation" (27).

The foreign words, passages, and references in Oe's novel
are not quite inlaid stones set into the text. They are perhaps
amusing to the Japanese reader. (They certainly are to one
nonJapanese reader.) In the passage quoted above, *penis* is
written in *katakana* rather than in English. But two pages
later, during the continuation of the same conversation, the
Japanese text is marked by the interjection of the English

words *gonorrhea, urethritis, inflammation of the urethra, burning, burning,* and *expensive* written in Roman letters (29–30). What is the function of these words written in Roman characters into the Japanese text? If the rather euphemistic terms for venereal disease indicate Takashi's attempt to explain, in English, his ailment to an American nurse, the repetition of *burning* and the term *expensive* serve no such purpose. There are, of course, Japanese words for *burning* or *expensive.* Similarly, in chapter 6, "Football a Hundred Years Later," Natsumi, reading Natsume Sōseki's diaries, remarks to her husband how aptly the English words that Sōseki has used in his diary to describe himself seem to fit Mitsusaburo: "languid stillness, weak state, painless, passivity, goodness, peace, calmness" (162). The irony of such a description of Mitsusaburo is obvious. And, in fact, Sōseki was describing his own state during an attempted recovery from the stomach ulcers that ultimately killed him. On a distinctly literary and intertextual level, Natsumi's comparison suggests yet another parallel between passivity and death. Or, when Mitsusaburo recognizes the limitations of his relationship to the valley and his childhood memories, the absence of another "truer" self that should be the basis for his behavior, he claims his own "identity"—the "identity" of a rat. And each time it is used, *identity* is written in Roman letters. Is it just his own remoteness from the traditions of his village and from his past that metamorphizes and objectifies Mitsusaburo, that provides him with the "identity" of a rat? What is this textual "identity"—a foreign concept inlaid into the Japanese dialogue— Mitsusaburo as the Japanese variation on Freud's rat man? Unlike *Kusamakura*'s narrating artist, who proposes an ironically facile synthesis of the languages, ideas, signs, and cultures of "East" and "West," this is a rather more ironic comment on the unsynthetic presence of the foreign in Japan—in her language (the text in Roman letters), her culture (the passage from Sartre that opens chap. 12 or the "Koreanization" of village tradition), her society and internal politics (the origins of the textual uprisings of 1860, 1871, and 1945), and her society and foreign politics (the security treaty demonstrations of 1959–1960).

Like the almost ominous penetration of the modern Japanese language and text by foreign words and discourses, or like the bogeyman *chosokabe* that haunted the childhood of Mitsusaburo, "existing everywhere in time and space," there is a narrative sense of history that is also threateningly present everywhere in time and space, permeating the presumably isolated discourse of the Japanese text. It is immediately the history of the Nedokoro family and their role(s) in the life of the valley. But it is also, if not so overtly, the larger history of a Japan that, as a latecomer to capitalist and imperialist power, straddles uneasily a great many of the boundaries between "West" and "non-West," developed and developing country, "third world" and "first world," "traditional" and "modern" society, subject and subjected culture. In this "powerful forest" of contradictions, the narrative is, like Mitsusaburo himself, absented from and of "truth." *Man'en gannen no futtobōru* is an unwilling narrative of impossibility.

But in this recognition of textual impossibility, Ōe's fiction recalls the gesture of Natsume Sōseki's *Kusamakura*—that gesture of resistance, in what appears to be only *Kusamakura*'s "haiku playfulness," to the increasingly narrow and constricting formulation of the modern Japanese state. *Man'en gannen no futtobōru* is the grimly solemn acknowledgment of the impossibility of recreating the past, whether it be of Sōseki's narrative gesture or of some quasi-traditional ritual of (non)meaning.

The dystopia of *Man'en gannen no futtobōru* is the impossible attempt to withdraw from history as it is the equally impossible attempt to remember the meaning of history. Hatzis's *To Diplo Biblio* and Kanafānī's *Rijāl fī al-shams* attempt to locate a provisional "use value" in a literary rendition of history; Ōe's fiction shares the negative critique of the former two texts but stops on the threshhold of their narrative implications. The narrative lays down one mask—the quasi-historical role of the Nedokoro family in the valley or Mitsusaburo as burrowing rodent—only to take up another—Takashi as myth or the surviving Nedokoro heir in pith helmet and khaki, speaking in Swahili, writing in English (and thinking in Japanese?) under the hot African sun. The desperate resistance of Sōseki's *Kusamakura* is transformed into the grimly desolate character of Takashi's heroics or Mitsusaburo's survival. So, in what might be its most "traditional" stance, for *Man'en gannen no futtobōro* there is a recognition of what is ultimately the linguistically constructed and performed play of "reality." There is no final unmasking to lay bare the "real." But the "new" masks that are raised bring with them even more ominous implications than the earlier equations of passivity with death. For, rejecting passivity and death, choosing life and action is also, for this text, choosing a disturbingly romanticized imperial stance.

It is presumably though his survival on whatever terms that is the crucial point of Mitsusaburo's story. And the dominant image in this narrative of disturbing and bizarre images is that of the "tenderness of the color red." It is the color of blood, of murder, of suicide, of the head of Mitsusaburo's best friend, of Takashi's torso shredded by the blast of a shotgun, of the dogwood leaves that are "an only partially clear sign" as Mitsusaburo crouches in a septic tank hole at the beginning of the novel, and of Natsumi's eyes, bloodshot and inebriated since the birth of her deformed son. But it is the painting of hell in the village temple, commissioned by Mitsusaburo's great-grandfather, that graphically reveals the narrative insistence on the color red. For, in addition to, or perhaps because of, its other repeated meanings, red is crucially the color of consolation and of a kind of peace for the narrative survivors. The painting's fiery red rivers and forests engulfing the ghosts of the condemned men and women driven on into the flames by fierce demons elicit a calmness in Mitsusaburo; the tortured dead are "players in some solemn sport," "so used to the demons and the flames that they are not frightened anymore." If the linguistic rendering of the beautiful natural world in Sōseki's *Kusamakura* elicited actual paintings, the linguistic renderings of the tortured human world in Oe's *Man'en gannen no futtobōru* elicit a textual painting—the hell picture. And Ōe's novel trains or educates an audience that is (finally) able to read the painting—Mitsusaburo. At the conclusion of the narrative, he recognizes the flaming red "tenderness" of the hell painting as "the color of consolation for people who try to continue quietly living their more gloomy, insecure and obscure daily lives and help them forget the threat of those terrifying people who confront and overcome their own hell head on" (393). This passage suggests the continued survival of textual discourse and author in the face of the ("terrifying") tendency of Japanese writers to resolve their textual, social, or personal "hells" in suicide as much as it does the continued survival of Mitsusaburo the fictional character.

Violence and death in *Man'en gannen no futtobōru* are almost a substitute for textual meaning. Or, more properly, they perform and display the mutilated body of textual meaning. The bloody string of violated corpses in this text is a most graphic demonstration of the vacating of the subject and of meaning. The "traditional" Japanese cultural practice that presumably suggests the absenting of meaning and of the centrality of the subject in the "delicate traces" of a haiku or the ritual gestures of a Noh actor are here, in this contemporary Japanese text, transmuted into what amounts to the ritualization of violence. For the violence of this textual hell is almost gratuitous; it is a violence, an incest, a rape, or a grotesque suicide that scarcely shocks or startles. If this textual violence does violence to anything, it is not just to some moral sensibility or propriety. It is perhaps that aestheticization of violence and violation that so strongly marks the "internationally Japanese" work of Kawabata Yasunari, in *Yukiguni* (Snow country) or "Nemereru bijo," ("The sleeping beauties") or of Tanizaki Jun'ichirō, in "Shunkin sho" ("Portrait of Shunkin") or *Kagi* (The key) to which the hell and violence of *Man'en gannen no futtobōru* addresses itself. Violence or death in a text by Kawabata or Tanizaki are frequently a gesture to the implicit possibility of some direct meaning; in Ōe's novel, it is a textual demonstration of the absenting of narrative meaning, even in those narrative acts that so clearly attempt to create meaning.

In spite of, or in addition to, the determined attempts at resolution, both autobiographically on the part of the real author and textually on the part of the implied author, *Man'en gannen no futtobōru* is exemplary for its engagement in the crucial contradictions of contemporary Japanese society and culture. Perhaps no text has better managed to fashion a metaphor for the uneven, "gloomy," and "hellish" dilemma of what L. S. Stavrianos in *The Global Rift* calls "the Japanese exception." He concludes his chapter on the historical and economic factors that allowed modern Japan's relatively independent and autonomous development with the assertion that "the Japanese model is irrelevant to Third World countries today" (366). And certainly those possibilities that resulted in the Japanese exception—centuries of isolation rather than colonial rule and neocolonial exploitation, Japan's imperialist expansion, the relative laxity of import trade restrictions, and the comparatively more accessible technology of a century ago—are hardly available to third world economies or cultures today. But there is at least one sense in which the Japanese model is relevant in spite of its exceptional status. That is in the extent to which even being an inimitable "exception" has not excluded Japanese society or culture from the contradictions not only of modern capitalist development but of the importation and consequent unevenness of that development. *Man'en gannen no futtobōru*, in its fiction of an ominously pervasive family history; of an unrecoverable tradition; of a fragmented rodent subject, and a labyrinth of dreams, desires, texts, languages, and masks, lays claim to a more-than-national relevance. Perhaps it even asserts itself as a textual admonition of the possibility of imminent farce, or at least irony, in the repetition of history, whether that history is familial, cultural, of a class, national, or international.

Chapter 8

IN OTHER WORDS, IN OTHER WORLDS:
IN PLACE OF A CONCLUSION

> Perhaps the most insidious and least understood form
> of segregation is that of the word. And by this I mean
> the word in all its complex formulations, from the
> proverb to the novel and stage play, the word with all
> its subtle power to suggest and foreshadow overt action
> while magically disguising the moral consequences of
> that action and providing it with symbolic and
> psychological justification. For if the word has the
> potency to revive and make us free, it has also the
> power to blind, imprison and destroy.
> —Ralph Ellison, *Shadow and Act*

> . . . I pray you, in your letters,
> When you shall these unlucky deeds relate,
> Speak of me as I am, nothing extenuate,
> Nor aught set down in malice. . . .
> And say besides that in Aleppo once,
> Where a malignant and a turbaned Turk
> Beat a Venetian and traduced the state,
> I took by the throat the circumcised dog
> And smote him, thus.
> —Shakespeare, *Othello*

THERE IS SOMETHING as suggestive as it is ominous in Othello's injunction to Lodovico about constructing narratives. Othello's statement suggests what Ellison points to as the dual symbolic power of the word—to imprison and to set free. The supposition of a liberating discourse, of words and narratives that "revive and set free" does not negate, but in fact iterates, the opposite possibility—of words and narratives that blind, disempower, and make impotent. To propose discourse(s) of liberation is, implicitly at least, to recognize the possibility of discourses that enslave.

But Othello bases his injunction on an assumption of narrative efficacy—"speak of me as I am"—that Ellison would not seem to share. It is precisely this assumption, as much as his proverbial jealousy, that is the real source of tragedy in the play. The narrative of Lodovico, in which Othello and his actions will be represented to the Venetian city-state, is postulated as *capable of* recognizing and of portraying Othello truly, "as he is." Yet, Othello's directive is immediately qualified by what has already characterized, as he well knows, the narratives in which he is represented by and for Venice— "nothing extenuate, / Nor aught set down in malice." For Othello has already been accounted for by an "extenuate" narrative—the duke's pronouncement of Othello's necessity to Venice as her military machine[1] to the Senate and to Desdemona's father, Brabantio, who has come to lodge a complaint against the Moor for bewitching his daughter (the word as what Ellison calls "magical disguise"). Thus, the secret marriage of Othello and Desdemona is recognized and upheld as legitimate by the duke in spite of her father's protestations. Patriarchal familial order and authority is violated for the sake of state order and authority. And, in fact, there *are* extenuating circumstances—the threat of the "war-like" Turks approaching the island of Cyprus. The other narrative possibility to which Othello refers, one "set down in malice," is, of course, that of Iago. Iago as narrator tells a rather different tale of Othello than the duke, not an extenuate one but a narrative in which the Moor is "a black ram" "tupping your [Brabantio's] white ewe," a "Barbary horse," and a "Devil," "lascivious" and "gross." Othello, in the last scene of the last act, knows both of Iago's malicious narratives and of what are, in contrast, the extenuate ones of the duke. And yet Othello in-

[1] This apt phrase in reference to Othello's function for the Venetian city-state is Robert McDonald's.

sists in conclusion, as he has throughout the play, on the at least potential efficacy of narratives. He insists that he is what he is and can be represented as such in narrative. In this insistence he is the polar opposite of Iago, who acknowledges from the beginning of the play that he and his narratives are false— "I am not what I am" (I.i. 65).

Perhaps it is not suprising then that Othello's final prescription to Lodovico is one that Othello himself cannot follow. The narrative Othello constructs to represent his own relation to the Venetian state is a schizophrenic one. He is both the "malignant and turbaned Turk," "a circumcised dog" who threatens the state *and* he is the state's loyal defender. And so, Othello the defender of the state stabs Othello the "traducer" of the state. "True" narratives, "true" representations, are, it seems, deadly in Shakespeare's play. And their fatal effects are not limited only to Othello. For it is not only the Moor's dead body that marks the play's closing scene. The bodies of Iago's wife Emilia and of Desdemona also bear witness to the risks of believing in and speaking the "truth." It is for telling Othello the truth about his actions that Iago kills Emilia. And, as she dies, Emilia makes explicit the cost of "speaking true" and its relation to her murder: ". . . as I speak true. / So speaking as I think, I die, I die" (V.ii. 249–50). Desdemona, too, dies for believing (perhaps naively) in the ability of true narratives—that she has *not* been unfaithful to Othello—to counter false ones—Iago's narrative of deceit, unfaithfulness, and adultery.

The bearing of this early-seventeenth-century English play on the modern "third world" or "non-Western" novel is perhaps only a metaphorical one. But, in fact, the belief in the efficacy of "pure" and "true" narratives to vanquish false, exploitative, and deadly ones is problematized in the six novels discussed here, as is the schizophrenia of Othello's final, fatal narrative. In the earlier novels of Papadiamandis, Haqqī, and Sōseki, the refusal or problematization of the "pure" and "true" narrative is more implicit. But it is explicit and almost militant in the work of the three later writers. Their multiple narratives are informed instead by a rather more complex, and even equivocal, relation to the possibility of true narratives. The novels of Hatzis, Kanafānī, and Ōe, in spite of their substantial differences, are grounded in something very similar to Ellison's profound reservation about the power of words (or narratives) to "revive and set free." What Othello, Desdemona, and Emilia do not recognize is an instructive contrast to the presuppositions of the novels discussed in the preceding chapters. For Shakespeare's characters fail to take sufficient account of their relationships to, and implication in, narratives *other* than the ones they have constructed. It is in this context that I would suggest there are no "pure" or parthenogenic narratives, only the fiction of them. Narratives—like language for some and history or ideology for others—always preexist; they are always already there before us. We are "born" into them without—contrary to the ideology of the capitalist marketplace—being able to pick and choose among them. The narratives in which we are engaged—psychological, familial, social, national, or global—are not arranged on a shelf for our leisurely consumption. Nor are we "safely" separate and apart from those narratives, languages, or ideologies. At any given moment we *are* represented in and by those narratives. Perhaps the most useful (and startling) notion toward which the six novels here gesture is the extent to which the representations of and positions in those multiple narratives cannot be altogether refused. They do, but not "truly" or completely, account for us. In the context of Shakespeare's play, Othello *is* Iago's (and Brabantio's) lascivious Moor and the Barbary horse. He is, after all, a Moor—a black, North African Arab, and one-time Muslim—in white, European, Christian Venice. He is also the duke's consummate war machine. Othello cannot altogether refuse the impact of those narratives on himself even though they are not narratives or narrative subject positions of his own making. But Othello is something else besides. He kills Desdemona based on a narrative of which the audience, Venice, and even arguably, Othello himself, is unaware. For, as Cassio, Iago, Emilia, and even Desdemona suggest, Venetian citizens do not kill adulterous wives. Nor does adultery necessarily arouse jealousy. It is the "foregone conclusion" of institutionalized love and sexuality—marriage—for aristocratic Venice. What then is the basis for Othello's murder of Desdemona? It is not based in the Venetian narrative(s). It is elsewhere, in an other world, one that is not articulated (or articulable?) in Shakespeare's play. Here then, it is also the repression or absence of alternative narratives that kills.

The implications for some sense of sacrosanctly autonomous subjecthood are crucial. It is a now familiar observation that the public and the private are not separate domains. But the "private"—the "self"—might well *be*, although not exclusively, the "public"—the self as represented by others *and* as spoken and constituted by "structures" of ideology. For if we speak narratives and languages—Ellison's "word"—we are also spoken *by* them; we construct and are constructed by them. This is the foregone conclusion most explicitly of the three contemporary novels of the last three chapters. It is this narrative observation that is the impetus for Costas's attempt in *To Diplo Biblio* to track the narratives of which he is a part—an impossible task for him alone and, arguably, only partially possible even in conjunction with others.[2] It is this narrative realization on which the narrative structure of *Rijāl fī al-shams* is built. The four Palestinians in that text are included in "narratives" of which they are unaware and in which they are unable to act. The inventory[3] that Costas attempts and only partially achieves is posited as the pressing task of the implied readers of Kanafānī's text. Otherwise, this

[2] See Martin Jay's suggestive article on this (im)possibility: "Vico and Western Marxism," *Vico: Past and Present*, 195–212.

[3] The sense of inventory here is Gramsci's. See Antonio Gramsci, "The Study of Philosophy: Some Preliminary Points of Reference," *Selections from the Prison Notebooks*, 324. Inexplicably, the English-language translation leaves out the concluding part of Gramsci's statement on the necessity of such an inventory. See Antonio Gramsci, *Quaderni del Carcere*, ed. Valentino Gerratana (Turin: Einaudi Editore, 1975), 2; 1363. The passage reads: "The starting-point of critical elaboration is the consciousness of what one really is, and is 'knowing thyself' as a product of the historical process to date which has deposited in you an infinity of traces, without leaving an inventory and therefore it is essential from the beginning to compile such an inventory."

narrative inability or absence is (textually) fatal. Ōe's Mitsusaburo, as well, is implicated in (familial) histories and narratives from which, initially, he seeks refuge and escape. This
attempt to flee the implications of not being in narrative control is situated, in a wonderfully ironic touch, in a septic tank
hole. But, in conclusion, Mitsusaburo emerges from his dank
hole(s) into the sunlight of Africa to take part in other (if questionable) narratives.

This same conclusion about the contradictory potential of
words and narratives is not quite so clearly defined perhaps
but it is there hovering at the margins of the three earlier
works as well. For Khadoula "the murderess" acts quite literally and even rationally on the realization that girl children
in turn-of-the-century rural Greece are a narrative "excess."
So she methodically sets about their elimination by removing
them from the mortal village narrative and, by extension, free-
ing them to an otherworldly narrative of a Christian afterlife.
Haqqī's Ismā'īl, confronted with the multiple narratives of a
global and national system for which he (like girl children for
Khadoula) is a sign of peasant (rather than gendered) excess
and underdevelopment, attempts not elimination but synthesis. Yet the foundation for Ismā'īl's synthetic and inclusive
narrative of "Easts" and "Wests," of peasants and intellectuals, is the realization (for the text if not for Ismā'īl as a character in the text) of conflicting narratives and of the tenuous
claim any one of them has as the "true" and authentic one.
Sōseki's *Kusamakura* takes a certain aesthetic delight in a multiplicity of narratives and in the extent to which textual (or
any other?) presence is a linguistic construct. But there is a
more grim figuration at the edges of that narrative. It finds
most explicit expression in Sōseki's later works but it is also
distinctly there in *Kusamakura*. *Kusamakura*'s narrating artist
attempts and fails not just to revel in aesthetic plurality—of
"East" and "West," of the visual and the linguistic, of the traditional and the modern. He also fails to construct and maintain what is his self-stated goal—an alternative transcendent
narrative that can escape the impingement of history, of the
urban, of an increasingly imperialist Japan. For Sōseki's text,

that pure and "untainted" alternative narrative is impossible, even on its own terms.

The proposition that narratives are multiple, that they are "fictional," and that they are also mutually conflicting and impinging—on one another and on the characters whom they speak and construct and by whom they are spoken and constructed—is the "foregone conclusion" not just of the novels here but of a good deal of contemporary fiction of the "third world" (although, this is not the exclusive property of "third world" narrative). This narrative multiplicity and conflict is precisely one of the challenges of the "third world" to the "first." The relationship between literary modernism, for example, and rising anticolonial movements, literary or social, in the colonized worlds has yet to be adequately addressed, but would surely be an instructive case in point. So too would be a reconsideration of the debates over whether or not notions of "postmodernism" can be descriptively or analytically applied to cultures other than those of West Europe or America.[4] It is in this context too that I would situate the generic travels to other worlds and in other words of the modern novel.

I have suggested here that the modern (West European) novel was initially perceived as foreign generically, literarily, and ideologically to much of the "third" or non-Western world and that the modern novel came as one of the accoutrements of Western colonial coercion and cultural hegemony. The movement of the modern novel to the "third" or non-European world, then, was inextricably linked to imperialism. But that very structure and terrain of the novel as a particular way of organizing narratives also became the site of opposition to Western hegemony. That movement is already implicit in the three earlier novels of Papadiamandis, Haqqī, and Sōseki. But the novel as oppositional becomes most apparent in the contemporary fiction of Hatzis, Kanafānī, and Oe. If the

---

[4] See Alan Wolfe, "Suicide and the Japanese Postmodern: A Postnarrative Paradigm?" and Gregory Jusdanis, "Is Postmodernism Possible Outside the 'West'? The Case of Greece," for interesting, insightful, and divergent discussions of the postmodern elsewhere.

earlier novels attempt to resist the challenge of Western hegemony by calling up the "traditional," the "indigenous," the "popular," or the transcendent, the later fiction critically qualifies that proposition of responding to hegemonic Western narrative(s) with constructions of "authentic" and "indigenous" ones. The notions of separate and autonomous development that underlie the earlier novels are rendered impossible (if in fact they were not so even for the early novels). The later novels construct narratives in which the very notions of "tradition," the "peasantry," "the individual," "modernization," "the intellectual," and the "worker" are critically reexamined and redefined. And like the earlier novels, they gesture toward the possibilities of a not-yet-spoken or seen future. Most literally, these novels pre-dict—speak before. The prefigure or presage the not-yet. They point at (un)real or (im)possible (literary) solutions to "only too real socio-historical dilemmas."[5]

It is not only the past of the non-Western novel that is marked by imperialism. The clear extension of the former proposition is that the modern *Western* novel—its formal characteristics, its structural framework, not to mention its content—is crucially and complexly linked to an expansive and decidedly imperial ideology. Here, I do not refer simply to those familiar and obvious novels of imperialism that take up the issue explicitly—Defoe's *Robinson Crusoe*, Conrad's *Lord Jim* or *Heart of Darkness*, Rudyard Kipling's *Gunga Din*— but to the more basic informing notion of the modern bourgeois West European and British and American novel itself.

A suggestive organizing metaphor for this relationship to the modern (and here particularly British) novel is Joseph Addison's essay, "Trade as a Civilizing Force," in the *Spectator* of Saturday, May 19, 1711.[6] It is not the obvious that is of particular significance in this context—that there are "not more useful Members in a Commonwealth than Merchants."

[5] See chap. 1.
[6] In Addison and Steele, *Selections from the Tatler and the Spectator*, 210–14.

Nor that trade is a singularly "civilizing force." Rather, it is
the narrative perspective from which Addison relates his proposition that seems particularly telling. As he walks among the
international merchants and goods of the Royal Exchange,
Addison describes his "secret Satisfaction" and the gratification of his "Vanity" (the libidinal overtones are unavoidable)
in the fact that "I am an Englishman." For the Royal Exchange
in London makes "this Metropolis a kind of *Emporium* for
the whole Earth." Whether or not merchants and their global
trade civilize, they do *organize* the world in a particular and
distinctly secular fashion—in "the private Business of Mankind." What gives Addison particular pride then is his distinctly British ability—"as I am an *Englishman*"—to peruse
the world laid at his doorstep. He is, through the auspices of
a (narrative) system that allows him the fiction of being at the
center of the world, a kind of voyeur. Addison expresses with
admirable forthrightness his responses and relations to a
world and its goods (both human and inanimate) laid at his
doorstep. His is a privileged narrative perspective from which
he can observe and recount without being known or necessarily observed himself: "I am known to no Body there but my
Friend Sir Andrew who often smiles upon me as he sees me
bustling in the Croud, but at the same time connives at my
Presence without taking any further Notice of me" (211). An
admirable understanding among gentlemen—and Addison is
rewarded for his perspective by "an infinite Variety of solid
and substantial Entertainments." Regardless of which particular text is designated as the "origin of the novel," this narrative perspective and organization seems to me crucial in the
construction of the modern "Western" novel. Addison's perspective as both narrator and purveyor is one here. He is both
the one who relates the narrative and the one who derives
pleasure, or at least the promise of pleasure, from the purlieu
that his narrative perspective affords. This latter position implies a certain reader of the narrative as well, at least minimally one that would share or comprehend his deferred narrative pleasure. Addison's essay also, of course, makes rather
explicit the relation between the construction of a particular

perspective and, in this instance, a flourishing merchant capitalism for which the world is a "natural" source of merchandise, while the marketplace is distinctly, and perhaps also "naturally," located in England. With a citation of classical "precedence" in an epigraph from Virgil, the global aspirations of capitalism are retrospectively naturalized in Addison's assertion that "Nature seems to have taken a particular Care to disseminate her Blessings among the different Regions of the World with an Eye to this mutual Intercourse and Traffick among Mankind, that the Natives of the several Parts of the Globe might have a kind of Dependance upon one another, and be united together by their common Interest" (211–12).

The modern, and here distinctly British, novel is a particular kind of prose fiction narrative that creates and represents narrative links in a world increasingly perceived as disparate, different, vast, and not immediately imbued with the divine. Addison's essay maps a necessary perspective on that world for the modern bourgeois novel, a perspective from which narratives can be constructed and related by a privileged narrator who sees and circulates among what is near at hand, but who is "unknown" and can retreat to a safe remove (of his own "private world" at home) if necessary. The very *goods* of the world—raw materials and commodities, their relationships to one another, to humans, to "Natives"—offer the promise of pleasure, of satisfaction, of gratification to the purveyor.

This is not to disregard the very real and radical break of this new bourgeois order with older aristocratic values and order. Addison imagines a statue in the Exchange of "one of our old Kings" come to life and surveying the scene below him: "In this case, how would he be surprized to hear all the Languages of *Europe* spoken in this little Spot of his former Dominions, and to see so many private Men, who in his Time would have been the Vassals of some powerful Baron, Negotiating like Princes for greater Sums of Mony than were formerly to be met with in the Royal Treasury!" (214, emphasis in the original). But if the vigor of the bourgeois challenge to the old estate and its more exclusively defined perspectives is apparent, so is the more ominous shape of things to come.

"Trade," Addison concludes, "without enlarging the *British* Territories, has given us a kind of additional Empire." The literal rather than symbolic expansion of that empire, economically and culturally, is only the next logical step. For, imperialism is, among other things, the postulation of value, of meaning, elsewhere and the subsequent search for its "location" and extraction.[7] The deformation and violence of this location-and-extraction mission is not diminished by the rather metaphoric language here.

Even the different and varied world of global goods, conveyed to and arrayed for the consumption of the purveyor within his own marketplace, is precisely a narrative construct, as Addison's essay so ably demonstrates. Addison's narrative perspective, and the nascent imperialism and commodity culture that it foreshadows, is predicated not on narrative in general but on a particular definition and organization of narrative. So the response to that definition of narrative by the novels of the last six chapters is neither general nor abstract. It is and must be more explicit—oppositional (on the terrain, in the words and worlds, of what it opposes) *and* simultaneously "other," different, (in other words and worlds).

The situation here is somewhat analogous to the characterization of popular Egyptian or Greek response to "modernization" (see chaps. 2 and 3). It is not so much against narrative (or modernization) in general as against a particular and disempowering definition and organization of narrative that these texts speak. Their comments on or in opposition to particular definitions of narrative are, at least initially, on the same terrain. But that, as Gramsci and Edward Said after him have suggested, *is* how counterhegemony functions—not on some other and unmarked terrain, conveniently distant in time and space, but on the same terrain differently.[8] Clearly,

---

[7] For an elaboration of this idea, see Mary Layoun, "Producing Narrative Value: The Colonial Paradigm," *Colonization in Race, Class, and Gender,* ed. Robert W. Lewis, spec. issue of *North Dakota Quarterly* 55.3 (1987): 190–203.

[8] Though Gramsci does not really elaborate on counterhegemony as such, it is a formulation that runs throughout his discussion of hegemony and the

that terrain outlines the shape of both the potential and the limitation in the construction of "other words" about "other worlds." And "differently" is a relative rather than an absolute practice. But the intervening resistance and opposition are not just transcendently theoretical and abstract—of the eye alone and above, across, or away from the ground. To the extent that they are on the ground as well, they affect and alter that ground. The proposition of limitations, narrative and otherwise, might seem a gross and disabling impingement on thought and action to a culture for which, in the ideologically dominant narrative, all things were possible for the self-designated autonomous subject. In that narrative of power, the entire world was the "home" of, the theater for, men's thought and action. (The allocation, either theoretically or practically, of quite the same mobility and ease was not postulated for women.) But it is not news (it is not "novel") for cultures that either never shared that narrative of omnipotence or that had it rather methodically denied or excised by colonialism. It continues to be a rather less "novel" and startling proposition for societies and cultures—and their narratives—that were and are excluded from that fiction of "naturally" autonomous and dominating power. Manipulating narratives, playing—but in absolute earnest—the various available narrative positions against one another in the attempt to sneak in a few new positions in the hope that they will change the dynamics of the narrative—this participatory narrative production is an essential part of what the novels discussed here (but not only these texts) are about. These novels "manipulate" or "play with" multiple narratives and narrative positions. They take up the figures and forms of the "West" and in their multiple "retelling" alter them, sometimes almost imperceptibly. They attempt to retell the narratives of the "West" *and* at the same time to speak other narratives

---

subaltern in the *Prison Notebooks*. Said's work, especially *The World, the Text and the Critic*, consistently and suggestively investigates the relations and their implications between state(s), institution(s), texts, and critics. But also, his *After the Last Sky* seems to me a compelling (individual) literary/ textual practice of counterhegemony.

that—to the extent that they are of other worlds—are necessarily in other words. In that context, it is not only the "third
world" recognition of the impinging imperial narratives of the
"first world" that is at issue. For, that recognition of limitations of and impingement on the fictional narratives of an absolute autonomy was an almost inescapable part of living under colonial rule (if not necessarily for the colonizers a part of
exerting that rule over others). The "master" in and of the
master narratives—of Addison's global goods and marketplace, of an older imperialism, of neocolonialism, or a contemporary multinational variation of that older imperialism—
is, at least potentially, disabled, limited, and impinged upon
by these other narratives of others. But rejecting the master
narrative(s)—a crucial one of which for the "third world" was
imperialism—is not to reject narrative per se. It is to demand
redefinitions of narrative, of agency, of the subject and autonomy. One of the essential differences in the master narrative
of imperialism is what positions are available to which characters. It is, in other words, the grossly unequal relations, the
imperialism, that underlies the narrative distribution of
power. And then a crucial point of counternarratives, like the
point of counterhegemony, is not just, I would insist, to turn
the tables—to remain within the same paradigm but with imperial power located elsewhere. It is to (attempt to) end imperial power. Not necessarily to end narratives but particular
narrative constructions in which the agency, autonomy, and
perspective of some are constructed on the backs of others.
And in that process of reforming or of actively dismantling
master narratives, there are no assurances about the shape of
that redefined meaning. For that, there are no foregone conclusions. As Gayatri Spivak has suggested in a consideration
of ideology and the politics of interpretations, there is no necessary foreclosure on meaninglessness.[9] To consider the possibility of new meaning, or new narratives, is to entertain the
negative possibility of meaninglessness. It is not though to
banish meaning. But those resituated narratives are not made

---

[9] Spivak, "Politics of Interpretations," *In Other Worlds*, 128.

just as we like, under circumstances of our own choosing. But with limitations, within the terms and circumstances of pasts that we did not shape, we can alter them. That we must is the conclusion of virtually all of the texts discussed above. It is a conclusion that can stand as well for my own here.

In this context, the recognition in other words and worlds—and in the "first world" too—that there is no single narrative that is "truly representative" is a most necessary one. Not to recognize it—as the truncated narratives of Othello, of Emilia and Desdemona, of Khadoula, of *To Diplo Biblio*'s unnamed writer, of Anastasia's "birds" and Skouroyiannis's bear, of the three Palestinians suffocated in a water tank, of Mitsusaburo's friend, brothers, and great-uncle suggest—is deadly.

There is no perpetually open and fluid text as there is no pristine and perpetually potential precedent space or time in which all things are forever possible. At any given moment, intervention—narrative or otherwise—is contained by the terrain and the narratives on or in which it takes place. It is this sense of impingement that informs the novels here, though in different ways and with different textual results—the impingement of an imperial and hegemonic "West" that encompasses the "rest" (not to mention the peoples inhabiting the West itself) in narratives that are "not entirely of their own making, that are not constructed under circumstances just of their own choosing."

In the narrative construction of words and worlds that are other to, different than, but not separate from, the "West," these novels gesture toward the deformative narratives of imperialism and neocolonialism *and* toward the deformation of internal, of national, or "traditional" narratives. This narrative potential is one of those foregone conclusions, if you will, of the novels of Hatzis, Kanafānī, and Ōe. But it is presaged, it is there implicitly, in the earlier novels as well. I will not repeat the readings of those texts. But it was the foregrounding of this potential, which is at the same time a limitation or deformation, that was the impetus for my own critical narrative. What is striking in these texts, in addition to their foregone conclusions—something "prior" to their textual beginnings—is their problematic narrative closure (their narrative conclusions). Papadiamandis's *The Murderess* concludes with the old woman judiciously (for the narrative) drowned in the sea. Ismā'īl in Haqqī's *Qindīl Umm Hāshim* disappears from sight in the synthetic glow of compromise. And the presumably transcendent musing of the artist/narrator of Sōseki's *Kusamakura* is ruptured and "completed" by the departure of a train off to the war front. The later novels attempt more overtly to violate narrative self-containment. Costas in Hatzis's *To Diplo Biblio* "understands" in the din of factory whistles with which the novel concludes. And if the Palestinians within Kanafānī's *Rijāl fī al-shams* do not "understand," it is clearly incumbent on the implied reader of the novel to do so. And Oe's Mitsusaburo in *Man'en gannen no futtobōru*, understanding the (familial) narratives of the past, sets out for Africa to create a "new" narrative (or, rather ominously but more likely, to participate in a rather older and arguably imperial narrative).

In this context of problematic fictional closure, the rhetorical function of nonfiction conclusions is familiar enough (but nonetheless scarcely unproblematic). Conclusions come at the end of, and sum up, a text, an argument, a legal pleading. Conclusions provide the narrative closure of nonfiction prose. They are, quite literally, a shutting off or closing in—the fixing of a boundary. So this conclusion has "summed up" some of the critical assumptions and observations of the preceding pages. But there is another sense of conclusion that I would like to evoke in closing. For, conclusions are also what you turn to first in looking at a new book, or even at a familiar one. Conclusions are a response (if not necessarily an answer) to the question "what's happening" and then to "so what?" It is to the question "so what?" that I have attempted to respond in conclusion. Actually, it is from that question that "travels of a genre" set out as well.

BIBLIOGRAPHY

Abu-Lughod, Janet. *Cairo: 1001 Years of the City Victorious.* Princeton: Princeton University Press, 1971.

Addison, Joseph and Richard Steele. *Selections from the Tatler and the Spectator.* Ed. Robert J. Allen. New York: Holt, Rinehart & Winston, 1970.

Ahmad, Aijaz. "Jameson's Rhetoric of Otherness and the 'National Allegory.' " *Social Text* 17 (1987): 3–25.

Ahmad, Eqbal. "From Potato Sack to Potato Mash: The Contemporary Crisis of the Third World." *Arab Studies Quarterly* 2.3 (1980): 223–34.

———. *Political Culture and Foreign Policy.* Washington DC: Institute for Policy Studies, 1982.

Ajami, Fouad. *The Arab Predicament: Arab Political Thought and Practice Since 1967.* Cambridge: Cambridge University Press, 1981.

Alāmi, Musa. "The Lesson of Palestine." *Middle East Journal* (October 1949): 373–405.

Allen, Roger. *The Arab Novel: A Historical and Critical Introduction.* Syracuse: Syracuse University Press, 1982.

Althusser, Louis. *Lenin and Philosophy.* Trans. Ben Brewster. New York: Monthly Review Press, 1971.

Amin, Samir. *The Arab Nation.* Trans. Michael Pallis. London: Zed, 1978.

Anderson, Perry. *In the Tracks of Historical Materialism.* Chicago: University of Chicago Press, 1984.

Antonius, George. *The Arab Awakening.* New York: Putnam, 1946.

Armstrong, Nancy and Leonard Tennenhouse, eds. *The Ideology of Conduct.* New York: Methuen, 1987.

Arvon, Henri. *Marxist Esthetics.* Trans. Helen Lane. Ithaca: Cornell University Press, 1973.

Augustinos, Gerasimos. *Consciousness and History: Nationalist Critics of Greek Society, 1897–1914.* New York: Columbia University Press, 1977.

Badawi, M. M. "Commitment in Contemporary Arabic Literature." *Journal of World History* 14 (1972): 858–79.

Badawi, M. M. "*The Lamp of Umm Hāshim*: The Egyptian Intellectual Between East and West." *Journal of Arabic Literature* 1 (1970): 145–61.

Bakhtin, M. M. *The Dialogic Imagination*. Trans. Caryl Emerson and Michael Holquist. Ed. Michael Holquist. Austin: University of Texas Press, 1981.

———. *The Formal Method in Literary Scholarship: A Critical Introduction to Sociological Poetics*. Trans. Albert J. Wehrle. Baltimore: John Hopkins University Press, 1978.

———. *Rabelais and His World*. Trans. Helene Iswolsky. Cambridge, MA: MIT Press, 1968.

———. *Speech Genres and Other Late Essays*. Trans. Vern McGee. Austin: University of Texas Press, 1986.

Barakat, Halim. "Arabic Novels and Social Transformation." *Studies in Modern Arabic Literature*. Ed. R. C. Ostle. London: Aris & Phillips, 1975.

Barrett, Michele, ed. *Ideology and Cultural Production*. New York: St. Martin's, 1979.

Barthes, Roland. *The Empire of Signs*. Trans. Richard Howard. New York: Hill & Wang, 1982.

———. *Image—Music—Text*. Trans. Stephen Heath. New York: Hill & Wang, 1977.

———. *S/Z: An Essay*. Trans. Richard Miller. New York: Hill and Wang, 1974.

Beasley, W. G. *The Modern History of Japan*. 2d ed. New York: Praeger, 1974.

Beinin, Joel. "Formation of the Egyptian Working Class." *MERIP* 94 (February 1981): 14–23.

Beinin, Joel and Zachary Lockman. *Workers on the Nile: Nationalism, Communism, Islam, and the Egyptian Working Class, 1882–1954*. Princeton: Princeton University Press, 1988.

Belsey, Catherine. *Critical Practice*. New York: Methuen, 1980.

Benjamin, Walter. *Illuminations*. Trans. Harry Zohn. Ed. Hannah Arendt. New York: Schocken, 1969.

Berger, John. *Pig Earth*. New York: Pantheon, 1979.

———. *Ways of Seeing*. New York: Penguin, 1972.

Berger, John, with Jean Mohr. *The Seventh Man: Migrant Workers in Europe*. London: Writers and Readers, 1982.

Bernal, Martin. *Black Athena: The Afroasiatic Roots of Classical Civilization*. New Brunswick, NJ: Rutgers University Press, 1987.

Bernstein, J. M. *The Philosophy of the Novel*. Minneapolis: University of Minnesota Press, 1984.

Berque, Jacques. *Cultural Expression in Arab Society Today*. Trans. R. W. Stookey. Austin: University of Texas Press, 1978.

Boullata, Issa J. "Encounter between East and West: A Theme in Contemporary Arabic Novels." *Middle East Journal* 30 (1976).

Burch, Noel. *To the Distant Observer: Form and Meaning in Japanese Cinema*. Berkeley: University of California Press, 1979.

Cavafis, Constantine. *Poiemata*, 2 vols. Athens: Ikaros, 1966.

Center for Contemporary Cultural Studies. *On Ideology*. London, 1978.

Chatman, Seymour. *Story and Discourse: Narrative Structure in Fiction and Film*. Ithaca: Cornell University Press, 1978.

Clawson, Patrick. "The Development of Capitalism in Egypt." *Khamsin* 9 (1981):77–117.

Cooke, Miriam. *The Anatomy of an Egyptian Intellectual: Yahya Haqqi*. Washington D.C.: 3 Continents Press, 1984.

Dakin, Douglas. *The Unification of Greece: 1770–1923*. London: Ernest Benn, 1972.

Dale, Peter N. *The Myth of Japanese Uniqueness*. New York: St. Martin's, 1986.

Davis, Lennard. *Resisting Novels: Ideology and Fiction*. New York: Methuen, 1987.

Dimaras, Constantine T. *History of Modern Greek Literature*. Trans. Mary Gianos. Albany: State University of New York, 1972. Trans. of *Istoria tis Neoellinikis Logotechnias*. Athens: Ikaros, 1964.

Doulis, Thomas. *Disaster and Fiction: Modern Greek Fiction and the Asia Minor Disaster of 1922*. Berkeley: University of California Press, 1977.

Eagleton, Terry. *Criticism and Ideology*. London: Verso, 1978.

———. "Ideology, Fiction, Narrative." *Social Text* 2 (1979): 62–80.

———. *Literary Theory*. Minneapolis: University of Minnesota Press, 1983.

Ellison, Ralph. *Shadow and Act*. New York: Vintage, 1964.

Etō, Jun. *Natsume Sōseki*. Tokyo: Keiso Shōbō, 1956.

———. *Sōseki to sono jidai* (Sōseki and His Time). 2 vols. Tokyo: Shinchōsha, 1970.

Fanon, Frantz. *The Wretched of the Earth*. Trans. Constance Farrington. New York: Grove, 1968.

Flora, Cornelia B., and Jan L. Flora. "The Fotonovela as a Tool for Class and Cultural Domination." *Latin American Perspectives* 5.1 (1978).

Fowler, Edward. *The Rhetoric of Confession: Shishōsetsu in Early Twentieth Century Japanese Fiction.* Berkeley: University of California Press, 1988.

Frye, Northrop. *Anatomy of Criticism.* New York: Atheneum, 1969.

Fukuzawa, Yukichi. *Autobiography.* Trans. Kiyooka Eiichi. New York: Schocken, 1972.

García Marquez, Gabriel. "The Soltitude of Latin America." *Granta* 9 (1983): 55–60.

Gluck, Carol. *Japan's Modern Myths: Ideology in the Late Meiji.* Princeton: Princeton University Press, 1985.

Goldberg, Ellis. "Bases of Traditional Reaction: A Look at the Muslim Brothers." *Peuples Mediterraneens* 14 (1981).

———. *Tinker, Tailor, and Textile Worker: Class and Politics in Egypt, 1930–52.* Berkeley: University of California Press, 1986.

Goldman, Lucien. *Towards a Sociology of the Novel.* Trans. Alan Sheridan. London: Tavistock, 1975.

Gramsci, Antonio. *Selections from the Prison Notebooks.* Ed. and trans. Quintin Hoare and Geoffrey N. Smith. New York: International Publishers, 1971.

Hall, Stuart. "Signification, Representation, Ideology: Althusser and the Post-Structuralist Debates." *Critical Studies in Mass Communication* 2.2 (1985): 91–114.

Halliday, Jon. *A Political History of Japanese Capitalism.* New York: Monthly Review Press, 1975.

Hanninen, Sakari, and Leena Paldan, eds. *Rethinking Ideology.* Spec. issue of *Argument-Sonderband* 3 (1984): 1–158.

Haqqī, Yahyā. *Qindīl Umm Hāshim* (The lamp of Umm Hāshim). Cairo: Dār al-Kitab, 1973.

———. *Umm al-'Awajiz* (Mother of the destitute). Cairo: Dār al-Kitab, 1984.

———. "Mother of the Destitute." *Modern Arabic Short Stories.* Trans. Denys Johnson Davies. London: Heinemann, 1967.

Harlow, Barbara. Introduction. *Palestine's Children.* By Ghassan Kanfani. Trans. Barbara Harlow. Washington DC: 3 Continents Press, 1986. iv–xiii.

———. *Resistance Literature.* New York: Methuen, 1987.

Hatzis, Dimitris. "Apo tin Exergesi ton Megaron os to Deutero Bra-

beio Nobel" ("From the revolt of the megarons to the second Nobel prize"). *Anti*, 26 October 1979.

———. "Apo ton Solomo sti Nea Poiesi" ("From Solomos to the
new poetry"). *Anti*, 29 February and 14 March 1980.

———. "Archaiokapilia, Ethnokapilia, kai Alles Diafores Kapilias"
("Archaeo-trafficking, ethno-trafficking, and various other kinds
of trafficking"). *Anti*, 28 April 1979.

———. *To Diplo Biblio* (The double book). Athens: Keimena, 1976.

———. "E Katharsi tis Radiofonias, Tileorasis, kai e Dianoisi mas"
("The purging of radio, television, and our intellectual life"). *Anti*,
30 January 1981.

———. "Kratos kai Eklissia" ("State and Church"). *Anti*, 17 February 1979.

———. *E Fotia* (Fire). Athens: Pleias, 1974.

———. "Hristougenniatiko Antidieigima sunkhronos Ethnografia"
("A Christmas anti-story as well as ethnography"). *Anti*, 21 December 1979.

Dimitris Hatzis. Spec. issue of *Anti*, 30 July 1981.

Hayman, David. "Toward a Mechanics of Mode: Beyond Bakhtin."
Novel 16.2 (1983): 101–20.

Haywood, John A. *Modern Arabic Literature: 1800–1970*. London:
Lund-Humphries, 1971.

Hibbett, Howard. "Soseki and the Psychological Novel." *Tradition
and Modernization in Japanese Culture*. Ed. Donald Shivley.
Princeton: Princeton University Press, 1971.

Hirai, Atsuko. "The State and Ideology in Meiji Japan." *Journal of
Asian Studies* 46.1 (1987): 89–103.

Hobsbawm, Eric and Terence Ranger, eds. *The Invention of Tradition*. London: Cambridge University Press, 1983.

Horkheimer, Max, and Theodor Adorno. *Dialectic of Enlightenment*. Trans. John Cumming. New York: Continuum, 1987.

Hourani, Albert. *Arabic Thought in the Liberal Age: 1798–1939*.
London: Oxford University Press, 1970.

Hulme, Peter. *Colonial Encounters*. New York: Methuen, 1986.

Hussein, Mahmoud. *Class Conflict in Egypt: 1945–1970*. Trans.
Michel and Susanne Chirman, Alfred Ehrenfeld, and Kathy
Brown. New York: Monthly Review, 1977.

Irokawa, Daikichi. *Meiji no bunka*. Tokyo: Iwanami Shoten, 1970.
Trans. Marius B. Jansen as *The Culture of the Meiji Period*. Princeton: Princeton University Press, 1985.

Jabra, Jabra I. "Modern Arabic Literature and the West." *Journal of Arabic Literature* 2 (1971): 76–91.

———. "The Palestinian Exile as Writer." *Journal of Palestinian Studies* 7.2 (1979): 77–87.

Jameson, Frederic. "A Brief Response." *Social Text* 17 (1987) 26–29.

———. "Ideology of the Text." *Salmagundi* (Fall 1976): 204–46.

———. "Imaginary and Symbolic in Lacan: Marxism, Psychoanalytic Criticism, and the Problem of the Subject." *Yale French Studies* 55/56 (1977): 338–95.

———. *Marxism and Form*. Princeton: Princeton University Press, 1974.

———. *The Political Unconscious*. Ithaca: Cornell University Press, 1981.

———. "Third World Literature in the Era of Multinational Capitalism." *Social Text* 15 (1986): 65–88.

Jay, Martin. *Marxism and Totality*. Berkeley: University of California Press, 1984.

———. "Vico and Western Marxism." *Vico: Past and Present*. Ed. Giorgio Tagliacozzo. Atlantic Highlands, NJ: Humanities Press, 1981.

Joseph, Roger. "The Semiotics of the Islamic Mosque." *Arab Studies Quarterly* 3.3 (1981): 285–95.

Jones, Sumie. "Natsume Soseki's *Botchan*: The Outer World through Edo Eyes." *Approaches to the Modern Japanese Novel*. Ed. K. Tsuruta and T. E. Swann. Tokyo: Sophia University Press, 1976.

Jusdanis, Gregory. "Is Postmodernism Possible Outside the 'West'? The Case of Greece." *Bulletin of Modern Greek Studies* 11 (1987): 69–92.

Kafatou, Sarah. "Politics in a Dependent Country: Contemporary Greece." *Socialist Review* (March–April 1979): 103–30.

Kanafānī, Ghassān. *Mawt Sarir Raqm 12* [*Death of Bed #12*]. Beirut: Dār al-Muthallath, 1961.

———. *Rijāl fī al-shams* (Men in the sun). Beirut: Dār al-Muthallath, 1963.

———. *Umm Saʾad*. Beirut: Dār al-ʾAwda, 1967.

———. *The 1936–39 Revolt in Palestine*. New York: Committee for Democratic Palestine, n.d.

Kazziha, Walid. *Revolutionary Transformation in the Arab World*. New York: St. Martin's, 1975.

Khaled, Leila. *My People Shall Live*. Ed. George Hajjar. London: Hodder & Stoughton, 1973.

Kilpatrick, Hilary. *The Modern Egyptian Novel*. London: Ithaca, 1974.

———. "Tradition and Innovation in the Fiction of Ghassan Kanafani." *Journal of Arabic Literature* 7 (1976): 53–64.

Kitching, Gavin. "The Theory of Imperialism and Its Consequences." *MERIP* (October–December 1981).

Kitayama Takashi. *Natsume Sōseki no seishin bunseki*. Tokyo: Okakura, 1938.

Kohler, Beate. *Political Forces in Spain, Greece, and Portugal*. London: Butterworth Scientific, 1982.

Kordatos, Yiannis. *Istoria tis Neoteris Elladas* [History of modern Greece]. Vols. 4, 5. Athens: 20 Aionas, 1958.

———. *Historia tis Neoellinikis Logotechnias* [History of Modern Greek Literature]. Vol. 2. Athens: Epikairotita, 1983. 2 vols.

Lacan, Jacques. *Ecrits*. Trans. Alan Sheridan. New York: Norton, 1977.

Lambropoulos, Vassilis. *Literature as National Institution: Studies in the Politics of Modern Greek Criticism*. Princeton: Princeton University Press, 1988.

Lawson, William. *The Western Scar: The Theme of the Been-to in West African Fiction*. Athens, OH: Ohio University Press, 1982.

Lenin, V. I. *Imperialism: The Highest Stage of Capitalism*. New York: International Publishers, 1984.

Lovell, Terry. *Consuming Fiction*. New York: Verso, 1987.

Lukács, Georg. *Realism in Our Time: Literature and the Class Struggle*. Trans. John and Necke Mander. New York: Harper & Row, 1971.

———. *The Theory of the Novel*. Trans. Anna Bostock. Cambridge: MIT Press, 1971.

Macherey, Pierre. *A Theory of Literary Production*. Trans. Geoffrey Wall. London: Routledge & Kegan Paul, 1978.

Marx, Karl. *The Eighteenth Brumaire of Louis Bonaparte*. New York: International Publishers, 1963.

McClellan, Edwin. *Two Japanese Novelists: Soseki and Toson*. Chicago: University of Chicago Press, 1969.

McKeon, Michael. *The Origins of the English Novel, 1600–1740*. Baltimore: John Hopkins University Press, 1987.

Miller, N. B. "Social Revolution in the Arab World." *Monthly Review* (February 1968): 20–32.

Miyoshi, Masao. *Accomplices of Silence: The Modern Japanese Novel*. Berkeley: University of California Press, 1974.

―――. "Against the Native Grain: Reading the Japanese Novel in America." *Critical Perspectives in East Asian Literature*. Seoul: International Cultural Society of Korea, 1981.

―――. "The Great Divide Once Again: Problematics of the Novel and the Third World." The Challenge of Third World Culture, Duke University, 25–27 September 1986.

Moosa, Matti. *The Origins of Modern Arabic Fiction*. Washington DC: 3 Continents Press, 1983.

Mouzelis, Nikos. "Modern Greece: Development or Underdevelopment." *Monthly Review* (December 1980): 13–25.

―――. *Modern Greece: Facets of Underdevelopment*. London: Macmillan, 1978.

Natsume Sōseki. *Sōseki zenshu* [Sōseki's complete works]. 18 vols. Tokyo: Iwanami, 1984.

Noet, Noel. *Histoire de Tokyo*. Paris: Presses Universitaires de France, 1961.

Ōe, Kenzaburo. *Zensakuhin* (Collected works), Series I. Tokyo: Shinchōsha, 1967. (I did not have access to the more recent series of Ōe's *Zensakuhin*, series II, during the final writing of this chapter.)

―――. *Kojintekina taiken* [*A Personal Matter*]. Tokyo: Shinchōsha, 1964.

―――. *Man'en gannen no futtobōru* (Football in the first year of Man'en). Tokyo: Kodansha, 1971.

―――. *Teach Us to Outgrow Our Madness*. Trans. John Nathan. New York: Grove, 1977.

Papadiamandis, Alexandros. *Ta Apanda* (The collected works). Ed. N. D. Triandafilopoulos. 3 vols to date. Athens: Domos, 1984.

―――. *Autobiographoumenos* (Autobiographical writings). Athens: Hermes, 1974.

―――. *Grammata* (Letters). Athens: Estia, 1934.

Papageorgiou, Kostas. Review of *To Diplo Biblio*, by Dimitris Hatzis. *Anti* (Opposition), 11 Dec. 1976.

Pappas, Peter. Review of *To Diplo Biblio*, by Dimitris Hatzis. *Journal of the Hellenic Diaspora* 4.4 (1978).

Poulantzas, Nikos. *The Crisis of the Dictatorships: Portugal, Greece, Spain*. Trans. David Fernbach. London: New Left Books, 1976.

al-Rā'ī, 'Alī. *Dirāsāt fī al-riwāya al-Misriyya* (Studies in the Egyptian novel). Cairo: al-Mu'assasa al-Misriyya al-'Amna, 1964.

Robert, Marthe. *Origins of the Novel*. Trans. Sacha Rabinovitch. Brighton: Harvester Press, 1980.

Rodinson, Maxime. *Israel: A Colonial Settler-State*. Trans. David Thorstad. New York: Pathfinder, 1973.

———. *Marxism and the Muslim World*. Trans. Jean Matthews. New York: Monthly Review, 1981.

Rubin, Jay. *Injurious to Public Morals: Writers and the Meiji State*. Seattle: University of Washington Press, 1984.

Sahinis, Apostolos. *To Neoelliniko Mythistorema* (The modern Greek novel). Athens: Ikaros, 1958.

Said, Edward. *After the Last Sky*. New York: Pantheon, 1986.

———. *Beginnings: Intention and Method*. New York: Basic Books, 1975.

———. "The Idea of Palestine in the West." *MERIP* (September 1978).

———. Introduction. *Days of Dust*. By Halim Barakat. Trans. Trevor Le Gassick. Washington D.C.: 3 Continents Press, 1983.

———. *Orientalism*. New York: Vintage, 1979.

———. *The Question of Palestine*. New York: Vintage, 1980.

———. *The World, the Text, and the Critic*. Cambridge: Harvard University Press, 1983.

Seidensticker, Edward. *Low City, High City: Tokyo from Edo to the Earthquake*. New York: Knopf, 1983.

Shakir, Mustafa. *al-Qissa fi Siriya hatta al-Harb al-'Alamiyya al-Thaniyya* (The novel in Syria prior to World War II). Cairo: n.p., 1957.

al-Sharqāwi, Abd al-Rahman. *al-Ard* (The Earth). Cairo, 1954.

Siddiq, Muhammad. *Man Is a Cause: Political Consciousness and the Fiction of Ghassan Kanafani*. Seattle: University of Washington Press, 1984.

Spender, Dale. *Mothers of the Novel*. London: Methuen, 1988.

Spivak, Gayatri Chakravorty. *In Other Worlds: Essays in Cultural Politics*. New York: Methuen, 1987.

Sprinker, Michael. *Imaginary Relations*. London: Verson, 1987.

Stasinopoulos, E. K. *Istoria ton Athinon* (The history of Athens). Athens, 1973.

Stavrianos, L. S. *The Global Rift: The Third World Comes of Age*. New York: William Morrow, 1981.

Sulaiman, Khalid A. *Palestine and Modern Arabic Poetry*. London: Zed, 1984.

Tillon, Germaine. *Algeria: The Realities*. New York: Knopf, 1958.

Todorov, Tzvetan. *The Poetics of Prose*. Trans. Richard Howard. Ithaca: Cornell University Press, 1977.

Turner, Bryan. *Marx and the End of Orientalism*. London: Allen & Unwin, 1978.

Vatikiotis, P. T. *The Modern History of Egypt*, 2nd ed. Baltimore: John Hopkins University Press, 1980.

Viglielmo, V. H. "Soseki's *Kokoro*: A Descent into the Heart of Man." *Approaches to the Modern Japanese Novel*. Ed. K. Tsuruta and T. E. Swann. Tokyo: Sophia University Press, 1976.

Wallerstein, Immanuel. *The Modern World System*. 2 vols. New York: Academic Press, 1974.

Watt, Ian. *The Rise of the Novel*. Berkeley: University of California Press, 1957.

Webb, Igor. *From Custom to Capital: The English Novel and the Industrial Revolution*. Ithaca: Cornell University Press, 1981.

White, Hayden. *Metahistory*. Baltimore: John Hopkins University Press, 1973.

———. *Tropics of Discourse*. Baltimore: John Hopkins University Press, 1978.

Williams, Raymond. *The Country and the City*. New York: Oxford University Press, 1973.

———. *Marxism and Literature*. Oxford: Oxford University Press, 1977.

Wilson, Michiko N. *The Marginal World of Oe Kenzaburo*. Armonk, NY: M. E. Sharpe, 1986.

Wolf, Eric R. *Europe and the People without History*. Berkeley: University of California Press, 1982.

Wolfe, Alan. "Suicide and the Japanese Postmodern: A Postnarrative Paradigm." *South Atlantic Quarterly* (Summer 1988).

Worsley, Peter. *The Three Worlds: Culture and World Development*. London: Weidenfeld and Nicolson, 1984.

Yoshida Rokurō. *Sakka izzen no Sōseki*. Tokyo: Shibundo, 1942.

INDEX

Abu-Lughod, Janet, 94
Addison, Joseph, 250–53, 255
Ahmad, Aijaz, 14
Ahmad, Eqbal, 76–77, 82
Ajami, Fuad, 102–3
Althusser, Louis, 14, 15, 16, 17, 18–19, 102
aware (compassion), in *Kusama-kura*, 118–20, 133, 136–37

Bakhtin, M. M., 4, 8, 224n
Barthes, Roland, *The Empire of Signs*, 112, 130
Bashō, *Okuno hosomichi*, 128–29, 131, 132, 133
Beasley, W. G., 11
Benjamin, Walter, 6, 51–52, 80
Berger, John, 39n, 47n, 153, 192, 193n, 206, 236
Bernstein, J. M., 6, 8
Berques, Jacques, 11, 75, 93–94

Cavafy, Constantine, 21
class conflicts: in early 20th-century Egypt, 66–67; of *E Fonissa*, 41–45, 46, 49, 53–54; in late 19th-century Greece, 30–31; as linguistic conflict, 27–29; of *Man'en gannen no futtobōru*, 220; in Meiji state, 132; in post-WWII Middle East, 181–82; of *Qindīl Umm Hāshim*, 75, 77, 85–87, 89, 93; of *Rijāl fī al-shams*, 186; of *To Diplo Biblio*, 161, 163, 164
colonialism. *See* imperialism
counterhegemony, 11–12, 13, 249–50, 253–55; of *Qindīl Umm Hāshim*, 98–99; as "resistance" in *Man'en gannen no futtobōru*,

232–33, 239–40; of Sōseki's prose, 115, 141–42. *See also* hegemony

Dimaras, C. T., 23, 24
Doulis, Thomas, 23, 24

Eagleton, Terry, 19, 20
"East" and "West," xi, 12–13, 147, 207, 248, 254–55, 256; in construction of modern Greek state, 29–34; in *E Fonissa*, 38, 45, 52–53; in *Kusamakura*, 130–31, 141–42; in *Man'en gannen no futtobōru*, 229–31, 233, 238–39; for the *nahda*, 58, 59, 64–65, 67; for post-1948 Arab world, 181; in *Qindīl Umm Hāshim*, 56, 65, 75–77, 85–89, 94–98, 101–4. *See also* "modern"; "three worlds"; "tradition"
Ellison, Ralph, 243, 244, 246, 247

fanariots, 27, 28–29
Fanon, Frantz, 14, 156–57

García Marquez, Gabriel, 20
Goldberg, Ellis, 49n, 72
Gramsci, Antonio, 11, 161, 164, 232, 247n, 253

Hall, Stuart, 16–17
Halliday, Jon, 108n, 112–13, 115–16
Haqqī, Yahyā, 10, 46, 51, 56–104, 105, 111, 137, 142, 143–44, 146, 180, 194, 220, 245, 248, 249, 257
Hatzis, Dimitris, 46, 146–47, 148–

Hatzis, Dimitris (*cont.*)
76, 178, 185–86, 188, 204–5,
233, 236, 239, 246, 247, 249,
256, 257
hegemony, xii–xiii, 7–8, 9, 11–12,
31–33, 40, 60, 81, 87, 141, 143–
45, 157, 231–33, 249–50, 256.
See also counterhegemony
Heikal, Mohammed Husayn, 73–
74, 194
history, in and as narrative(s), 46,
103, 118, 119–21, 129, 137–38,
141, 148–49, 165, 189–92, 199–
200, 202–3, 212–13, 216, 217–
19, 225–26, 227, 231, 233, 239.
See also memory
Husayn, Tāhā, 71, 73, 74–75

ideology, narrative workings of, 14,
15–19, 93, 102, 110, 115, 121–
29, 246, 247–48, 250–53, 255
imperialism, 8–9, 11, 13, 19, 108n,
113–14, 115, 132, 137, 145,
155–57, 236–37, 239–40, 249–
53, 255, 256
internationalism, 33, 146, 152, 166,
168, 170, 176, 185–87, 203–8,
236–37, 242. *See also* national/
nationalism
irony, 34–35, 43–44, 85–86, 90–
91, 121, 127, 131–32, 136–37,
141–42, 155, 160–61, 235–37,
242

Jameson, Frederic, 14, 15, 87, 102,
155n, 162, 179
Joseph, Roger, 97–98

Kanafānī, Ghassān, 146–47, 158,
176, 177–208, 233, 236, 239,
246, 247–48, 249, 256, 257
Kawabata Yasunari, 215n, 241
Kordatos, Yiannis, 24
kotzabasides, 27, 28, 29, 30–31,
41–42, 44, 49

Lacan, Jacques, 15, 155–56, 158
language, "problems" and "solutions," 23–24, 25–28, 40, 45–46,
47, 49, 61–62, 67, 84–85, 132,
146, 152, 156, 167, 175n, 178–
79, 210, 237–39
Lenin, V. I., 19
Lovell, Terry, 5, 6
Lukács, Georg, 6, 15, 81, 162

Marx, Karl, 17, 120
McKeon, Michael, 6
memory, 79, 135, 149, 150, 164,
168–69, 174, 190–200, 213, 218,
225, 239
metanationalism. *See* internationalism
migrant workers, 45–46, 146, 150,
153, 163–64, 166, 170, 176,
185–86
"modern," the, 9, 27–29, 39–40,
45–46, 52–53, 60, 63, 72, 76, 78,
94, 99–100, 102, 103–4, 105,
111–13, 117, 131, 133, 141,
146–47, 150n, 234, 236, 239,
248, 253. *See also* "East" and
"West"; the "three worlds"; "tradition"
modernism, 157n, 159, 161–62,
216n, 249
Mouzelis, Nicos, 26, 28, 31n, 170n,
175
Murasaki Shikibu. *See Tale of Genji*

nahda (literary renaissance), 58–62,
64–65, 81, 184
narrative closure, 38, 54–55, 88, 99,
101, 103–4, 118–20, 138, 173–
74, 201–3, 204, 221, 227–29,
233–37, 256–57
narrative perspective/voice, 6, 7,
34–35, 50–51, 52, 74, 78–81, 99,
117–18, 127–28, 134, 138–40,
149–51, 159–61, 167–68, 216–
17, 219, 251–53, 255
national/nationalism, the, 43, 47,

49, 54, 58, 61–62, 65, 67, 68–71,
115–17, 152, 168, 170, 176,
180–83, 183–86, 203–8, 222,
242, 256; cultural nationalism,
71–75, 166; and national literary
studies, 3–4, 13, 143, 145–46.
See also internationalism; *nahda*
Natsume Sōseki, 36n, 100, 105–43,
143–44, 146, 151, 160, 168, 218,
231, 235, 237, 239–40, 245, 248,
249, 257
novel: early, 7; and the national, 3–
4, 8, 31–32, 43, 61, 81–82; origins of, 4–7, 32, 60, 251; premodern narratives, 5, 9–10, 32,
52, 60–62. *See also* narrative closure; narrative perspective/voice;
subject; utopic; *and chapters on
specific novels*

Ōe Kenzaburo, 111, 146–47, 158,
176, 178, 207, 209–42, 246, 248,
249, 256, 257
Othello, 243–47, 256

Papadiamandis, Alexandros, 21–55,
81, 84, 89, 99, 100–101, 105,
111, 137, 142–43, 143–44, 146,
148, 154, 172–73, 245, 248, 249,
257
peasantry, 37, 42–44, 46–49, 52–
53, 58, 63, 66–67, 79, 82–84, 86,
88, 99–100, 110–11, 146, 190–
95, 196, 223, 229–31. *See also*
class conflicts
popular press/newspapers, 5, 22–
23, 30, 31–32, 59–60, 65, 126

realism, 5–6, 7, 151, 159, 161–62,
195
Rodinson, Maxime, 95, 180n

Said, Edward, 12, 14, 60, 144, 253
Spivak, Gayatri, 17, 155–56
Stavrianos, L. S., 108–9, 242
Steele, Richard, 6
story, 51–52, 78–81, 85, 93, 99
subject, 5–6, 7, 18–19, 87–88, 93,
100–101, 105, 106–7, 112, 127–
28, 131, 132, 134, 140–42, 146,
149, 152, 155–59, 163–64, 188,
189–90, 192, 200, 202–3, 207,
211–13, 226, 228, 232–34, 236,
238, 241, 247, 254–55

Tale of Genji, 10
Tanizaki Jun'ichiro, 215n, 241
"three worlds," the, xii–xiii, 8–9,
12–14, 108n, 146, 207–8, 236,
239, 242, 245, 249, 254–57. *See
also* "East" and "West"; "modern"; "tradition"
Tillon, Germaine, 189
"tradition," 24, 26, 29–30, 37–38,
39, 40, 45, 46, 48, 67, 71–74,
76–77, 78, 79, 81, 85, 88, 94–97,
99–100, 103–4, 105, 106, 110–
11, 115, 143–47, 148, 194–95,
210–11, 213–14, 220, 226, 231,
235, 239–240, 241, 248, 256. *See
also* "East" and "West"; "modern"; "three worlds"

utopic, the, 20, 48, 93, 99–100,
102, 103, 117–18, 125–26, 134,
144–45, 161, 171, 188, 206, 235

Wallerstein, Immanuel, 13
Watt, Ian, 5, 32
Worlsey, Peter, 13–14

NORTHERN MICHIGAN UNIVERSITY LIBRARY

3 1854 000 431 919

DATE DUE

DEC 20 1993

DEMCO 38-297